Cooperation without Submission

The Chicago Series in Law and Society
Edited by John M. Conley, Charles Epp, and Lynn Mather

Cooperation without Submission

Indigenous Jurisdictions in
Native Nation–US Engagements

JUSTIN B. RICHLAND

The University of Chicago Press
Chicago and London

The University of Chicago Press, Chicago 60637
The University of Chicago Press, Ltd., London
© 2021 by The University of Chicago
Published 2021
Printed in the United States of America

30 29 28 27 26 25 24 23 22 21   1 2 3 4 5

ISBN-13: 978-0-226-60859-4 (cloth)
ISBN-13: 978-0-226-60876-1 (paper)
ISBN-13: 978-0-226-60862-4 (e-book)
DOI: https://doi.org/10.7208/chicago/9780226608624.001.0001

Library of Congress Cataloging-in-Publication Data

Names: Richland, Justin B. (Justin Blake), 1970– author.
Title: Cooperation without submission : indigenous jurisdictions in native nation–
    US engagements / Justin B. Richland.
Other titles: Chicago series in law and society.
Description: Chicago : University of Chicago Press, 2021. | Series: Chicago series
    in law and society | Includes bibliographical references and index.
Identifiers: LCCN 2020053634 | ISBN 9780226608594 (cloth) | ISBN 9780226608761
    (paperback) | ISBN 9780226608624 (ebook)
Subjects: LCSH: Indians of North America—Legal status, laws, etc. | Indians
    of North America—Government relations. | Sovereignty. | Hopi Tribe of
    Arizona—Relations—United States.
Classification: LCC KIE1877 . R53 2021 | DDC 342.7308/72—dc23
LC record available at https://lccn.loc.gov/2020053634

For Sally Engle Merry & Marlene Sekaquaptewa

Contents

Figures

A Note about Transcripts, Orthography, and Terminology

I include both original transcripts of audio recordings I produced and transcripts of official proceedings for which I only have access to archived texts.

The portions of transcripts that appear in this book employ several conventions typical of linguistic anthropological studies (Duranti 1997). For all the transcripts, names or initials of speakers occur in the left column. Where a language other than English is in use, the original utterance appears in bold italics and represented by one clause per line; each clause is translated with an English gloss immediately below it.

Throughout the book, all Hopi utterances and terms are represented using an orthography from the *Hopìikwa Lavàytutuveni: A Hopi Dictionary of Third Mesa Dialect* (Bureau of Applied Research in Anthropology 1997). Also note the following additional conventions:

–	A dash indicates that speech was suddenly cut off during or after the preceding word.
?	A question mark indicates a marked rising pitch.
.	A period indicates a marked falling pitch.
[	Brackets mark the onset of utterances spoken in overlap with other talk.
( )	Parentheses indicate transcriber's notes.
=	An equals sign indicates speech that continues without pause but has been broken up to account for an interjected utterance from another speaker.

Utterance numbers divide interactional discourses in a turn-by-turn progression. Within each numbered turn, lines divide turns at talk by phrase.

Finally, a note on terminology. The question of how best to name those contemporary political and legal entities by which Indigenous Peoples organize themselves remains a lively topic of debate in Native American and Indigenous Studies. To honor the spirit of that debate, and as a non-Native scholar who wishes to pay heed to the different ways Indigenous persons themselves name their contemporary political systems, I interchangeably use the terms "Native Nations," "Indigenous Nations," "Tribes," "Aboriginal Peoples," "Native Peoples," and "Indigenous Peoples" throughout the book. Likewise, I also interchangeably refer to individual actors or their statuses as "Native American," "American Indian," "Native," "Indigenous," "Aboriginal," or by the individual's particular Tribal affiliation. Across all these usages, I mean to consistently emphasize the status of Native Nations as sovereign, self-determining political and legal entities whose citizens identify as the original inhabitants of territories that today are geopolitically enclosed (partially or wholly) within the boundaries of the United States of America.

PART 1

Introduction

Cooperation without Submission

Introduction

This book considers the historic and ongoing relationship between the United States and those Native Nations whose territories and reservations are now located within that settler nation's borders. More specifically, it is my attempt to describe an often overlooked and misunderstood dimension of those relations; namely, the way they are enacted and made meaningful by those Tribal leaders who undertake them and the non-Native officials with whom they engage as part of their everyday governance.

In my twenty-five years working mostly for the Hopi Tribal Nation but also with other Tribes and Tribal advocacy organizations, I have regularly been struck by a fact at once routine and in need of restating; that is, while more dramatic events like the 2017 confrontation at Standing Rock Sioux Nation over the Dakota Access Pipeline rightly bring to the fore Indigenous Nations' interests and relations vis-à-vis the United States (Estes 2019; Estes and Dhillon 2019), the majority of the work that goes into navigating the complex relationships between Tribes and the United States happens in more routine day-to-day governance. It is work that takes place in the neon-lit rooms of US executive branch offices in Washington, DC, or in bland regional federal buildings, or in the multipurpose conference centers of Tribal government buildings. They also occur occasionally as public meetings at town halls, school gyms, resort casinos, and bingo parlors. The work is often unremarkable engagements and bureaucratic back-and-forth that rarely make the local diner-counter conversation circuits, let alone the national press.

The invisibility of these events has meant that most Native Nation–US engagements are rarely understood as sites for the enactment of Tribal sovereignty, Tribal governance, and/or resistance to settler colonial impositions. Moreover, what might count as expressions of Tribal self-determination in these contexts often looks different from how they appear in moments of more spectacular confrontation. Instead of raised fists and body block-ades, enacting self-determination in these quiet contexts involves a subtle but determined insistence by Tribal advocates on the enduring viability of their People's interests and the norms, knowledge, and relations that consti-tute them. This insistence is often the impetus behind Tribal representatives' willingness to engage US officials in the first place. And it is a ground they do not cede, even when non-Natives misunderstand their reasons for engaging or when the outcomes of their engagement fall short of their Tribes' goals.

I call this commitment "cooperation without submission," which is based on what my mentor, Hopi linguist, lawyer, and anthropologist Emory Sekaquap-tewa, once said about his People's principles of sociocultural and political or-der. At first glance, the phrase seems to express a simple contradiction. How can there be "cooperation" between two or more political agents without each yielding some aspect of their respective autonomy? Further reflection only yields more complexity, for "cooperation" offered up without autonomy is not cooperation at all; it is coercion. At this point, the phrase not only starts to sound tautological but also bears a striking resemblance to some of the clas-sic themes of Euro-American political liberalism, the stuff of sovereignty and social contract theory deliberated by Hobbes, Locke, Rousseau, and their fol-lowers and critics.

But Sekaquaptewa insisted that he learned this lesson elsewhere. He ar-gued that his view is based on the teachings he received about the coordina-tion accomplished by the clans and ceremonial societies that constitute Hopi society, and particularly how they come together for Hopi Peoples' mutual benefit and ongoing well-being. Of particular import is that this coordina-tion is conditioned on the mutual respect for each clan's particular norms, knowledge, and relations (what they call *navoti*, traditional sacred knowledge or knowledge gained through hearing) and the strict prohibitions against sharing that navoti with anyone not a member of that clan or not initiated in its ceremonial societies. It is this commitment to decentralized social power and authority—to the notion that each Hopi clan has its own ways of valu-ing, knowing, and relating to the world—that cannot not be challenged by the other clans that have thrown in their lot together. It is the ongoing rela-tions of respect for each partner clan's authority and the vigilance against imposing the norms and knowledge of one on any other that constitutes the glue holding Hopi society together rather than pulling it apart (Ishii 2001; Sekaquaptewa 1972).

It is my argument in this book that, although he never claimed it, Seka-quaptewa's theory both suggests an abiding principle of Hopi sociality and characterizes an impetus that Hopi—and indeed many other Tribal Nations—rely on when engaging their non-Native counterparts in US federal agencies and other settler colonial organizations and institutions: many Native Nations have a similarly distributed, decentralized theory of sociopolitical authority and practices of self-governance. This, coupled with their shared experience of centuries of Euro-American settler colonialism—which invariably makes them unrecognizable and erases their sovereignty and authority even when claiming to work for their benefit—is why I argue that Sekaquaptewa was speaking about a Hopi theory of sociopolitical order and engagement that has resonances with the experiences and commitments of other Native Nations' engagements with the United States.

I believe that cooperation without submission (hereafter, CWS) can be understood as an Indigenous theory of jurisdiction. It describes an actively accomplished sphere of authority that Indigenous leaders (and advocates for Native Nations) invoke and enact as expressions of their ongoing sovereignty in the practices of their everyday self-governance. It is a jurisdiction entailed and produced in the details of the legal language—*juris-diction* (literally law-talk)—that Native Nation leaders and representatives deploy when undertaking the government-to-government relationship with the US settler state. I argue that US agencies and organizations have long passed laws and policies that claim an interest in Indigenous norms, knowledge, and relations. More often than not, however, they treat Indigenous lifeways as objects to be inquired about, evaluated, and made meaningful according to US regulatory and scientific criteria. Ironically, they do not see them as the foundational and constitutive elements of Indigenous everyday practices of self-determination, or of that which is accomplished through Indigenous juris-dictions of CWS. The results are therefore all too predictable. That is, US agents and agencies continuously make unrecognizable the reasons Native leaders and advocates engage with them in the first place, and constantly misdiagnose why federal laws and policies fail Tribal Nations more generally. This has been true since the first relations with Native Nations.

To understand this, we need to consider the legal and political histories of US relations with Native Nations and the criticisms leveled against US and other settler colonial regimes governing their relations with Indigenous Nations. This will be taken up in finer detail in chapter 2, but I offer a cursory discussion of it here. I will then introduce readers to the kinds of scenes of Native-US engagements I analyze in this book by using two specific examples from the hundreds of hours of ethnographic data I have gathered in working with the Hopi Cultural Preservation Office. The details of these two events allow me to highlight the theories and methods of legal language analysis and linguistic anthropology that I apply to Native-US engagements throughout the book. These include, in particular, the theories and methods that I gather under my notion of legal language as juris-diction. I end this chapter with an overview of the general structure of the book, including summaries of the chapters that follow.

It has been almost two hundred years since the 1831 Supreme Court decision in *Cherokee Nation v. Georgia*,[1] in which were announced some of the foundational principles of federal Indian law. Chief among these were: (1) that Tribes are "domestic dependent nations" retaining certain inherent rights of self-determination and internal governance, while ceding other aspects of their sovereignty to the United States, including absolute title to their Aboriginal lands and resources;[2] and (2) that to the extent that US settler colonialism infringes on Tribal sovereignty, the federal government bears a "trust responsibility" to Tribal Nations. That is, whenever the United States enacts policies affecting Tribal Nations, it must do so in a manner that comports with Tribes' best interests.[3] These remain, ostensibly, the two organizing principles of US policies toward Tribal Nations to this day, including those that are supposed to animate the details of regulatory and administrative processes that have constituted the front line of Native-US engagements (Getches et al. 2016; R. Miller 2015).

Even those unfamiliar with the history of US policies toward Native Americans will know that this relationship is one in which the "best interest" of Tribal Nations has usually been defined by federal actors in ways that effectuated the further loss of Tribal Nations' political, economic, and sociocultural autonomy. This certainly was the case from the mid-1800s to early 1900s, when the prevailing policies called for the breaking up of collective Tribal land holdings, the cultural assimilation of Native Peoples through forced reeducation, and the erasure of Tribal Nations' political relations to the United States (Pommersheim 2009; Wilkinson 1987). It is also true of the policy from the late 1950s to the late 1960s, which attempted to end the unique relationship between certain select Tribes and the US, to additionally allow several named state governments to assume criminal jurisdiction over Tribal lands in their borders, and to do both without any effort to secure Tribal consent for these tectonic policy shifts. Scholars of federal Indian law and Tribal governance understand both periods as the long dark nights when

---

1. Cherokee Nation v. Georgia, 30 U.S. (5 Pet.) 1 (1831).

2. *Cherokee Nation* at 2.

3. *Cherokee Nation* at 2.

Tribal Nations suffered the greatest losses at the hands of a US government that was ostensibly acting in their best interests (Getches et al. 2016; Wilkins and Stark 2018).

But some argue that settler colonial depredations have also been enacted on Native Nations between the 1930s and 1950s and again from the late 1960s until now, when the nominal commitments of US policy toward Native Nations have been the acknowledgment of Tribal rights to self-governance. These periods are characterized by laws that ended prior assimilative policies and inaugurated processes for "recognizing" and "reorganizing" Tribal Nations, while later encouraging them to exercise their rights to self-determination by exerting greater control over the day-to-day operation of federally funded programs. While these policy eras express a greater commitment to Tribal sovereignty, they have more recently come under criticism for actually doing more to erode genuine Tribal self-governance. The critique is that they fail to genuinely acknowledge and be open to the decision-making authority of Tribal Nations over their own futures, while at the same time hiding behind virtuous-sounding policies the United States' role in continuing to deprive Tribal Nations of their rights (Bruyneel 2007; Coulthard 2014; Deloria and Lytle 1983).

In light of this, colonialism in the United States, Canada, Australia, and other settler nation-states has been described as uniquely committed to the elimination of Indigenous Nations (Veracini 2010, 2015; Wolfe 1999, 2006). And this is true "whatever settlers may say" (Wolfe 2006, 388). One of the founding theorists of settler colonialism, Australian anthropologist Patrick Wolfe, quotes Deborah Bird Rose when he writes that "to get in the way of settler colonization, all the native has to do is stay at home" (388). Given this, he argues:

> Settler colonialism has both negative and positive dimensions. Negatively, it strives for the dissolution of native societies. Positively, it erects a new colonial society on the expropriated land base—as I put it, settler colonizers come to stay: invasion is a structure not an event. (388)

This concept of settler colonialism has found fertile ground in Native American studies, Indigenous studies, and the anthropologies concerned with both. It discloses how and why struggles like the resistance of the Standing Rock Sioux Tribal Nation to the Dakota Access Pipeline arise not just when US policies are explicitly oriented to the elimination of Tribal Nations but also in periods when those policies proclaim US support for Tribal self-governance and economic development. Wolfe's theory contextualizes Indigenous resistance as a legitimate response both to overt acts of settler violence

and to the equally insidious settler impulse to "maintain the refractory im-
print of the native counterclaim," a perverse drive to cultivate an "'indigenous
aura' to reflect and justify the settler state's independence from what was the
mother country" (Wolfe 2006, 389).

In a similar vein, historian Philip Deloria (1998) describes this refraction
as the kind of "playing Indian" on display from the earliest days of the US's
pre-revolutionary era into the present. It is evident in the acts of colonial reb-
els in the Massachusetts Colony, who disguised themselves as Mohawks and
destroyed tea shipments from the United Kingdom in what is now known as
the Boston Tea Party. But it is also present in the seemingly more benign appropriations by the Boy Scouts of America and its ersatz Indian themes, which
arose at the very same time that US policies were lashing Native Peoples with
the deepest cuts of forced assimilation. And it continues in the various mas-
cot controversies that continue to embroil sports culture in the United States
(King and Springwood 2001). A great irony of the interest that non-Native
individuals and institutions have long displayed for Native Nations and their
norms, knowledge, and relations is that their interest has almost always come
at the expense of Indigenous Peoples themselves.

The irony is no less dramatic, and the appropriation no less serious, when
the "playing Indian" is less obvious. For example, some of the theoretical and
analytic apparatuses I use in this book are schools of thought whose unique
efflorescence can be at least partly traced to the norms, knowledge, and relations gained from early Euro-American encounters with Native Nations and
their theories of sociality and governance.[4]

I am not the first to notice these influences nor to acknowledge their erasure. In *Native Pragmatism: Rethinking the Roots of American Philosophy*, Scott L.
Pratt (2002) argues that philosophical pragmatism owes its reputation as a
"distinctively American philosophy" (xvii) as much to lessons learned from Native American rejections of non-Native encroachment as to rejections of European political and conceptual traditions. Pratt argues that the lessons learned
from Native Americans are precisely those of what he calls an "indigenous attitude" (38) formed in the crucible of engaged response to the ethnocentric chauvinisms of European thought of the day. This attitude sought to replace European emphases on objectivism, certitude, and progressive rationalism with
perspectives that bear a striking resemblance to Indigenous intellectual principles, like the Narraganset concept of *wunnégin*, that emphasize practical ethics,

---

4. My approach to the study of law and society is deeply informed by American legal realism (ALR), and my pragmatic approach to the study of language owes just as much to American
philosophical pragmatism (from which ALR springs).

epistemological diversity, and the generation of meaning and understanding as immanent in the relational engagements of everyday life (Pratt 2002). Pratt is clear that the influence was not direct. Rather, he traces how these concepts and the works of Indigenous leaders such as Teedyuscung (Delaware) and Sagoyewatha (Seneca) overtly influenced early Euro-American thinkers and political actors such as Roger Williams and Benjamin Franklin. Later, this influence reached the writings of nineteenth-century figures such as Jane Johnston Schoolcraft (Ojibwe), John Ross (Cherokee), and Lydia Marie Child. It was through these genealogies that certain notions of the ethics of an everyday relational epistemology, and the ideas of practical, autochthonous governance it underwrote, came to bear intellectual fruit in thinkers that include William James, Charles Peirce, and John Dewey, among others (Pratt 2002).

As I show in greater depth in chapter 6, a similar influence can be traced through the work of the American legal realist Karl Llewellyn. His groundbreaking work on the "law-ways" of the Northern Cheyenne was completed at nearly the same time as he led the charge in a legal realist–inspired reform of US commercial law through the drafting of the Uniform Commercial Code. For scholars like Llewellyn, whether they recognized it or not, their "playing Indian" proved to be serious business indeed.

To the extent that my own thinking in this book, and in other writings, has been inspired by the insights of both philosophical pragmatists and legal realists, one might say that my attention to the commitments of CWS is not only unsurprising but long past due. For whatever may have come before, I myself cannot escape the debts I owe to Indigenous theories and the relations invariably formed in and through those theories that have come down to me. Nor should I. For what kind of relations are adequately compassed merely by acknowledging their history? Recognizing the debts owed to Indigenous thought, as I do here, may be a necessary first step, but recognition in and of itself is inadequate to the ongoing relations that these and other engagements inaugurated long ago.

Indeed, by itself, simply "recognizing" Indigenous Peoples and their impacts on US society may actually work to further harm the very Native Nations that settler colonial actors think they are honoring. That at least has been the lesson from those critical theorists who have extended this insight into the various modes of settler colonial misappropriation. This is particularly true for those who seem to hold out the promise of productive political relations with Native Nations but in fact preserve and extend settler dominion over them. Yellowknives Dene political scientist Glen Coulthard (2014) and anthropologist Elizabeth Povinelli (2002, 2011) have argued that even the acts and policies of so-called political recognition do more to eliminate genuine relationality with Tribal Nations than promote them.

Coulthard directs his critique at Canada's prevailing policies toward Indigenous First Nations that, in the wake of several landmark political and legal confrontations, were officially enshrined in a 1982 amendment to the Canadian Constitution as the "recognition" of "existing aboriginal and treaty rights." Thirteen years later, Canada extended this policy by declaring its recognition of First Nations' "inherent rights to self government" more generally (Coulthard 2014).

For Coulthard, the problem with these policies lies in the ways the settler state maintains control of when and under what criteria its recognition of Indigenous rights will be granted (Coulthard 2014, 30). He takes aim at the defenders of the Canadian multiculturalist recognition regime for not understanding how notions of equality and dialogue—on which recognition is premised—fail to account for the ways in which the material structures of settler colonialism remain the taken-for-granted benchmarks of what counts as productive evidence of "legitimate" Indigenous self-governance. Indigenous norms, knowledge, and relations that are not consonant with theories of labor, capital, and market rationalism at best will be ignored or deemed unworthy of recognition and at worst will be met with violence. As he writes, insofar as "recognition" is treated as "something that is ultimately 'granted' or 'accorded' a subaltern group or entity by a dominant group or entity . . . [it] prefigures its failure to significantly modify, let alone transcend, the breadth of power at play in colonial relationships" (30–31).

Even so, scholars of indigeneity have also noted that Indigenous Peoples have not stood pat or otherwise capitulated to the ever-constricting binds that settler colonialism seeks to impose on their sovereignty and the normative orders that undergird it (Barker 2017; Byrd 2011; P. Deloria 2004; Lyons 2010; Rifkin 2010, 2017; Riley 2007a, 2007b; A. Simpson 2014; L. Simpson 2017; Vizenor 1999, 2008; Weiss 2018). One of the most compelling forms of this argument in recent years, as it applies to the North American context, comes from Khanawà:ke Mohawk scholar Audra Simpson's concept of "indigenous refusal" (A. Simpson 2014). In her book *Mohawk Interruptus: Political Life across the Borders of Settler States*, Simpson gives an account of the ways in which Native Nations contest settler colonial intrusions and erasures not just in moments of spectacular conflict but also in everyday practices. These often move orthogonally to the cunning binaries of legal recognition and elimination that have characterized settler state policies toward them. As she writes:

> Refusal comes with the requirement of having one's political sovereignty acknowledged and upheld, and raises the question of legitimacy for those who are usually in the position of recognizing: What is their authority to do so? Where does it come from? Who are they to do so? (A. Simpson 2014, 11)

Simpson's concept of refusal offers an important corrective to those who might read critiques of settler colonialism as painting a fatalistic picture of the totalizing abjection of Indigenous subjectivities and agency. This is true whether those refusals appear in the galvanizing moments of confrontation, like those deadly ones that took place in 1990 between Indigenous activists and Quebecois provincial police (A. Simpson 2014),[5] or in the quiet evasions that First Nations make to overly intrusive inquiries from anthropologists. They even emerge in how Simpson chooses to represent the lives of her fellow band members; that is, in many ways, as utterly the same as many other contemporary, semiurban communities across Canada and yet as unapologetically and irreducibly Indigenous (A. Simpson 2007, 2014).

Refusals, Simpson thus argues, are not just responses to settler colonial domination and dispossession but also generative acts, large and small, that do more than stop those efforts in their tracks. They indeed upset settler colonial logics of recognition and representation, whether anthropological, legal, or otherwise. But Indigenous acts of refusal orient their interruptions beyond resistance and toward a kind of Indigenous *insistence*. There is a necessity and import to Indigenous normative orders, epistemological presumptions, and relational calculi, and they bring their own authoritative logics to contemporary sociopolitical moments. In an earlier publication, Simpson describes the ethnographic encounters that ground her theory of refusal:

> The people I interviewed do know the different forms of recognition that are at play, the simultaneities of consciousness that are in work in any colonial encounter (including those with me) in the exercising of rights and that knowledge translates into the "feeling side" of recognition. . . . What is theoretically generative about these refusals? They . . . tell us something about the way we cradle or embed our representations and notions of sovereignty and nationhood; and they critique and move us away from statist forms of recognition. (A. Simpson 2007, 78)

For Simpson, Indigenous refusals neither ignore the discourses of recognition politics that shape Native lives in settler colonial contexts nor are dictated by the ways in which they serve as responses to settler colonialism. Refusals are also more than a move in a language game whose rules are set by the settler state. They serve as the productive limit of settler colonialism by both speaking back to and exceeding the terms by which the United States "grants" recognition and insists upon defining indigeneity.

---

5. It was a dispute between the Kanehsatàt:ke band of Mohawk and the leaders of the town of Oka, who wanted to develop a golf course on a deeply sacred place in which many Mohawk ancestors had been buried.

In this way, while refusals do not entirely eschew the discourse and dia-logue of Native-settler relations, they also do not embrace their presumptive terms either. They instead are used for opportunities to work toward setting a different ground on which to meet and the terms up for consideration in those meetings. By extension, I argue, this includes the government-to-government relationship. Refusals might be thought of as generative limits, in the spirit of Chickasaw critical theorist Jodi Byrd. Borrowing from Choctaw novelist and scholar LeAnne Howe, Byrd explains that *haksuba* in Choctaw "can mean . . . to be stunned with noise, confused, deafened" and "a cacophony, whether joy-ous or colonialist," and, quoting Howe herself, as a "chaos [that] occurs when Indians and non-Indians bang their heads together in search of cross-cultural understanding" (Byrd 2011, xxvii). But as Byrd is careful to point out, haksuba is ". . . a generative, creative force, or a potentially destructive one" (xxvii).

Oftentimes, the cacophonies raised by Native acts of engaged refusal fail to achieve unequivocal non-Native appreciation of Indigenous Peoples rights and claims. This failure resembles the ironies of Indigenous expressive cre-ativity that Ga-waabaabignakaag Anishinaabeg/White Earth Nation Ojibwe critical theorist Gerald Vizenor (2019) has recently argued remain utterly lost on the Euro-American researchers who see Native discourses and narratives as "specimens" to be collected. This orientation blinds these scholars to the manner in which, in the actual moments of their performative production, these Indigenous speech acts (like storytelling, but also political and ritual oratory) point to and comment on, often ironically, the specific historical and political contexts in which they emerge and to which they contribute. And this is true whether those moments involve back-and-forths between Indigenous interactants, or in Native engagements with their non-Native counterparts, or both. In all these contexts, when Euro-American interlocutors analyze In-digenous speech acts primarily as instances of a genre of "Native" talk—that is, objects of their observational judgments and evaluative matrices—without also reckoning with their historical and political specificity, their significance for the Indigenous People speaking them in the real-time moments of their everyday lives are lost to non-Native ears. Thus it can often appear that Native speech acts fail to hit their marks when it is assumed that non-Indigenous apprehension of them is their primary goal.

Following Byrd (2011), it is not clear that these cacophonous speech acts are only successful if they achieve non-Native apprehension. While that may be one goal of their enactment in face-to-face engagements, it is not the only or even primary one. Indeed, if Native Nation actors and advocates have learned anything over the years of experiencing US officials' promis-ing care but delivering crisis, it is to expect non-Native misapprehension and even active "unrecognition"—an affirmative effort at making Native Nations unrecognizable (see chapter 5). And yet Native Nations persist in engaging them anyway. Native acts of engagement might thus be thought of in the terms that Scott Richard Lyons (2010; Ojibwe/Mdewakanton Lakota) calls "x-marks." Taking his inspiration from the inherently ambiguous x-marks by which Native Nations' leaders signed treaties with the United States, he considers the manifold ways in which Native Nations and their members put their imprimatur on the world in everyday acts of engagement that are necessarily indeterminate. Describing the x-mark as a "sign of consent in a context of coercion" (1), Lyons explains:

> The x-mark signifies power and a lack of power, agency and a lack of agency. And yet there is always the prospect of slippage, indeterminacy, unforeseen consequences, unintended results; it is always possible, that is, that an x-mark could result in something good. Why else, we might ask, would someone bother to make it? (3)

I wonder if the Hopi theory of CWS—particularly when extended to Hopi engagements with non-Native actors and when considering acts of other Indigenous Nations' engagement with settler colonial agencies—is calling for a kind of haksuba or x-mark. Can acts of CWS be thought of as modes of Indigenous refusal that do not require Indigenous removal from the scenes of engagement with the settler state but rather demand just the opposite? That is, could cooperation without submission be understood as acts of official Native-US engagement that insist on the kind of stunning noise (Byrd 2011), interruption (A. Simpson 2014), ironic inversion (Vizenor 2019), or mark of assent that does not connote agreement but, first and foremost, an enduring Indigenous *insistence*?

Perhaps, even further, could we posit that when Native Nation actors and officials are engaged in acts of CWS, they are working out relations to reshape both their own futures and those of their non-Native counterparts? Could they be undertaking a version of what Joseph Weiss has described as the everyday practices of "future-making" (Weiss 2018, 184)? For example, Weiss engaged with Haida citizens and leaders undertaking protests and producing public art in the settler Canadian context, but also in their quieter moments of fishing and family time. In both cases, he argued, their actions and orientations showed them constituting their present activities in temporal arcs of meaning and possibility that "engaged in processes of imagining, negotiating, and constituting these possible futures both for themselves and the larger social world(s) of settler Canada" (14). Could this be true of acts of CWS emergent in Native Nation–US engagements as well?

In the chapters that follow, I suggest that this is precisely the potential in extending the notion of CWS as a commitment to Indigenous juris-diction. It helps explain why Native leaders and actors insist on these engagements even when US agents, again and again, make the ends Native Nations seek out such engagements unrecognizable. It helps explain the failures that repeatedly result from these meetings when US agents, whatever their intentions or claims in working with Native Nations, insist on viewing Indigenous norms, knowledge, and relations as objects in their settler evaluation rather than as the foundation of Indigenous juris-diction. Finally, it gives a unique perspective on the ethical demands always already imposed on those of us whose theoretical and analytic commitments are informed by schools of thought (like American legal realism and American philosophical pragmatism) that fail to reckon with the accrued debts our theories owe to Native intellectual traditions from which they draw and the Nations that strive to continue to enact them today. By extending a theory of CWS as a commitment to the Indigenous juris-dictions of all Native Nations, we give greater complexity to our understanding of why Native Nations and their actors continue to engage with their non-Native counterparts. These are not acts of capitulation but of self-determination. The impetus for their undertaking and the efficacy by which they are judged is not premised on whether non-Natives can understand why Indigenous Peoples take them up. Even still, we who are non-Native can and must endeavor to open our futures (Weiss 2018) to the ongoing relations that Native Nations nonetheless invite us into through them and the obligations that we thereby owe in return.

In this spirit, I offer the following interlude, which relates two experiences I had in my work with officials from the Hopi Tribal Nation. I think they exemplify how Tribal officials engage their non-Native counterparts in acts of cooperation without submission, acts that become discernable in the details of everyday practices of Tribal governance. Both were experiences that, upon later reflection, I think were the moments that I first started to understand the implications and applications of my mentor Emory's notion of cooperation without submission.

*

INTERLUDE: READING THE SIGNS FROM THE HOPI CULTURAL PRESERVATION OFFICE

A version of the Burger King logo was taped to a wall in the Hopi Cultural Preservation Office (HCPO). Stewart Koyiyumptewa, the current program manager of the HCPO and also its former archivist, had found a digital

FIGURE 1.1. Sign at HCPO, Hopi Tribal Headquarters, Kykotsmovi, AZ. Sign created by Stewart Ko-yiyumptewa. Photo by Hannah McElgunn, used with permission.

version of the logo of the fast-food chain on the internet and pasted it into a word processing document. After printing it out, he used a red marker to draw an *X* through it. Surrounding the logo, he typed: "HCPO Motto: This Isn't Burger King. You Can't Have It Your Way!" The sign was meant to humorously but forcefully invoke, with an ironic twist, Burger King's popular catchphrase, "Have It Your Way," from the 1980s and 1990s ad campaign (figure 1.1).

Leigh Kuwanwisiwma, who served as the director of the HCPO for nearly three decades before retiring in 2018, had mentioned this sign during several meetings I had with him over the years. He always brought it up within the context of relating yet another story of a non-Native scholar or government official who had come to the Tribe expecting to get easy approval for this or that project involving Hopi cultural resources, only to have their request rejected. Since the early 1990s, the HCPO has been responsible for governing research on the Hopi reservation about Hopi culture and society to ensure both that such research is conducted in conjunction and collaboration with the Hopi Tribe and that the researcher advocates for Hopi cultural property rights off the reservation as well.

To this end, and pursuant to Hopi Tribal laws,[6] the HCPO has been the lead agency in the Hopi Tribal government charged with representing the Tribe in negotiations on the management and repatriation of Hopi material and immaterial cultural property under the control of non-Native universities, institutions, and agencies. Since the early 2000s, it has represented the Tribe in a host of engagements with its federal counterparts pursuant to the

6. Hopi Tribal Resolution H-70-94, May 23, 1994.

United States regulatory regimes of "meaningful tribal consultation,"[7] an expansion of a process inaugurated under the Native American Graves Protection and Repatriation Act of 1990.[8] Today, through executive orders, presidential memoranda, and a slew of federal regulations, all federal agencies are required to develop and deploy procedures for "regular and meaningful consultation and collaboration with tribal officials in the development of federal policies that have tribal implications."[9]

As one might expect, however, notwithstanding the rules and laws governing these official engagements and consultations, HCPO officials have often found that what their non-Native counterparts expect from consultation is little more than a Hopi rubber stamp for the plans that they have drawn up and are often peeved when the Hopi refuse to give it. Hence, the "You Can't Have It Your Way" sign. It reminds non-Native officials and others (including researchers like me) seeking to consult with the HCPO that they should never assume cooperation simply because some government agency (or affiliated institution) or individual is on a tight timeline or considers their own project worthwhile or performs minimum outreach to the HCPO.

Indeed, the sign presumes that a researcher has already done the minimal work of physically visiting HCPO's office in person. Many do not even do this; it's not a trip many non-Hopi would make if they weren't meaning to go specifically to the Aboriginal territory of the Hopi People, in the remote high desert mesas of Northeastern Arizona. To get there, you first have to travel more than the one hundred odd miles northeast of the city of Flagstaff, Arizona, crossing the southwestern corner of the Navajo Reservation along BIA Route 2, which is a single-lane road that takes you from the hamlet of Leupp to Kykotsmovi, Arizona, the home of the headquarters of the Hopi Tribal Nation's government. To gain entrance to the Honanie Administration Building, a 1970s cinderblock building, you must log in with the security guard at the main doors. But you are admitted only if someone already expects you, or the guard knows you from prior visits.

After you are granted access, you wind your way across dusty linoleum floors and past fluorescent-lit office cubicles. You arrive at the director's office in the section designated for the Department of Natural Resources, of which it is a branch. If Leigh Kuwanwisiwma (the director at the time of my visits)

7. Executive Order 13,175, Consultation and Coordination with Tribal Governments, 65 Fed. Reg. 67,249 (November 6, 2000).

8. Native American Graves Protection and Repatriation Act, Pub. L. No. 101-601, 25 U.S.C. 3001 et seq., 104 Stat. 3048 (1990).

9. Executive Order 13,175, 65 Fed. Reg. 67,249 (November 6, 2000).

was in, his door would be open. But he was often out doing the business of the HCPO, and so stopping by on the fly, as I often did, was no guarantee I would find him, or Stewart Koyiyumptewa, or anyone else, and so I would have to come back another day. Travel plans must account for these possibilities, and you either stay in the home of Hopi friends and colleagues or you manage to secure one of the few rooms at the only motel nearby. However, there are few vacancies as it is filled with tourists or other researchers or visiting government officials who are better than you at making motel reservations.

On the day I first saw the sign, Kuwanwisiwma was in Flagstaff for a meeting with representatives of the Museum of Northern Arizona about the status of the collection of Hopi cultural property being held for the Tribe in a repository for repatriated materials. Most of the other HCPO staff were also gone, having traveled southeast to the Tonto National Forest for a consultation with representatives of the US Forest Service concerning the impact that a proposed US policy change would have on Hopi ancestral sites in the forest (discussed in chapter 4). While the old saw that "all politics is local" certainly applies for the Hopi, it is best to remember that their presence in the region reaches back centuries longer than any other extant people, and demands their maintenance and care for ancestral sites that blanket a territory spanning hundreds of miles in every direction. Thus, for HCPO staff, the politics of the local—and the demands that they engage regularly with non-Native agencies and institutions that exert power over parts of it—means a lot of time away from the office.

When I finally saw the "You Can't Have It Your Way!" sign, it reminded me of an event I had recently participated in with members of the HCPO, this time on a consultative trip to the Field Museum of Natural History in Chicago. While there, I happened upon a different form of Hopi signage hanging in an unlikely place. I was in the Field's cavernous underground storage facility: the fluorescent-lit and climate-controlled Collections Research Center. This is where the museum keeps its three-hundred-thousand-plus holdings of Native North American material culture, second in the world by a non-Native institution. The first is the Smithsonian Institution in Washington, DC. The Field's collection includes a substantial collection of Hopi material, most collected in the late nineteenth and early twentieth centuries. With nearly thirty-four thousand accessioned items, it is the largest for any Native Nation in the Field's collection.

It was when we arrived in the section with the Hopi materials that I became aware of what I could not see as much as what I could. It turns out that on a prior visit, the HCPO had respectfully insisted that, as the first step in repatriation negotiations, the vast majority of the Hopi materials be removed

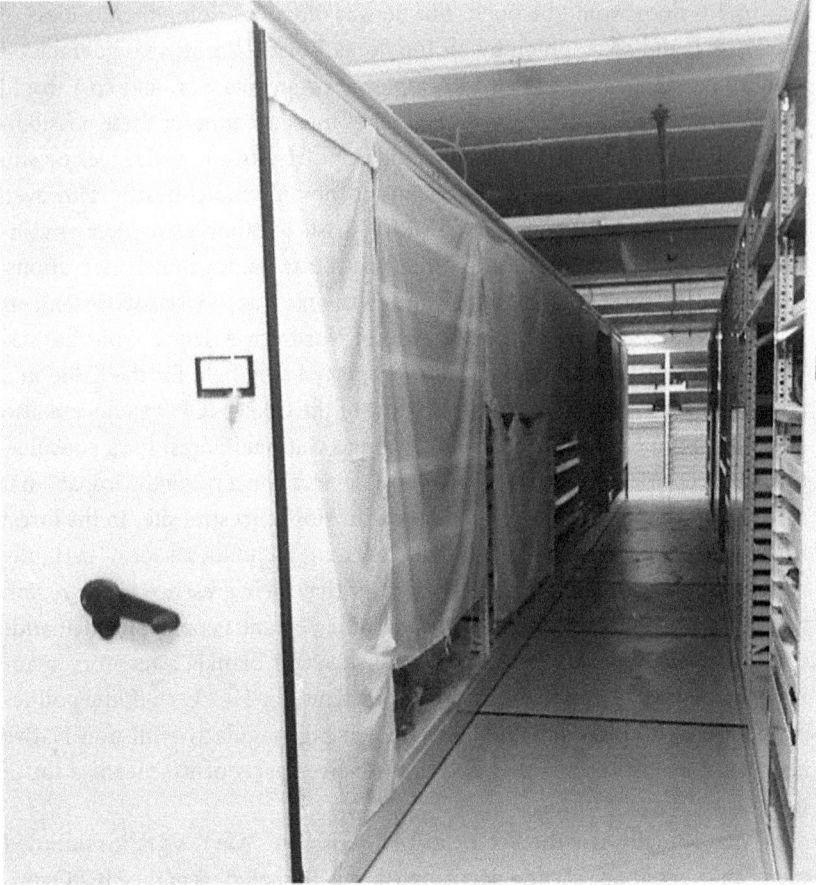

FIGURE 1.2. Hopi prayer feather, Field Museum Collections Resource Center, Chicago, IL. Photo by Justin B. Richland, used with permission of the Hopi Cultural Preservation Office and the Field Museum of Natural History.

from casual sight and contact by museum visitors and staff. And this applied not just to the items on display, but even those that remained in storage. And the Field complied. Today, the items still sit on their shelves but behind loosely hanging sheets of white fabric. In some instances, the materials are in locked cabinets. While the concealment of Hopi material in and of itself might seem remarkable, I was also aware of the things that the Hopi clearly wanted people to see. In particular, I noted a single downy feather, likely from a turkey, dangling from a bright white cotton string, affixed to a large move-able storage case, in place of what would have most likely been a descriptive placard noting this case as holding Hopi material (figure 1.2). The sign that

I saw is a Hopi prayer feather, a *paho*, which is tied by Hopi to any variety of human and nonhuman actors that animate Hopi life, and into which its maker would have quietly spoken his intentions for the good health, well-being, and hope for right relations between the person placing the prayer and the being receiving it.

When I asked how the feather got there, I was told that HCPO officials had left it on a previous visit. I was also told the paho had not been recorded or otherwise accessioned as a part of the museum's official collection of Hopi

FIGURE 1.2. (*continued*)

material. This struck me as important; instead of becoming part of the Field's order of things, it is allowed to abide on its own terms, a symbol of Hopi normative orders and commitments. It is a marker of significance, expressing the Hopi's ongoing, Indigenous *insistence*. As Audra Simpson (2014) explains of her experiences with her Khanawà:ke Mohawk relatives, this Hopi prayer feather is a generative refusal right there in bowels of the Field Museum, at the very heart of the settler colonial logics that long ago wanted to turn their norms, knowledge, and relations into objects of scientific evaluation. The unaccessioned prayer feather flips those efforts on their head, at least partly, and instead gives voice to a Hopi claim that returns Hopi norms, knowledge, and relations to their place as the foundational elements of their Indigenous juris-diction. It explains what you need to understand about what resides on the shrouded shelves and in the locked cabinets, and about the relationship to these items that the Hopi feel obliged to enact. Much like the "You Can't Have It Your Way!" sign, understanding the significance of the paho requires that you already have some familiarity, even if cursory, with the HCPO and its work with the Field Museum. But you would also have to have some familiarity with Hopi culture and society more generally. You would need some experience and appreciation for how their duties and obligations to the beings on those shelves also express values and norms about the sacred and the secret, what can be known and what must remain not-known, and the expectations of ongoing obligations of respect and mutuality that go with all who would come together for the care and handling of those beings.

I discuss these two signs, the "You Can't Have It Your Way!" in the director's office and the prayer feather in the Field, here in relation to the work that the HCPO engages in with non-Native individuals, and federal agencies, and institutions that seek access to, or control of, Hopi material culture. Together, they speak to a nuanced orientation that the Hopi government, and Hopi generally, have always had toward settler colonial actors, institutions, and epistemological projects with which they have dealt since regular Hopi-US engagement began. Both signs speak, albeit in different registers, of a staunch insistence on the part of the HCPO to determine how Hopi culture, information, representation, and dissemination of knowledge should be accessed, and by whom. At the same time, both reveal a cooperative and collaborative impulse too. To say "you can't have it your way" does not foreclose all possibilities for engagement of Hopi on non-Hopi programs. And a paho hanging in the Field Museum is as much an invitation to right relations between the HCPO and those non-Natives immediately responsible for the care of the Hopi culture in their possession as it is a message to the beings being cared for.

*

The Problem of Cooperation, Even without Submission, in Native Nation–US Engagements

My experiences working with Native Nations other than Hopi have suggested to me that CWS and its unrecognizability by non-Natives appear to be operating in many Tribal engagements with the United States, and are exemplified in key moments in the history of those relations. This book is about the underlying Indigenous theories and practices that inform the ways in which Native Nation leaders choose to engage with non-Native agencies and institutions more generally.

Indeed, I find this idea resonates with a key insight made many years ago by Lakota Standing Rock Sioux scholar, critic, and leading activist for American Indian rights Vine Deloria Jr. In *Behind the Trail of Broken Treaties: An Indian Declaration of Independence* (1974), he argued that whatever else he and other advocates for Native Nations are calling for, they "are not seeking a type of independence that would create a totally isolated community with no ties to the United States whatsoever. On the contrary . . . the movement of today seeks clear and uncontroverted lines of political authority and responsibility for both tribal governments and the United States" (162).

Deloria's book was itself inspired by the events surrounding the weeklong Trail of Broken Treaties Caravan, in which over a thousand Native advocates and activists traversed the United States in October and November 1972, ending in Washington, DC, where they attempted to present the Nixon administration with their Twenty Points Position Paper (V. Deloria 1974). Among its twenty points, the paper called for the restoration of treaty-making between Native Nations and the United States, creation of commissions to oversee the drafting of new treaties, resubmission of treaties that were drafted but never ratified by Congress, and laws ensuring an "Indian right to interpret treaties" whenever the meanings of treaty provisions are in dispute (American Indian Movement 1972). Interestingly, in the online version of the text, under the document title, is a subtitle: "We want to have a new RELATIONSHIP with you . . . an HONEST ONE!" Though it is unclear whether this subtitle was part of the original text or a later addition, either way it lends credence to Deloria's argument, as well as to the arguments in this book, that so much of the advocacy for Native Nations' rights to sovereignty and self-determination is about rethinking relations with the United States, not severing them entirely.

Alas, the Nixon administration refused to accept the Twenty Points Position Paper. In response, about five hundred of the caravan participants occupied the offices of the Bureau of Indian Affairs in the Department of the Interior in protest. The damage done to federal property by the occupiers during the ensuing five-day standoff received national media attention. Unfortunately, explains Deloria, this attention largely "overshadowed the real issues of caravan—which were highlighted in the Twenty Points" (V. Deloria 1974, vii)—a problem that was only exacerbated when the response from the Nixon administration reflected a thorough "lack of understanding of the history of the relationship between the United States and . . . Indian tribes" (ix), particularly when it assumed that the Twenty Points Position Paper constituted a call for "a renunciation of citizenship . . . or secession" (vii).

This book considers the call for renewed and reinvigorated Tribal-US treaty-making relations that the Twenty Points Position Paper, and Deloria's reading of it, first highlighted. But it also explains how misunderstandings like those in the Nixon administration and the confrontations that ensued describe a recurring pattern—past and present—in the details of Tribal-US engagements. This book explores how the specific kinds of claims to sovereignty and relationality that Deloria writes about emerge not only in events such as the spectacular weeklong caravan in 1972, in the Pacific Northwest fish-ins of the early 1960s, in the American Indian Movement's occupation of Alcatraz in 1969, or in the incident at Wounded Knee in 1973, but also in the practices of everyday Tribal governance and engagement with US agencies.

It is well known that Deloria doubted that the efforts of those undertaking the work of Tribal governance, particularly in negotiations with the United States, could accomplish the real political changes needed to adequately support Native Nation self-determination (V. Deloria 1969). This skepticism holds true for various reasons. First, insofar as Native Nation engagements with the United States turn on whether or not the federal government acknowledges those with whom it is engaging as officially representing their Nation, Deloria rightly noted that the act of "recognizing some men as chiefs and refusing to recognize others" has long been a weapon in the ongoing US settler colonial drive to "divide and conquer" Native Nations (219). Second, he was also rightly concerned that the everyday work, and its quotidian approach to this or that policy, means that the overarching questions of sovereignty, self-determination, and rights claims never get fair airings. As he wrote, Tribal leaders' efforts "provided a consistent but ineffective voice against government policy—consistent because they maintained the validity of the tribe's national status . . . ineffective because they foreswore all recognized methods of raising the political issues" that needed raising (V. Deloria 1974, 28). Add to these specific concerns the fact that Tribal governments, like all governments everywhere, have always been susceptible to accusations of nepotism, cronyism, and self-dealing (e.g., Dombrowski 2001; Orr 2017; Wilkinson 1999), and we begin to see how complicated the assessment of the motivations of Tribal officials can be.

With this as a backdrop, there are thus admittedly a number of risks inherent in the project that unfolds in the pages that follow. In addition to the objections raised by Deloria and others after him (Orr 2017; Wilkinson 1999; cf. Wilkinson 2005), one might rightly object that I, as a non-Native scholar, am precisely not the person to represent the perspectives and commitments of Tribal actors and officials, many of whom can and do regularly speak on their own behalf. This is a fair criticism, and one to which my only response is that the analysis I am offering here is not, should not, and cannot be read to overwrite the perspectives, commitments, and positions that Indigenous actors caught up with the everyday work of Native-US engagements are actively undertaking. Nor does it claim to weigh in on the effectiveness of strategies of Indigenous engagement in the examples I describe throughout as instances of CWS. Such questions seem to me to tread too close to questions of rectitude and propriety that are for Tribal actors and those they represent to answer in the unfolding dialogues by which they work out the contours of their self-determination. They are not for non-Tribal members, and certainly not non-Natives, to decide, and I do not do so in this book.

Then there is the risk that in describing this Hopi theory of CWS, and in endeavoring to see how it might play out in other contexts of Tribal-US engagements, I am glossing over considerable cultural, social, and historical differences among the many Tribal Nations. Only 574 Tribes—a fraction of the total number in the United States—are acknowledged by the US government and thus share official government-to-government relationships. Each of these Tribes is deeply committed to its particular Tribal differences and distinctions and protects them vigorously (Rosser 2006). The applicability of theories of CWS across Tribes in this book is then also a reasonable criticism. However, my use of Hopi theories of sociopolitical action as a way to gain insight into the actions not only of Hopi Tribal representatives but also of others is not to erase the details of other Tribal practices but rather to raise awareness and invite closer engagement with them. I deploy an Indigenous theory of sociopolitical action not as an object of analysis but as the analytic framework itself. I hope that Hopi theories of cooperation without submission suggest the utility in approaching the everyday work of contemporary

Tribal governance, in the fullness and particularity with which that work always unfolds, and with the careful and sensitive attention it deserves. Failing to appreciate such work as an active, ongoing accomplishment of Tribal self-governance, however partial and open-ended, strikes me as yet another way to erase the agency and complexity of contemporary Tribal life.

Finally, there is the risk that in attending to the details of discourse and interaction that make up the everyday engagements between Tribal and US agents, notions of CWS paint a Pollyanna-ish picture of Tribal-US relations. It risks depicting these relations in a manner that ignores the harsher realities of some aspects of contemporary Tribal life and that still sees Indigenous Peoples suffering from poverty, early mortality, violent crime, and other indicators of precarity at three, four, and even five times the national average (Indian Health Services 2019; Perry 2004; Proctor et al. 2016). This does not even include the abjection, deprivation, and outright destruction that have been accomplished over the centuries-long history of these relations. There is thus a risk in undermining the difficult, dangerous, and courageous stands that individuals and group activists—from Tekoomsē ("Tecumseh," Shawnee) to Goyaałé ("Geronimo," Chiracaua) to the American Indian Movement to the activists at Standing Rock—have been forced to take to show the fundamental illegitimacy of settler colonial states like the United States, and the ultimate ineffectiveness that comes when Indigenous Nations endeavor to engage with them in any relations other than those of steadfast and enduring refusal. I would never want the words on these pages to be taken to ignore the suffering that Native Nations have endured under US laws and policies. Instead, and what I think is the underlying impulse undergirding Indigenous juris-dictions of CWS, is that Native *insistence*, past and present, has never been defined by, nor locked into, the terms of engagement set by the logics of settler colonialism. Instead it is founded on an Indigenous generativity that, however refracted through the shameful effects of federal mistreatment or otherwise distorted by the non-Native efforts at making them unrecognizable, nonetheless perdures. And this too is true, to again paraphrase Patrick Wolfe, "whatever settlers may say" (Wolfe 2006, 388).

A Linguistic Anthropological Approach to Law: Juris-diction

My approach to the promise and peril of Native Nation–US engagements as sites for the enactment of a domain of Indigenous authority grounded on principles of CWS comes from my background as a linguistic anthropologist and scholar of legal language. The methods and theories in which I have been trained start from the truism that Robin Conley (2016) noted: "Language is simply what law is made of" (6). The most sacred legal edicts (such as the US Constitution or a judge sentencing a criminal defendant to death) and the most pedestrian (such as when a cop lets a speeding driver off with a warning) are always, at bottom, linguistic accomplishments.

But there is something deeply foundational to the ways in which law's power and authority is operative in the details of legal language. As Conley, O'Barr, and Riner (2019) have explained, "[T]he abstraction we call [legal] power is at once the cause and effect of countless linguistic interactions taking place every day at every level of the legal system" (15). As such, they and others have argued that to understand the exercise of actual legal power and authority requires we take seriously moments of legal engagement and what gets accomplished in and through the observable communicative details of their actual accomplishment (Conley, O'Barr, and Riner 2019; Mertz 1994, 2007; Richland 2013).

While there is more than one way to undertake this kind of research on and analysis of legal language, my experience working on these issues in the contexts of Native Nation law and governance leads me to focus on the language practices that constitute the granular interactional and textual backsand-forths that, like steps in a dance, incrementally build up in the actual engagements between Tribal leaders and their counterparts in US agencies. In those contexts, I have been struck not just by the ways in which US legal power and authority are expressed and enacted in the interactions of Native-US engagements but also by how often those discursive acts are met with expressions and enactments of Indigenous legal power and authority. What is more, while Native leaders and advocates appear in many ways to calibrate their contributions to those of their non-Native counterparts, the details of their talk and text actually show them insisting on the enduring vitality of their Indigenous norms, knowledge, and relations in ways that speak past them as well. It is this concatenation of interactional stances—Indigenous actors simultaneously signaling their cooperation with US regulatory practices of consultation and their refusal of the imposition of settler colonial legal logics in favor of enacting their own discourses of power and authority—that I describe as acts of cooperation without submission.

Importantly, I believe CWS explains what Native leaders and advocates are doing when they engage their non-Native counterparts and why they continue to do so despite knowing, after so many years of frustration, that US agents are likely to make Indigenous cooperation in these moments unrecognizable, and to Native Nations' disproportionate detriment. I believe that when understood in light of the details of actual consultative interactions, CWS is best understood as the discursive enactment of a domain of Indigenous authority that endures whether or not settler colonial actors recognize it. It is a domain premised on Indigenous norms, knowledge, and relations that are neither reducible to the logics of US legal power nor assailable by those who would enact that power. Indeed, CWS is approachable only by those willing to coordinate their actions in light of them. It is this quality of the talk and text that constitute CWS I therefore foreground by describing them as contributing to enactments of *juris-diction*, and it is to this notion I now briefly turn.

For me, juris-diction derives its analytic value from the role that language plays in the specific execution of a legal institution's claim to and performance of its authority. It is a play on the notion of jurisdiction, whose conventional meaning in law concerns the breadth, reach, and articulation of a given legal body's power and authority vis-à-vis other institutions in the system to which it belongs, or between one state legal system and another. In its most familiar use, the modern legal notion of jurisdiction in Euro-American law carries with it a reference to some geospatial expanse, a territory over which the laws of the nation-state (or some subnational or seminational component thereof) are understood to be in force. There is also another sense of jurisdiction in modern Anglo-American law that concerns the *kinds* of issues and types of persons over which the law has the authority to act. At least in the United States, this type of jurisdiction is partly a product of the fact that the federal government is a limited government arising from a federation of the states, each with its own laws. But it is also the product of a much longer history of English common law, going back to the sixteenth century, when the courts of common law (or Kings Court) were but one type of institutional authority to which English subjects could take their disputes. Other courts—such as those of canon law (involving Church doctrine), chancery (concerned with matters of equity), and admiralty (involving issues of international maritime laws)—operated alongside the Kings Court and were understood to have their own exclusive jurisdiction over different kinds of social persona, reckoning with different issues and searching for different ways of resolving them. Determining whether a litigant's complaint was a dispute at common law, equity, canon law, or the like involved a decision on not only which institutional authority could hear the case but also on the status of the person (as a subject of the crown, a member of this guild, or an adherent of that faith) and the different possible remedies this person, as a complainant, sought. It also meant that claimants could sometimes escape the judgment of one court by claiming the legitimate protection under the exclusive jurisdiction of another, such as when a subject could seek sanctuary under canon law by claiming in an ecclesiastical court that they were at risk of religious persecution by the application of a law enforced by the Kings Court (Coke [1644] 2002; Hale 1971).

Today, the common law systems of the United Kingdom and the United States have expanded to enfold some of these separate jurisdictions (such as equity, in the United States), while in general the rise of the modern "modular" nation-state has fundamentally smoothed over what historically was much more of a partial and often patchworked jurisdictional space-time (Cormack 2007; Dorsett and McVeigh 2012). Still though, remnants of this competition for jurisdiction continue to play out, at least partly, in how the jurisdictional lines and limits of courts are figured according to the "subject matter" at issue in a dispute. Such tensions can be felt in the variety of technical and rhetorical devices by which issues of jurisdiction are raised when courts are called upon to decide the scope of their authority (McVeigh 2007).

It is perhaps little surprise then that the notion of jurisdiction has been taken up by legal theorists more recently as both a mode and an object of critical inquiry into law's meaning-making and authoritative force by considering the details of its everyday operation and constitutive practices (Berman 2002; Cabatingan 2016; Constable 2014; Cormack 2007; Cover 1983; Dorsett and McVeigh 2012; Douzinas 2007; Ford 199; Kahn 2017, 2019; Maurer 2013; McVeigh 2007). These new theorists of jurisdiction offer a shared insight: it is in the details of legal praxes that governmental institutions in their lawmaking, -applying, and -executing capacities pose questions of their own authority to themselves, and to profound effect. It is precisely the practice orientation in the new jurisprudence of jurisdiction that I believe offers a way of thinking about how the use of language operates at the heart of law's macrosociological power and authority generally, and in Native-US engagements specifically.

Sociolinguist Émile Benveniste (1973) provides an etymology of the word "jurisdiction" as combining the Latin roots for law (*iuris*) and speech (*dictio*) in a way that both points up the performative, relational character of legal speech (speaking the law) and makes reference to the normative, informational content of that speech (law's speech). For contemporary scholars, this double sense of jurisdiction suggests the reflexive qualities by which law (like and through language) is spoken into existence not only in foundational legal speech acts, such as preambles of constitutions, but also in more mundane legal speech moments, such as when litigants petition a court to decide on its authority to hear their case, or in the opening statements of legislation, regulatory opinions, or executive orders that recite boilerplate language. It is in such moments that the scope and force of law, as constituted of language that speaks its performative authority into existence (what might be called *jurisdiction*, to foreground its conceptualization as law-language-in-use), presupposes its power generally (that is, it has some power over something) and asks after the particular limits of that power as it may apply to the case at hand (Cormack 2007).

The notion of legal language as *juris-diction* thus offers a useful corrective to exclusively macrosociological or abstract theories of law and legal power, especially those of sovereignty, such as in the political theological works of Giorgio Agamben (1998, 2005) and Carl Schmitt (2006). Both have gained significant attention of late. But where these political theological approaches to the question of sovereignty focus on the essence of sovereign power, they tend to reproduce a distinction between constitutional moments and the practices of everyday legal language. What a theory of *juris-diction* reveals is that maintaining the distinction between these two modes of constitutive legal power is actually part of the way in which legal actors use legal language in their everyday work to simultaneously enact the sovereign authority of the state institutions they participate in and mask the otherwise breathtaking nature of their efforts as just the ho-hum operation of routine legal processes.

Bradin Cormack (2007), a scholar of law and literature who writes on English literature from the period of modern common law's nascency, captures the matter nicely when he explains that his work is an endeavor "to resist the terms of a conversation . . . that has made sovereignty seem more stable than it is" (9). For him, "jurisdiction helps counter the almost irresistible tendency to make sovereignty have meaning only as political theology, by making it instead, as the real effect of a more mundane process of administrative distribution and management" (9).

When understood as *juris-diction* (see Constable 2010), the notion reveals how language practices are central not only to legal action but also to the broadest claims of the sovereign authority law presupposes and entails. By attending instead to juris-diction, I argue, analyses of the production of sociolegal power and authority are redirected toward understanding sovereignty as an active undertaking, and moreover one that is getting (re)constituted in the unfolding, unstable pragmatics of the present. Through the notion of *juris-diction*, sociolegal scholars can analyze everyday instances of legal discourse and text in which contingencies of lawmaking are laid bare when legal actors actively engage in wrangling over the scope and content of the authority of the legal institution with which they are caught up. As such, it makes possible the potentiality of legal authority as not yet settled and moreover as embedded within and against a field of other sources of authority. The scope and extent of sovereign power imagined through moments of legal language as juris-diction are hence always pointing to its limits and what may exceed those limits.

Juris-diction turns analyses away from questions about the *source* of legal authority and instead toward questions about the *scope* of legal institutions' and actors' authority over a specific case under consideration. It orients attention to quotidian matters of everyday legal texts, discourses, and practices. This reveals both the lawmaking by actors in legal institutions and how that lawmaking is elided behind what is described as the "merely" procedural and doctrinal applications of well-established legal praxes.

Indeed, analyzing the authority of legal institutions as a kind of jurisdiction reveals how that authority is produced even when interlocutors decline to exercise legal power over a particular case. When legal actors decide that the legal institution they engage with (through language) has no authority to act, the force, authority, and legitimacy of that legal institution is nonetheless enacted. That this is true suggests the extent to which the actors engaging with each other in and through the language of law are already speaking law's social force into existence, and in ways that simultaneously presuppose and make it unavailable for critical assessment of the source of that power. A theory of juris-diction reveals precisely the way in which, pragmatically speaking, law's power and authority are grounded (both in lawmaking and law-preserving capacities) in nothing but the language being used by legal actors. It is in this sense that Costas Douzinas (2007) writes that "the function of jurisdiction [is] . . . to bring the sovereign to life and give [it] voice and then . . . to conceal sovereignty by confounding its creative, performative aspect with the declaration of the law" (26).

A theory of Indigenous juris-diction reveals what is at stake in failing to attend to the way in which leaders of Native Nations, as representatives of sovereign nations, approach their interactions with US agents and continue to work out their ongoing government-to-government relations. Whether the "unrecognition" comes from the US counterparts in these meetings or from critics of Tribal engagement viewing them from a sidelong glance, failing to see Tribal engagements as enactments of Indigenous *juris-diction* through CWS misses the extent of what is at stake in proposed policy changes or regulatory decisions. Of course, policies change, regulatory decisions matter, and legal outcomes have real impacts. But as moments of Indigenous jurisdiction, they also stand for an invitation to much larger arcs of relation, and the meaningful contours of duty, obligation, and expectation that might be worked out in the unfolding government-to-government relationship between Tribal nations and the US settler state. And this is true whether the engagements take place in the seemingly routine details of a US Forest Service consultation or in the high-stakes discussions with the Office of Federal Acknowledgment about a Tribal petition for federal recognition. It is true in the face-off between Tribal leaders forcefully but respectfully defending their treaty-based land rights against US officials pressuring them to cede these rights. And it is true in the arcana of the interpretation of the tax code as it applies to Tribal development projects (all discussed in later chapters). As I endeavor to show in these and other contexts, Tribal leaders' choices to engage or not, to refuse or accede, are better understood when seen through the lens of the knowing, norming, and relating that constitutes Indigenous jurisdictions of CWS.

Outline of the Book

This book is divided into four parts. Part I includes the introduction, this chapter, and chapter 2, which offers an overview of the history of the laws and policies governing Tribal-US relations and the meaning that Tribal actors have given to their engagements with the United States. This overview, and the specific attention paid in that chapter to the enduring ambiguity that attends Tribal Nations' political status vis-à-vis the United States as "domestic dependent nations,"[10] lays the groundwork for understanding how the everyday practices of Tribal actor engagements with their US counterparts might usefully be analyzed in light of the Hopi theory of cooperation without submission. This includes the promise and peril for Tribal Nations that have always attended these engagements.

Part II offers two chapters with deep consideration of the Hopi sociopolitical contexts and effects that inform and illuminate the political theory of cooperation without submission. In chapter 3, I show how Hopi norms of social ordering insist on a kind of dispersed authority, mutuality, and coordination among the different Hopi clans, which is premised on the idea that no one segment of Hopi society can claim legitimate knowledge or power over all the others. I then show how CWS, founded on Hopi theological traditions and rhetorical forms, has become a model for contemporary Hopi Tribal governance both in internal operations and in how Hopi leadership engages with the United States. I also suggest the way I think CWS might be thought of as Hopi sovereignty-in-the-making.

In chapter 4 I show how CWS unfolds in the details of a specific consultation I observed in summer 2013 between members of the Hopi Cultural Preservation Office and non-Native archaeologists representing the US Forest Service (USFS). In furtherance of the idea of CWS as Hopi sovereignty-in-action, accomplished through language and interaction, the juris-dictional dimensions of CWS are observed through a detailed analysis of how Hopi actors narrate the significance of the Hopi cultural properties that are the

10. *Cherokee Nation* at 2.

ostensive subject of the consultation. In particular, I argue that when the Hopi leaders describe the import of the sites that are currently in control of the USFS but are slated for a type of excavation to which the Hopi object, they are telling the story of the ways in which these sites were occupied historically, are occupied now, and the demands that both occupations make on the Hopi in the present. Skillfully representing the narrative time and space of their story to envelope the present storytelling moment, Hopi officers' discursive contributions actually push back against the USFS plans by enacting the very relations of respect and care that the Hopi want observed for those sites, and even invite the USFS to partner with them in maintaining that care. That is, they enact Hopi juris-dictions and then invite the Forest Service to adjust their own jurisdiction to theirs, and in a way that would allow for the type of CWS that is the hallmark of Hopi sovereignty-in-action.

Part III of the book, comprising chapters 5 and 6, moves away from the detailed analyses of Hopi engagements with US actors to evaluate the utility of extending CWS to other Tribal Nations in their everyday engagements with US agencies and other non-Native institutions. The chapters reveal that US agents show an abiding interest in discerning the norms, knowledge, and relations that constitute Indigenous law, politics, and everyday life. Yet in assessing the validity and significance of these norms, knowledge, and relations only through US settler colonial evidentiary criteria, the effect is to simultaneously undermine Indigenous self-determination and extend US jurisdiction over them. It is yet another example in the long history of non-Natives in the United States "playing Indian" (P. Deloria 1998), with US agents claiming an interest in Native *ways of being* but having less appreciation for the *persons* whose lives these ways animate. Both chapters focus on regulatory breakdowns that can be traced to US actors not understanding that Tribal representatives undertake these interactions as ongoing acts of CWS.

Chapter 5 considers the dire consequences that Tribal Nations face when US agents subsume the juris-dictional logics of Tribal norms, knowledge, and relations to the evidentiary evaluations of US regulatory processes. In this chapter, I consider the bitter ironies that take place when US agents not only fail to comprehend the contours of contemporary Tribal sovereignty but do so in ways that affirmatively make them "un-recognizable." By this I suggest something other than that these processes contribute to the erasure of Tribal nations and their juris-dictions. Instead, I argue that they miss them altogether, constituting instead a distorted and distorting picture of Tribal norms, knowledge, and relations that stands in their stead, one that is both measured by non-Native evaluative logics and invariably found to come up short. And all the while, US agents get to claim credit for engaging with Tribal nations in a government-to-government relationship. In the face of this, the norms, knowledge, and relations that contribute to the ways in which Tribes themselves enact their juris-dictions never stand a chance. I observed the tragic consequences of this process as it emerged in the real-time unfolding of an engagement between the leaders of a Tribal Nation and federal agents at the Office of Federal Acknowledgment (OFA), the agency tasked with determining whether Tribes are to be "acknowledged" by the United States as Nations. Both the office and its acknowledgment process have come under severe criticisms, leading to radical reforms five times in the OFA's thirty-year history. The most controversial regulatory requirements of the OFA's acknowledgment criteria turn on questions of what counts as the necessary relations among Tribal members sufficient to establish that they constitute a Tribal Nation, now and in the past. The final decision of the OFA permanently determines (in)eligibility for federal acknowledgment, and thus a government-to-government relationship with the United States. The net effect is that the settler colonial logics of relationality become the metrics for evaluating whether a Tribal Nation meets the criteria of a "state," including exercising normative authority over its members. In this specific example, the determination, which took the OFA decades to decide, is tragic for the Tribal petitioner, who in "failing" to meet the US criteria not only does not gain federal acknowledgment but experiences firsthand the ways in which their community and its juris-dictions are actively made un-recognizable by the process and the effects of that effort. Of course, none of this means that Tribal nations like VRTN or others engaging their US counterparts give up on their juris-dictions and the *insistence* in their Indigenous sovereignty they enact through it. And this is perhaps why they continue to seek out those engagements, and the government-to-government relationship more generally, even when that means participating in a federal acknowledgment process has been one of the most troubled regulatory regimes in federal Indian law, one whose troubles are likely to continue.

Chapter 6 extends the theory of Indigenous juris-diction and the ways it is made un-recognizable by non-Native officials in two ways, one analytically and one substantially. For the former, this chapter considers how Tribal norms, knowledge, and relations were made un-recognizable in a recent line-item amendment to the Indian Tribal Governmental Tax Status Act, a provision of the US tax code, hindering (or outright stopping) sorely needed major Tribal economic development projects.[11] The amendment added a regulatory

---

11. The Indian Tribal Governmental Tax Status Act of 1982 (Title II of Pub. L. No. 97-473, 966 Stat. 2605, 2607, as amended by Pub. L. No. 98-21, 97 Stat. 65, 87 [1983-1 CB 510, 511]), codified at 26 U.S.C. § 7871.

hurdle to Tribal governments that want to issue tax-exempt municipal bonds to potential investors for development projects, a barrier not imposed on non-Native municipalities.

The text of the amendment appeared neutral on its face and seemed to mirror similar language in other federal legislation that authorized federal agencies to treat Tribal Nations as states for the purpose of enacting certain regulatory requirements. But the amendment was the brainchild of a US congressman who staunchly opposed Tribal gaming. An analysis of the amendment's legislative history and actions taken by the congressman and other proponents to influence Internal Revenue Service regulatory rulings interpreting how the provision is applied to Tribal Nations reveals how the force and authority of legal texts can be influenced by the juris-dictional machinations that bring them into effect.

I highlight the effects of the Tribal Tax Status Act amendment by using a classic theory of sociolegal scholarship and analyzing the legislative text through its appropriation of Native American norms, knowledge, and relations. It shows how the early American legal realism of Karl Llewellyn, and in particular his theory of the so-called trouble case method and his application of it to the drafting of the Uniform Commercial Code,[12] owes a deep debt to Indigenous jurisdictions, and especially to the Northern Cheyenne Nation, whom he studied. That Llewellyn's scholarship continues to shape contemporary sociolegal understanding of the relationship between legal language and legal action, particularly around the analytic acuity of notions of "custom" and including the effects such concepts have on legislative texts and their drafting, only further reveals the enduring but still overlooked influence that Indigenous juris-dictions have on settler colonial law and science. Llewellyn's work has no direct bearing on the amendment in question, but I invoke it to foreground how an analytic approach using the influence of Indigenous juris-diction offers a unique angle from which to see how the amendment, and the extent to which its effects turn on an interpretation of the term "customarily," works to make un-recognizable contemporary Tribal Nations and their sovereignty.

I then substantially extend the theory of Indigenous juris-diction by discussing how Tribal officers at a conference I attended in 2009 wanted a way to counteract how the amendment defined what a Tribe could and could not be in ways that *claimed* a concern for Tribal norms, knowledge, and relations but actually *appropriated and evaluated* them for its own purposes. I argue that the Tribes' responses compelled not just refinements of relevant legal

---

12. Llewellyn led the UCC effort from its initiation in 1941 until his death in 1962.

discourses and their interpretations but also, and even more significantly, the creation of a community's meaning and knowing through defining what a Tribal Nation is for the purposes of US taxation principles.

Part IV is composed of one chapter, and it contains the summaries and conclusions from the preceding chapters. In chapter 7, I return to the ways in which cooperation without submission can be understood as a Hopi theory of political order, emergent from the Tribe's own traditions of power, knowledge, and authority. CWS can be seen in interesting ways in Hopi dealings with non-Natives, including, for example, Forest Service agents. I describe how this Hopi Indigenous theory might be extended to other Native Nations dealings with US settler colonial agencies, and how the failures of those engagements is attributable to the ways in which US agents are unable, or unwilling, to appreciate Native Nations' commitment to those normative, epistemological, and relational orders as expressions. of cooperation without submission.

2

Beyond Dialogue: A Brief History of Native-US Engagement

Introduction

In 2012 the National Congress of American Indians (NCAI)—the oldest and largest advocacy group for Native Nations in the United States—published a report on the status of US agencies' implementation of an executive order signed by President Bill Clinton on November 6, 2000: "Consultation and Coordination with Indian Tribal Governments."[1] That order, and a memorandum signed by President Barack Obama in 2009 meant to shore it up,[2] required all federal agencies to develop and implement protocols for "engaging in regular and meaningful consultation and collaboration with tribal officials in the development of Federal policies that have tribal implications."[3]

The NCAI report found that as of 2012, "several agencies had yet to fully implement their policies," despite being three years past the statutorily mandated deadline to do so. The NCAI nonetheless encouraged "all agencies . . . to implement comprehensive tribal consultation policies in a timely manner," but underscored the point in a manner that could also be read as arguing against Tribal consultation as an end in itself: "The fundamental request of the National Congress of American Indians . . . has been that the federal government go *beyond dialogue* and truly take action to meet its responsibilities to Indian Country" (National Congress of American Indians 2012, 4, emphasis added).

1. Executive Order 13,175, Consultation and Coordination with Tribal Governments, 65 Fed. Reg. 67,249 (Nov. 6, 2000).

2. Presidential Memorandum for the Heads of Executive Departments and Agencies on Tribal Consultation, 74 Fed. Reg. 57,881 (Nov. 5, 2009); see also Eitner 2014; Routel and Holth 2013.

3. Executive Order 13,175, 65 Fed. Reg. 67,279.

This was not the first time I had heard this demand from Native leaders that the United States go "beyond dialogue." It was not even the first time I had heard this in reference to Tribal consultation. I was at the annual conference of the NCAI in October 2009 when it was announced that President Obama planned to sign the memorandum on Tribal consultation. The conference was held in the blessedly air conditioned Palm Springs Convention Center, in California, which—as is typically the case for the Coachella Valley in early October—was still getting midday temperatures in the triple digits. I remember thinking the cooling was necessary, not just because of the heat outside but also because of the emotions being generated in the main conference hall, which was packed with hundreds of conference attendees, NCAI executive leadership, and representatives from the Obama administration.

I also remember being impressed by the broad representation of Native Nations among the attendees, which included multiple delegates from most of the (then) 564 federally recognized Native Nations,[4] and others from various Tribal nongovernmental organizations and Tribal advocacy groups. I was equally impressed by the high-caliber officials from the Obama administration who had come to address them.

Standing at the elevated podium, Larry Echo Hawk of the Pawnee Nation, the newly appointed assistant secretary of Indian affairs, and Kimberly Teehee of the Cherokee Nation, President Obama's senior policy advisor for Native American affairs, both spoke with passion and force about the renewed commitments and opportunities the Obama administration would offer Native Peoples. At the time, Echo Hawk and Teehee were already seasoned political operatives specifically in the world of Native Nation–US affairs, having both served in various top positions in the Democratic National Committee during the Clinton years. While Echo Hawk was not the first Native American appointed assistant secretary of Indian affairs, Teehee's position was the first of its kind for a presidential administration, a signal intended show that Obama sought a more vigorous engagement with Tribal Nations than what had come before.[5]

4. Since 2009 an additional ten Tribal Nations have been officially acknowledged by the federal government and thus share a government-to-government relationship. This brings the total number of federally recognized Tribal Nations at the time of this writing to 574. See Indian Entities Recognized by and Eligible to Receive Services from the Bureau of Indian Affairs, 85 Fed. Reg. 5462 (Jan. 30, 2020).

5. As a sign of her ongoing stature in Native Nation–US relations, Teehee was recently appointed the delegate-designee of the Cherokee Nation to the US Congress. The position was created by a provision in the 1785 Treaty of Hopewell and the 1835 Treaty of New Echota between the United States and the Cherokee, in consideration for the reduction of and later removal

Part of the reason Teehee was there was to announce Obama's first White House Tribal Nations Conference, called for November 5, 2009. Obama would eventually choose the opening of that conference to stage the ceremonial signing of his memorandum on Tribal consultation. In public remarks he would make later about the 2009 event, which was attended by representatives of nearly four hundred Tribal Nations, President Obama would boast that it was the "largest gathering of tribal leaders in our history."[6] It is noteworthy, I think, that both the Clinton and George W. Bush administrations also made statements following their versions of these Tribal Nation summits, in which they celebrated theirs being the "first" and "largest" convening of Tribal leaders in the country's history.[7] This rhetoric is suggestive. It is as if simply convening a meeting with Native Peoples and their leaders is seen as significant enough to US officials that it should count for something, regardless of whether or not any real lasting policy announcements or commitments by the administration to Tribal Nations actually happen.

I wonder if this disparity of value and meaning was on the minds of at least some of the members of the NCAI executive committee seated onstage with Teehee and Echo Hawk. If Teehee had hoped that her announcement of the coming conference in Washington was going to be met with universal appreciation, she would have been disappointed. After the opening remarks, Tribal delegates were given an opportunity to ask questions of Echo Hawk and Teehee at two microphones placed at either side of the meeting hall. The questions and comments ran a wide spectrum, from some attendees expressing their conditional support for the new administration to others speaking of their concerns about the alarming rates of social ills disproportionately

---

from their Aboriginal homelands in the American Southeast. However, the position remained unoccupied until Teehee was appointed to the position by Cherokee Principal Chief Chuck Hoskin, Jr., in August 2019. Chandelis Duster, "Cherokee Nation Names First Ever Delegate to Congress," *CNN*, September 3, 2019, https://www.cnn.com/2019/09/03/politics/cherokee -nation-names-delegate-kimberly-teehee/index.html. (Accessed June 24, 2020.)

6. Barack H. Obama, "Remarks by the President at the Tribal Nations Conference" (The White House, Office of the Press Secretary, Washington, DC, December 5, 2012).

7. William J. Clinton, "Remarks to the Community at Pine Ridge Indian Reservation, July 7, 1999," *Public Papers of the Presidents of the United States, William J. Clinton, 1999, Book III, July 1–December 31, 1999* (Washington, DC: United States Government Printing Office, 2001), 1149; George W. Bush, "Remarks on the Opening of the National Museum of the American Indian, September 23, 2004," *Public Papers of the Presidents of the United States, George W. Bush, 2004. Book II, July 1–September 30, 2004* (Washington, DC: United States Government Printing Office, 2007), 2175.

FIGURE 2.1. Kimberly Teehee (left) and Juana Majel Dixon (right) at the 2010 annual meeting of the National Congress of American Indians. Photo Courtesy of National Congress of American Indians.

facing Tribal citizens.[8] For each speaker, Teehee respectfully listened, occasionally nodded, and sometimes took notes.

Delegate and NCAI executive committee member Juana Majel Dixon of the Pauma Band of Mission Indians, an elder stateswoman of California and National Native affairs, took an opportunity to speak up. From the stage, and leaning out to be seen among then NCAI president Jefferson Keel of the Chickasaw Nation and other members of the executive committee, Majel Dixon turned her chair and her microphone to pose a comment and concern to Teehee (see figure 2.1). She first expressed her own cautious optimism that the Obama administration would indeed usher in a new era of cooperation, but she then cautioned about the coming Tribal Nations Conference: "We have had a lot of these 'listening sessions' but a listening session is not a consultation. We need real consultation."[9] Teehee did not directly respond to Majel Dixon's comment, or to any other comments posed to her in that session, so it is hard to know whether or not her silence was felt in the room as a particularly charged rebuke. What I do recall is that the comment drew the largest response from the audience, as a long round of applause and chorus of cheers filled the darkened hall, sending a clear signal of support for Majel Dixon's gentle rebuke of the Obama officials.

8. Tribes across the United States face lower employment and two to three times higher crime and domestic violence than the national average.

9. Quote is from my contemporaneous notes.

When I read in NCAI's 2012 report on the status of executive branch implementation of Tribal consultation processes, I think its demand that US agencies to go "beyond dialogue" with Tribes in Indian Country echoes the caution that Majel Dixon expressed at the 2009 meeting. Judging by the reaction it received, I doubt the wariness is all that unusual, at least among Native leaders. Anyone with only a cursory understanding of the history of Native Nations and their relations to the United States knows that it has been one largely characterized by dispossession, deprivation, and deceit at the hands of a settler colonial government that, most gallingly, often claims to be acting in the name of Native Peoples' best interests (Deloria and Lytle 1983; Wilkinson 1987). In the face of yet more policy pronouncements calling for greater communication and coordination between Tribal Nations and the United States, Majel Dixon's exasperation with listening sessions and the NCAI's demand that the United States finally move beyond dialogue are both ways of saying that the federal government has for too long been all talk and no (good) action.

In retrospect, the pushback on both was prescient. Two comprehensive federal government reports issued in the wake of the NoDAPL/Mni Wiconi confrontation at the Standing Rock Reservation drew similar conclusions in 2017 and again in 2019. Both reports focused on federal agency practices of Tribal consultation undertaken in the course of approving large-scale infrastructure projects and review of the processes of those agencies required by US laws to comply with federal permitting protocols. For the 2017 report, the Departments of the Interior, Justice, and the Army issued joint findings and conclusions, and summarized the comments provided by Tribal leaders at a series of eight regional meetings held across the United States in October and November 2016 and comments submitted during a period of open comment.[10] All told, the 2017 report canvassed representatives of fifty-eight federally recognized Tribal Nations and eight Tribal advocacy nongovernmental organizations, and submissions from one hundred other nations (*2017 IAJ Report on Tribal Consultation*, 2). In March 2019, the Government Accountability Office (GAO) issued its own report in response to a request from Congress to supplement the 2017 report.[11] The GAO relied heavily on the same oral and text submissions gathered for the 2017 report, but also conducted interviews with representatives of eight additional Tribes, met with representatives of Tribal historical preservation offices at their national conference in summer 2018, and spoke to the heads of twenty-one federal agencies.

---

10. *2017 IAJ Report on Tribal Consultation*.
11. *2019 GAO Report*.

In the seas of ink spilled in the drafting of these reports—and the letters, transcripts, tables, and graphs created along the way—the conclusions give the sense that, at least from the perspective of Tribal representatives, the problems of consultation remain essentially the same as they were in 2009. For example, according to the 2017 report: "Tribes expressed their experiences with Federal agencies treating government-to-government consultation as a 'box-checking' procedural exercise." It noted that Tribal representatives described "feeling powerless to influence the direction of infrastructure projects in the beginning stages, or to prevent the ultimate damage or destruction of their resources" (*2017 IAJ Report on Tribal Consultation*, 11–12). In a key section of the executive summary, the report states:

> While each Tribe's comments were unique to their respective experiences, Tribes spoke with one voice as to the need for improvement in how and when Federal agencies engage Tribes prior to authorizing or otherwise initiating Federal infrastructure decisions. . . . Tribes noted that often agencies neither treat Tribes as sovereigns nor afford Tribes the respect they would any other governmental entity—let alone treat Tribes as those to whom the United States maintains a trust responsibility or as those who hold reserved rights through treaties that granted the United States vast amounts of territory. Tribes emphasized that the spirit with which consultation is conducted is essential. (2)

For its part, the *2019 GAO Report*, which had the added task of making concrete recommendations for remedying the consultation process to Congress and the executive branch, identified a number of key factors hindering the effective communication of Tribal interests to US agencies. These included the timeliness with which Tribes were first contacted for input, clearly communicating how Tribal input was to be evaluated and implemented (if at all), and the respect their input was to be given as the expression of a sovereign entity in a government-to-government relationship with the United States (*2019 GAO Report*, 2). The report recommended that the agencies under consideration adopt protocols for training their officials in the history of US law and policy toward Native Nations, including especially the government-to-government relationship. However, the general thrust of its more concrete suggestions involved making efficiency recommendations for streamlining and centralizing the procedures for communicating with Tribes and between agencies when working with the same Tribe on a single project. In many ways, then, the original demand made by Majel Dixon to Teehee in 2009 remains unmet. Whether described as the need for "real consultation" or for engagement to move "beyond dialogue," the call to action being raised by Tribal leaders, then and now, is more nuanced than the bald resistance and refusal that is often attributed to Indigenous acts of resistance. Indeed, the NCAI's 2012 report and the two follow-up governmental reports from 2017 and 2019 each evaluate the status of federal agencies' implementation of consultation practices so as to promote the development of more robust policies for administrative engagement with Tribal Nations.

How to make sense of this? What would Native Nation–US engagement "beyond dialogue" look like? What is the history of their relations such that, from the perspective of Tribal Nations, engagement is necessary but by itself is insufficient? How might Tribal actors undertaking engagement work see their efforts in that light? In short: What does "meaningful tribal consultation" mean for Tribal actors doing the everyday work of Tribal-US engagement, and how does that meaning reveal both the promise and peril that has always come with such work (Eitner 2014; Haskew 2000; Routel and Holth 2013)? When the NCAI demands that federal agencies' engagements with Tribal Nations move beyond dialogue, is it demanding that those engagements be appreciated for what they mean for Native Americans; namely, meetings in which the ongoing government-to-government relationship is always opened up for reconsideration, and matters of sovereignty are always at stake? This is to argue not for platitudes about giving space for "Native voices" but to genuinely question what these meetings are truly about and to insist that Indigenous norms, ways of knowing, and relational commitments must inform them and their outcomes. I wonder whether the call for moving beyond dialogue is an insistence that the everyday practices of Native Nations–US engagement must produce relations premised on Indigenous juris-dictions of CWS.

In this chapter, I argue that the question of the relationship between Native Nations and the United States is the original, unresolved, and (perhaps) unresolvable question animating the field of US law and policy, both past and present. CWS is one way of describing the abiding arguments for Indigenous juris-diction, and the sovereignty accomplished through it, that Tribal leaders undertake in the everyday work of engagement with the United States and its representatives. Indeed, the extent that it is even possible to talk about a shared orientation across the vast diversity of cultural, historical, and socioeconomic conditions and experiences of the 574 Native Nations that the United States officially recognizes (let alone the hundreds of other Native Nations that do not have government-to-government status) is the result of a similar response to the settler colonial laws and policies that have governed the nearly 250 years of interaction with the United States since its founding. Of course, the particularities of the responses Native Nations have mounted at different places and times of everyday engagement reflect much of that sociohistoric, cultural, and economic diversity. Additionally, these Nations' leaders historically have been only partially responsive to the specific demands of the settler regimes while at the same time speaking from and to the particular interests, arcs of meaning, and commitments of the Indigenous communities they represent.

Yet these responses also reveal a remarkable similarity across time and space, suggesting a shared commitment to refuse the "with us/against us" dichotomy that many want to attribute to their engagement with the US settler government. I believe that Native Nations' actions suggest the manifold ways they insist on a uniquely Indigenous juris-diction, one that partakes of some version of a theory of CWS in which it is understood that Indigenous participation is both premised on and productive of outcomes that must express their sovereignty and the ever-unfolding norms, knowledge, and relations that ground it.

When such engagements fail, it is not first and foremost because of bad actions by US agents, or because the leaders of Tribal Nations were duped by or complicit in US agents' actions, or because the terms of final agreements fall short of serving Native Nations' interests in ways that were promised. All of these elements may, of course, be in play in any Tribal-US engagement—and as I will show below, often have been. And after all, Native leaders are neither more nor less susceptible to bad judgment or the bad intentions of others than are non-Indigenous leaders.

Rather, I argue, Native-US engagements fundamentally fail at the outset if and when, despite laws and policies that at least nominally call for it, US officials in these interactions are unable (either willfully or out of ignorance) to appreciate what these engagements mean for Tribal officials. These engagements are "meaningful tribal consultations" when they are constituted as sites for enactment of Indigenous juris-dictions of cooperation without submission. They are sites for the presumption and production of relations between sovereign nations that are necessarily open-ended and subject to renegotiation every time the two sides meet across a Washington conference room table, or a working lunch in a converted bingo hall, or even on a windswept ridge at a site of archaeological and ceremonial significance.

This is why I describe Native-US relations as not just the original *and unresolved* issue of US law and policy toward Native Nations but perhaps as never *entirely resolvable*. To resolve the question of Native-US relations is to assume, at least from a view within the Indigenous juris-dictions of CWS, that relations can be defined once and for all, as if sovereignty, Indigenous or otherwise, can be settled in advance of the input from future generations of Native and non-Native leaders. But it is precisely the open-ended, unresolvable quality that I think best captures the beating heart of Indigenous juris-dictions of CWS. It is why Native Nation leaders are often willing to return to engagements with their US counterparts despite a history riddled with failure, disappointment, and dispossession. It is also why such consultations are always about more than the talk that constitutes them. They are, in the words of the NCAI report, always both dialogic and beyond dialogue at the same time.

What follows in this chapter is a consideration of some of the laws and policies that have governed Native Nation–US engagements for the last two and a half centuries. From the earliest years when treaty-making was the primary mode of engagement between Tribes and their non-Native settler counterparts to the present federal regulatory regime of so-called meaningful Tribal consultation and official US policies of Tribal self-determination, Native Nations have been battered by the shifting winds of a US settler colonialism that has relied on the ambiguity of the status of Native Nations and what engagements with them could and should mean. At the same time, and upon closer look, the question of the meaning of these engagements for Tribal Nations, and the relations they presume and produce for Native Peoples generally, seem to be always alive in the everyday details by which those engagements are accomplished. They are kept alive by the juris-dictions of the Native leaders and advocates who enact them.

As a result, even though US officials regularly fail to appreciate it, the juris-dictions by which Tribes enact the unfolding shape of their relations with them remain an Indigenous *insistence*, like the Hopi prayer feather in the bowels of the Field Museum, awaiting non-Native counterparts in settler agencies and institutions to meet them on those terms. It is this "spirit," I believe, that Tribal leaders were referencing in their comments for the GOA's 2019 report; a "spirit" of Native-US relations in the mode of cooperation without submission.

Unfortunately, the spirit that Native Nation representatives have always brought to these engagements—a spirit that might also be understood as a kind of treaty-making after treaty-making had been abolished by the Congress—has too often been lost on their US counterparts for various reasons that can be explained when read against the worst ethnic chauvinisms of US settler colonialism. To see how this plays out in the details of legal and political language shaping these events, consider first the interactions that shaped one crucial moment of Native Nation–US engagement. This was a set of meetings that took place in 1892 on and near the reservation of the Kiowa, Comanche, and Apache Tribes in what is now Western Oklahoma.

✳

INTERLUDE: THE MEANING OF NATIVE-US ENGAGEMENT
IN THE JEROME COMMISSION HEARINGS

In 1899 the US Senate Committee on Indian Affairs received an alarming report about a matter before it: a proposed agreement awaiting US congressional ratification that would permanently dismantle the reservation of the Kiowa-Comanche-Apache Tribes (hereafter, KCA). The agreement would give every Tribal member a 160-acre allotment and pay the KCA Tribes another $2 million for opening the remaining 2.5 million acres of land to Euro-American settlement. It was the product of terms drafted by a three-man commission that had been appointed by Congress for these purposes. This commission had gone to Fort Sill and Anadarko, on the KCA's reservation in what is now Southwest Oklahoma, in September and October 1892, to hold hearings with the leaders of the three Tribes. At the end of those meetings, the commission claimed to have secured the signatures of three-quarters of the adult male members of the KCA and to have successfully negotiated the terms of what would come to be known as the Jerome Agreement.

But the report before the Senate Committee in 1899 alleged that almost as soon as the agreement was signed, the KCA leaders had rescinded their assent to it. They did so, the report claimed, out of protest against the fraud, deception, and misrepresentations that the commissioners and their staff had subjected them to, and which they did not discover until after they had signed. The report was composed of a number of letters from former agents of the Bureau of Indian Affairs, anthropologists from the Bureau of American Ethnology, and other scholars, leaders, and advocates describing their knowledge of the events around the Jerome Agreement. As a whole, they wrote in support of the complaints raised by the Tribal leaders, especially Lone Wolf of the Kiowa, and suggested Congress either void the Jerome Agreement or substantially alter it to better represent KCA expectations and interests.

As compelling as these letters are, even more compelling is the accompanying transcript purporting to be a contemporaneous record of the hearings held between the commission and Tribal leaders during that sweltering three-week period in the late summer of 1892. That transcript is instructive as it reveals the complex and competing ways in which the Native and non-Native interlocutors approached the meeting and how different their goals appeared to be right from the outset.

It begins with a statement from the commission's head, former Michigan governor David H. Jerome, explaining that they had been appointed by President Benjamin Harrison "to come out and trade with the Indians about their lands."[12] But the Tribal leaders—including Lone Wolf of the Kiowa, Quanah Parker for the Comanche, and Whiteman for the Apache—knew full well why the men of the Jerome Commission had called the meeting. Word had reached them of the meetings the commission had already held with many of the other Tribes in the region that, like theirs, had signed treaties with the United States guaranteeing them the use of certain reservation lands in what, until recently, had been called Indian Territory.[13]

The KCA leaders also knew that the commission had come pursuant to the Dawes Severalty (or General Allotment) Act of 1887.[14] Through that legislation, Congress ordered the breakup of collectively held Tribal reservations, the allotment of a certain portion of those lands into individually held plots (of up to 160 acres), and the opening up of the remainder for settlement by non-Native citizens. For the representative leaders of the KCA Tribes, this meant something quite specific; any change to the boundaries of the KCA reservation would have to meet the terms of the 1867 Treaty of Medicine Lodge that had created it just twenty years earlier. Article 12 of that treaty explicitly provided that "no treaty for the cession of any portion of the reservation . . . shall be of any validity or force . . . unless executed and signed by at least three-fourths of all the adult male Indians occupying the same."[15]

Thus, in an effort perhaps to quell their concern, Jerome opens the meetings by greeting his counterparts and explaining that "while we come here

---

12. Letter from the Secretary of the Interior, in response to Resolution of the Senate of January 13, 1899, Relative to Condition and Character of the Kiowa, Comanche, and Apache Indian Reservation, and the Assent of the Indians to the Agreement for the Allotment of Lands and the Ceding of Unallotted Lands, S. Doc. No. 77 at 2, 8, 55th Cong. (3d. Sess. 1899) (referring to copy of a report of the proceedings of the councils held by the commission that made the agreement of 1892, S. Doc. No. 77 at 8; cited hereafter as S. Doc. No. 77 (1899)).

13. Nineteen Tribes in total had been engaged by the Jerome Commission from 1889 to 1893, including the Cherokee, Choctaw, and Chickasaw, whose forced relocations between 1830 and 1850 from Georgia to west of the Mississippi River is a well-known tragedy in US history. The Cheyenne and Arapaho would also suffer US violence in the lesser-known but equally tragic Sand Creek Massacre of 1864, which also included the Kickapoos, Ponca, Potawatomi, Osage, Shawnee, and Sac and Fox, to name only the larger Tribes (Hagan 2003).

14. Dawes Severalty Act of 1887 (General Allotment Act), Pub. L. No. 49-119; 25 U.S.C. ch. 9 §331 et seq. (Feb. 23, 1887).

15. Art. 12, Treaty of Medicine Lodge, 15 Stat. 581 (1867).

this morning as strangers . . . we hope before we get ready to leave . . . that we will go away the friends of the Indians."[16] He then speaks at length about the manner in which he and his fellow commissioners would approach the hearing, making a point of saying, in the racialized paternalism of the day: "The commissioners are not here to deal sharply with the Indians or to wrong the Indians or do anything that a father would not do with his child. . . . We are here to talk to you patiently, slowly, and quietly."[17]

He repeatedly emphasizes this point throughout the two days of meetings, commenting that "the Government does not desire these Indians to give up anything they now have unless it gives them something that it thinks is better for them than what they now have."[18] As this latter statement lays bare, the paternalism is not only a matter of rhetoric. At least as Jerome describes it, the US "desire" in passing the Dawes Act is to act in a manner that it thinks is in the Native Nations' best interest. The point of sending this commission is to consult with Tribal leaders about their views on these matters, but with the idea that the final decision rests exclusively with the settler government. Of course, as mentioned, this stood in direct conflict with the terms of Article 12 of the Treaty of Medicine Lodge.

After Jerome spoke, the two other commissioners take their turns. Alfred M. Wilson has only a few words, reiterating much of what had been said, but, interestingly, emphasizing to the KCA leaders that they should take their time to "talk about it amongst yourselves, and if you think the road we point out to you is not the best, come back tomorrow and tell us what is best."[19] If Wilson's stance seems to open the door to KCA decision-making authority in this process, the third commissioner to speak, Judge William Sayre, quickly slams it shut.

He states that after nearly a hundred years of treaty-based reservations held by the United States in trust for Tribal Nations, the federal government has now decided on a different approach. "The Great Father studied these things and thought them over in Washington," Sayre tells them, "and concluded that the reservation plan was not the best one, but that the Indian must take his land in allotment."[20] Then, as if this put too fine a point on it, Sayre makes his meaning plain: "The President has not made an order for the

16. S. Doc. No. 77 at 8 (1899).
17. S. Doc. No. 77 at 8 (1899).
18. S. Doc. No. 77 at 8 (1899).
19. S. Doc. No. 77 at 8 (1899).
20. S. Doc. No. 77 at 8 (1899).

people upon this reservation to take allotments . . . The power resides in the Great Father to make the order any time."[21]

It is telling, I think, that even before the Tribal representatives had a chance to speak, the introductory statements of the three commissioners already show how the Euro-American cultural chauvinism toward Native Nations and their knowledge, relations, and norms could be simultaneously beneficent and belligerent by promising friendship and threatening force. Even more telling is that, either way, commissioners never really contemplated that the KCA had genuine self-determining, decision-making authority in the matter of the allotment of their lands. And this is true no matter what US law or treaty might have otherwise provided. It is well known that US leaders and agents at the time regularly used such patronizing rhetoric in the texts and talk that constituted their engagements with and about Native Nations. What is perhaps less appreciated is how much this led officials like Jerome, Wilson, and Sayre to miss that representatives from Native Nations were engaging with them as leaders of the sovereign Nations that even US laws and treaties, like the 1867 Treaty of Medicine Lodge, recognized not twenty years earlier.

As might be expected, the leaders of the KCA took a rather different tack. Tabanaca of the Comanche is the first to step forward. He tells the commissioners that he "had been to Washington and received advice on building houses and making farms," and that while he himself would follow the decision of others in his Tribe, he personally did not "think that this trade can be accomplished soon."[22] Next to speak is Quanah Parker, a well-known figure in the area who, as the son of a Comanche man and Irish woman, had parlayed his abilities to move between both Native and non-Native communities in the area into considerable personal wealth and status by leasing Comanche Tribal lands to Euro-American ranchers (Hagan 2003). Parker explains to the commission that he, Lone Wolf of the Kiowa, and Whiteman of the Apache had also recently traveled to Washington to speak personally with the commissioner of Indian affairs, who was also the head of the Bureau of Indian Affairs. That commissioner had informed them that "there will be three men out to see you. They may want to buy the land. They have not got any money, but want to buy it with mouth-shoot."[23]

We can see just how much the commission seemed to underestimate the leaders of the KCA Tribes when we take note of Jerome's response to this statement. Jerome takes Parker's comment as a critique and objects to

---

21. S. Doc. No. 77 at 10 (1899).
22. S. Doc. No. 77 at 11 (1899).
23. S. Doc. No. 77 at 11 (1899).

the notion that the commission is not empowered to make good on a land sale. Of course, Parker was right, inasmuch as Congress would first have to approve any agreement reached between the commissioners and the KCA Tribes. While this seems like a technical matter, that is true if we only view this Native-US engagement as an act of US bureaucracy. When viewed from the perspective of the leaders of an Indigenous self-determining nation, it is understandably troubling that those US officials with whom they were asked to negotiate could not guarantee in specific monetary terms what the nation they claimed to represent was willing to pay them for their land.

Parker then presses him for the details of the offer. Jerome, however, refuses to answer Parker's direct question as to how much they are offering to pay per acre for KCA reservation land. Before Jerome can provide more than a few words of objection, Parker reveals his full understanding of the distribution of powers in the federal system by acknowledging that whatever terms the commission might agree upon at this engagement, "Congress had not made any appropriation for it."[24] Thus, it could not be guaranteed.

Parker then tells the commissioners that while others might be "in a hurry to sell their land," he is counseling caution. "I have talked to my people like this: Do not go to this thing like you were riding a swift horse, but hold up a little . . . do not go into this thing recklessly." He then exhorts the same to the commission: "To say to the people that the country should be opened up now is too quick."[25] But Parker does not object to the idea outright, and even admits that he thought it would be a good move in time. This echoes a sentiment expressed by other KCA leaders who, in the opening hours of the engagement, all agree that while an allotment deal might be reached, it would happen only if sufficient time were taken by all sides to come to a mutual understanding of agreeable terms.

Alas, and despite Commissioner Wilson's assurances that the Tribal leaders would have time to talk over the proposed agreement with each other and their fellow Tribal citizens, the subsequent actions of the US agents suggest a haste that belied Wilson's words. For example, when Parker decides to travel back to his community at the end of the first day, before the meetings are over, but to return within two days before they are concluded, his actions are met with derision by Jerome. "I hope Mr. Parker understands that this business is of more importance to him and his people."[26] Apparently, whatever time the KCA leaders would have to consider the offer from the United States or

24. S. Doc. No. 77 at 11 (1899).
25. S. Doc. No. 77 at 13 (1899).
26. S. Doc. No. 77 at 10 (1899).

consult with their peoples, it was not going to be enough to allow any interruptions to the commission's timeline. If the commissioners' actions with the other Nations they met with on their tour through the Indian Territory is any indication, they likely expected to have an agreement in hand by the time they finally adjourned this engagement. Note the irony in this, given that Jerome had only moments before been forced by Parker's questioning to admit that whatever agreements were reached or promises made, they would still have to be taken back to Washington for congressional approval and the securing of funding appropriations, a process that would take months, if not years. All of this prefigures by more than a century the complaints of Native leaders about contemporary Tribal consultation meetings being called by US agents, impatient to keep US timelines but with little regard for the schedules of Tribal leadership, and often only in the late stages of their proposed policy developments. Then, as now, it seems like all the US agents really wanted from Tribal leaders in these consultations was an Indian rubber stamp for their already-decided-upon plan.

The KCA leaders, however, are unwilling to go along, or so it seemed. As the second day of meetings unfolds, other KCA leaders come forward with their comments, many of which cohere around a rising suspicion that the US intentions are not as solicitous as the commissioners claim. This fact is corroborated when it becomes clear that the KCA leaders are laboring under a misconception about the expiration year of the 1867 Treaty of Medicine Lodge, and the commissioners are quick to turn it to their advantage. In short, the KCA leaders believe the treaty would expire in 1897, and state as much in the meeting. While they are not ready to agree to anything in 1892, they suggest that the ensuing five years would provide ample time for them to work toward a compromise agreeable to all involved.

Jerome's response to this is almost certainly misleading. On the one hand, he points out that, contrary to their understanding, the Medicine Lodge Treaty does not expire in 1897. Indeed, he says that "when they talk about the treaty expiring at the end of thirty years they are mistaken; it does not expire."[27] While true, the implication of this is not only that there was no reason to wait until 1897 to come to an agreement but also that the terms of the treaty would remain in force, even after an agreement was reached. Jerome continues: "[T]here is no intention on the part of the Government or of Congress to have these Indians move off this reservation at any time, but in the

---

27. S. Doc. No. 77 at 12 (1899).

plan that will be presented to you by the commissioners, it is that you may live upon this reservation as long as you live if you so desire."[28]

There is much that this statement leaves unsaid and (perhaps knowingly) concealed. In fact, while it was true that the US government had no plans to forcibly remove KCA members from the lands on which they then resided, it would still fundamentally change the way in which land was being held and potentially abrogate the Medicine Lodge Treaty along the way. That is, it would convert the KCA lands from a collective reservation held in trust by the United States into allotments of 160-acre parcels to which each member would hold title (Hagan 2003). The remainder, approximately 2.5 million acres, would then be purchased by the United States and subsequently opened up to non-Native settlement. The effect of this conversion would, among other things, expose KCA Tribal members to various forms of property taxation, debt foreclosure (should individuals seek to borrow against the value of the land), and the overweening interest of land speculators looking to capitalize on the opening of the Oklahoma Territory. The latter would contribute, in the aggregate, to one of the most jaw-dropping consequences of US policy of allotment: the transfer of 65 percent of Indigenous land holdings (around 90 million acres) into the hands of non-Natives in less than forty years (Deloria and Lytle 1982).

While Jerome was not lying when he said that KCA could remain in place for as long as they wished, he nonetheless omitted just how profoundly an assent to allotment would alter the KCA land holdings to something that would become unrecognizable.

This problem was not lost on Lone Wolf, the principal chief of the Kiowa, who would, as was typical for a Kiowa leader of his stature, be one of the last leaders to speak (B. Clark 1994; Hagan 2003). Acknowledging what he had heard in the conversation, Lone Wolf starts by thanking the commissioners for telling them "of the good intentions of the Government" and "making them so plain to us that each Indian present this afternoon understands every word of it."[29] Despite their goodness, or maybe because of how plainly the government's intentions seemed anything but good, Lone Wolf pivots, stating that "this commission made us feel uneasy":

> Being thus made uneasy about our country we have decided that the road that was made a long time ago is about the best that we can travel, and because this road was made for us by the Government, through its representatives, and in the sight of the Great Spirit, that is why we do not wish to do anything

28. S. Doc. No. 77 at 12 (1899).
29. S. Doc. No. 77 at 18 (1899).

that is disrespectful about the treaty and in four years from now they would be ready to listen to the commissioners that are sent by the Great Father at Washington.[30]

Wrapping up, Lone Wolf implores them, "I ask this commission not to be unkind to their friends before them, not to force them, not to say anything that will make them feel bad. All we ask is that you listen to Quanna [*sic*] Parker's, Lone Wolf's, and Whiteman's pleadings." He ends by stating the decision that the three of them had been authorized to deliver: "[T]he Comanches decided not to sell the country, and the Kiowas decided not to sell the country, and the Apaches decided not to sell the country. And I do not wish the commission to force us. That is all."[31]

Nevertheless, eight days later, the commission left not only with the three leaders' assent but also with signatures of 456 of the adult male Tribal members and the certification of the Indian agent. How this was accomplished, despite the objections and concerns expressed by KCA leaders just days earlier, and the controversies that ensued, has been the subject of exhaustive research and commentary by scholars, advocates, and others from the moment the agreement was declared finished. Quanah Parker, Lone Wolf, and other leaders who originally signed the document would repudiate it and ask to have their names removed just days later (B. Clark 1994; Hagan 2003). The leaders would later state both to Congress and in proceedings before the US Supreme Court in *Lone Wolf v. Hitchcock*[32] that it was nothing short of deceit and misrepresentation that led them to sign. As distressing as the mounting evidence of such double dealing was, equally—or perhaps even more—distressing was the willingness of both Congress and the Supreme Court to ignore the facts. Most destructive of all was the legal rationale that the Court would provide in its decision in *Lone Wolf*, namely, a theory of congressional absolute "plenary power." The upshot was that it made the legislature's authority to set federal Indian policy, including unilateral violations and abrogation of treaty rights, virtually unreviewable by US courts.

The Court's opinion in *Lone Wolf* remains to this day the law of the land (Singer 2002).[33] What makes it particularly ignominious is the flimsy regard in which it held long-established legal principles of Native Nation–US relations. Principles that had, before then, given actual legal teeth both to the

---

30. S. Doc. No. 77 at 19 (1899).
31. S. Doc. No. 77 at 19 (1899).
32. Lone Wolf v. Hitchcock 18 U.S. 553 (1903).
33. Singer quotes Sioux Nation of Indians v. U.S. 601 F2d. 1157, 1173 (Ct. Cl. 1979).

sovereignty of Tribal Nations and the obligations that the United States took
on to support Tribal self-determination through its treaties and trust responsibility generally.

But is it possible to discern, even in the laws and policies that preceded
the Jerome Commission by many decades, how settler colonial beneficence
and belligerence seem to stand cheek-by-jowl and perhaps even be constitutive of the fundamental ways in which the US has always approached Native Nations? Do federal laws and policies reveal, for example, that despite
proclaiming an interest in and commitment to accommodating Indigenous
norms, knowledge, and relations, that insofar as Euro-American agents seem
always to orient to Indigenous lifeways as objects of their evaluation and assessment, rather than as the foundations of their Indigenous authority, they
have routinely failed to see how Tribal leaders endeavored to engage them,
just as KCA leaders did, as representatives of sovereign self-determining nations enacting their juris-dictions of CWS?

Before turning to the details of the *Lone Wolf* decision and how its outcome exemplifies why contemporary Tribal advocates like the NCAI are so
skeptical of the value of engagement with the United States that does not
move beyond dialogue, it is necessary to consider the development of the US
laws and policies that laid the groundwork for that ignominious decision. Of
particular import, and to which I now turn, is how matters of Native-US relations get worked through acts of law and policy that emphasize the import of
understanding the details of actual moments of interaction and engagement
between the parties.

A Brief History of Federal Indian Relations and the
Meaning of Legal Text and Talk

Questions on the relationship between Native Nations and the United States
and questions on what role matters of meaning and interpretation plays in
their engagements have been central to what is often called federal Indian
law, ever since its foundations were first laid in the eighteenth and nineteenth
centuries. The original executive order—under Clinton—inaugurating the
"meaningful tribal consultation" regime is titled "Presidential Memorandum on Government-to-Government Relations with Native American Tribal
Governments." It directs:

> [E]ach executive department and agency shall consult, to the greatest extent
> practicable and to the extent permitted by law, with tribal governments prior
> to taking actions that affect federally recognized tribal governments . . . [to]

assess the impact of Federal Government plans . . . on tribal trust resources and assure that tribal government rights and concerns are considered during the development of such plans, projects, programs, and activities.[34]

Importantly, the policy behind the memorandum is explicitly based on the "unique legal relationship" the United States claims with Native Nations.[35] And yet, hinting at problems that many have argued are an enduring characteristic of the nearly 250 years of that relationship, the memorandum also describes a need to once again "clarify our responsibility" and commitment "to building a more effective day-to-day working relationship reflecting respect for the rights of self-government due the sovereign tribal governments."[36] That is, something about the uniqueness of the legal relationship between United States and Tribal Nations may at once be the source of its potential and its pitfalls. It is a push-pull that turns precisely on the ways in which the "meaning" of those relations get worked out, not just in abstract policy declarations but also in the everyday practices of real-time government-to-government engagement.

As such, while the particular processes of so-called meaningful Tribal consultation may be new, the principles of US settler colonial governance and the contradictions of the exceptional modes of relationship on which it relies go back much further (Eitner 2014; Routel and Holth 2013). In many respects, meaningful Tribal consultation is just the latest procedural elaboration designed to address and enact the contours of a relationship between Native Nations and the United States. The question of the character and commitments entailed by that relationship and the roles that meaning plays in the moments of real engagement between the sovereigns and their various representatives have been the central fulcra on which the whole of US law and policy toward Native Nations has teetered for well over two centuries.

For those familiar with federal Indian law (i.e., the body of constitutional provisions, legislation, case laws, and regulations that govern US relations with Tribes), it is well known that the uneven story of Tribal Nations' legal recognition as sovereign nations in the United States has always been dominated by how to characterize the relationship between the two. With a settler nation that distinguishes itself by its liberal social contract and democratic republican origins and with Indigenous Nations that both preexist the United States and stalwartly choose to hold themselves apart from it, working out

34. Presidential Memorandum on Government-to-Government Relations with Native American Tribal Governments, 59 Fed. Reg. 22951 at 22952.

35. 59 Fed. Reg. 22951 at 22952.

36. 59 Fed. Reg. 22951.

their ongoing relationship remains fundamental to determining their re-spective rights, authorities, and responsibilities. No wonder determining the "meaning" of those relations in the details of this or that treaty or statute, Supreme Court decision, or executive order is likewise central to the laws, policies, and regulations that have come to define federal Indian law.

Space here does not permit addressing all the shifting dimensions of Na-tive Nation–US relations that have occurred over the two and a half centuries of federal Indian law. For such an overview, I direct readers' attention to the many comprehensive legal and political histories that have been written over the years (e.g., Blackhawk 2019; Fletcher 2016; Getches et al. 2016; Goldberg et al. 2015; Riley 2017; Wilkins and Lomawaima 2002).

Instead I focus specifically on the way treaty-making has affected Tribal-US relations, and how the meanings that Native and non-Native actors at-tach to treaty-making impact US actors' understanding of Native Nations, their juris-dictions, and enactments of their sovereignty. I have in mind the early treaty-making practices that defined their relations before and after the founding of the US settler state, and continue to define those relations to-day, despite the unilateral abolishment of treaty-making by Congress in 1871. I turn to a discussion of three foundational cases in US law that articulate the status of Native Nations vis-à-vis the United States, including the role that treaty-making played for the Supreme Court as it articulated that status. These cases, sometimes referred to as the Marshall Trilogy, show the Court grappling with the demands of justifying the realpolitik of US settler colo-nialism with its ideals of a constitutional representative democracy and the treaty-making that gets done in its name. Chief Justice John Marshall char-acterized Tribal nationhood vis-à-vis the United States as inherently unique, contradictory, and ambiguous—captured by his description of them as "do-mestic dependent nations"[37]—and how this status, and the Euro-American ethnocultural chauvinism on which it is based, obligates the United States to attend to and always act in a manner consistent with the "best" interest of Tribal Nations.

I will end by returning to the Kiowa-Comanche-Apache Tribes' engage-ments with the Jerome Commission, particularly as taken up by the US Su-preme Court in the infamous case *Lone Wolf v. Hitchcock*. Some commenta-tors and critics have called this "among the worst decisions ever made by the Supreme Court and . . . arguably the most unjust decision of all time in the field of federal Indian law" (Singer 2002, 37). I do this to show how time and again US agents and actors have either made principles unrecognizable or

---

37. Cherokee Nation v. Georgia 30 U.S. (5 Pet.) 1 (1831) at 2.

cynically manipulated to their own ends. This has happened since the initial acknowledgment of Tribal sovereignty through practices and notions of Native Nations–US treaty-making, and in the space seemingly allowed to heed the meaning that Tribal Nations bring to engagements with their US counterparts.

Tribal-US Relations and the Meaning of Engagement through Treaty-Making

In the earliest days of the American Republic, US agents relied on a practice of treaty-making used by England and its North American colonies when seeking to enter into formal relations with Native Nations (Fixico 2008). Treaty-making is perhaps the best known, and valorized, mode of engagement between Native Nations and the United States and its Euro-American predecessors. This is true not only in the US non-Native popular imagination but also in how relations between the United States and Native Nations are conceptualized in US law and policy. Given that the Euro-American practice of treaty-making is undertaken between representatives of sovereign nations, the fact that English (and then US) officials engaged with Native Nations through the making of treaties suggests that Indigenous populations were likewise regarded as self-determining sovereign nations (Prucha 1997, 2000). Native Nations and their representatives were seen as capable of entering into reciprocal agreements for sales of land and land use, exchange of economic resources, exclusive trade rights, military partnership, and, in some instances, mutual rights to enforce their laws against the citizens of the other. Evidence of these rights and expectations can be found in all 374 ratified treaties and 16 agreements that the United States signed with Native Nations in the first hundred or so years of the Republic (Fixico 2008; Prucha 1984, 1997).

Treaty-making holds particular significance for Native Nations as well. Federal Indian legal scholar Kristen Carpenter (2008) has written extensively on the importance of treaties specifically and of matters of meaning and interpretation in Native Nation–US relations more generally. In her arguments for what she calls "interpretive sovereignty," she writes: "It is still true that in 2008 treaties affect issues of taxation, jurisdiction, civil rights, and hunting and fishing that affect American Indians and other US citizens" (115). This is because treaties are political compacts between two governments, and, like all treaties, they are recognized in Article IV of the US Constitution as the "supreme law of the land."[38] It is also the case that the particularities of their

---

38. Constitution of the United States of America, Article IV, cl. 2.

content and context present unique problems of meaning and interpretation that have considerable legal consequences.

Carpenter's call for a research agenda of "interpretive sovereignty" is an effort to address the unique challenges "of language, culture, and power" that treaties pose (Carpenter 2008, 115). The challenges are the foundational ambiguity—an example of Jodi Byrd's *haksuba* (see chapter 1) perhaps—of Native-US engagement more generally. Indeed, a certain cacophonous quality is arguably inherent in the practice and form of Native Nation–US treaty-making. In most cases, the things we call "treaties" involved text artifacts meant to memorialize the terms agreed to in oral negotiations and ceremonial acts of reciprocity between Tribal representatives and their US counterparts. But for many Native Nations, the central form of an agreement was often the face-to-face negotiation itself, when the general terms of exchange and partnership were worked out and then ritually sanctioned, sometimes through the sharing of food or a smoke, and almost always through the exchange of gifts (Carpenter 2008; Prucha 1997; Williams 1997).

Raymond J. DeMallie (1980), historian of the Plains Tribes, writes that when it came to the treaty-making engagements, called treaty councils, between the United States and Nations like the Sioux, Comanche, and Kiowa, "the council was an end in itself. What was important was the coming together in peace, smoking the pipe in common to pledge the truthfulness of all statements made, and the exchange of opinions" (39). Likewise, in a study of Native Nation treaty-making in Canada and the United States, Lumbee legal scholar Robert A. Williams (1997) describes the Haudenosaunee (Iroquois Confederacy) reliance on the extension of its mourning rituals, called condolence councils, to treaty negotiations with Euro-American colonists (60).

The Haudenosaunee ceremony involved acknowledgment of past harms suffered by both sides, followed by the ritual wiping of eyes, ears, and mouths, so that the two sides would be prepared to negotiate in good faith, without sadness, regret, or revenge on their minds. This was followed by an exchange of gifts that served to seal, through promises of future trade and the discursive forging of kinship and other types of relations, the terms of a newly constituted community of interests, meanings, and commitments (Williams 1997, 60). Williams reports a similar sentiment stated by Ojibwe chief Mashipinashi at the negotiation of the Greenville Treaty of 1795 with the United States. The chief is recorded as saying, "I expect what we are about to do shall never be forgotten. . . . Remember, we have taken the Great Spirit to witness our present actions; we will make a new world, and leave nothing on it to incommode our children" (quoted in Williams 1997, 99). This last quote is reminiscent of what Lone Wolf is reported to have said to the Jerome Commission in his closing remarks to them at their meeting in 1892. Rejecting on behalf of the Kiowa People their offer to allot the KCA reservation, Lone Wolf announces that they will stay the course laid for them in the Medicine Lodge Treaty of 1867. And he justifies this "because this road was made for us by the Government, through its representatives, and in the sight of the Great Spirit, that is why we do not wish to do anything that is disrespectful about the treaty. . . ."[39] For Native leaders like Mashipinashi and Lone Wolf, the written text of a treaty was a secondary record, an echo, of the much more profound and powerfully performative moment of face-to-face agreement made in the solemnifying, sanctifying presence of the sovereign Great Spirit called by all to bear witness to it. It is arguably just this same spirit of sovereignty, which, while having theological roots in European political theory (Agamben 1998; Schmitt 2006), is here rendered in the secularized discourses of contemporary Tribal governance, that was being referenced in the *2017 IAJ Report on Tribal Consultation*, when it states that "Tribes emphasized that the spirit with which consultation is conducted is essential" (*Improving Tribal Consultation* 2017, 3).

At the same time, Tribal leaders engaged in treaty-making also appreciated the memorialization of these ritualized, sanctifying engagements in the material records that could be later brought out as proof of those original events. Williams (1997) recounts several examples in which the presentation and exchanges of material and sacred goods—to acknowledge the terms of their agreement—were understood as evidence of the sealing of an agreement that remained in the possession of both parties. One need only think of the Pueblo ceremonial canes, first exchanged between the Spanish and Mexican governments and the leaders of the Puebloan Nations of present-day New Mexico, with whom they negotiated relations. It was a practice later adopted in 1863 by President Lincoln to signify the United States' commitment to upholding the land grants that the Pueblos had secured from the Spanish and Mexico. The canes remain symbols of office for many Pueblo governors to this day.[40]

Most often, treaty-making involved performative engagements that meshed communicative elements of spoken and material forms together. Consider,

---

39. S. Doc. No. 77 at 19 (1899).

40. In the next chapter I describe an interaction in which a Hopi leader is asked to show a deeply sacred item, usually kept out of sight, and which gained its sacrality in part because it memorialized the terms of a peace agreement and land settlement between the Hopi Village of Walpi and certain Navajo communities with whom they had been at war in the nineteenth century.

for example, the *wampum*. Wampum is the Narragansett word for a small tubular bead, often purple or white, made from different parts of the quahog clamshell. The beads were woven onto lengths of hemp, bark sinew, or string into "belts" with designs of repeating formal patterns. The belts were regularly presented by the nations of the Haudenosaunee (Mohawks, Oneidas, Onondagas, Senecas, and Cayugas) to other nations—Indigenous, settler, and imperial—to solemnify the terms of an alliance agreed upon on the day of the wampum presentation ceremony. One well-known example comes from the Haudenosaunee and their presentation of the Guswentah (Two-Row Wampum) belt to Dutch colonists in what is now Upstate New York in the seventeenth century (Haas 2007; Williams 1997). The Two-Row Wampum features a white shell-beaded plane against which two parallel rows of purple shells run through the middle. The pattern signifies the parallel travels that the "vessels" of the Haudenosaunee and the Dutch take on the same river, moving freely side by side, without disruption from the other. Significantly, this meaning was produced not by the belt alone but also in its presentation and representation; that is, whenever the parties represented in the belt would physically come together. As Haas explains, wampum are hypertexts, whose arrangement of forms and color contrasts constitutes information structures of meanings retrievable only by those who were "part of the community with the cultural context for accurate retrieval of that information" (Haas 2007, 80). Wampum such as the Two-Row were thus meant to bear messages "spoken and woven" into them; messages that "are repeated each time an individual (re)presents the . . . wampum hypertext . . . to the community" (86). As such, the wampum is not a text that speaks for itself. Rather, it is "a living rhetoric that communicates a mutual relationship between two or more parties, despite the failure of one of those parties to live up to that promise" (80).

I suggest that the simultaneously "spoken and woven" aspects of these wampum bear the characteristics of the everyday accomplishment of Indigenous juris-diction through CWS. This is true inasmuch as its presentation and "reading" involve the contemporaneous calling into being of the constitutive reciprocal commitments and expectations that bind the two parties to it in a way that presumes that in so doing the two sovereign nations have the capacity to be bound and to appreciate the sanctity of their bond and its terms. In the case of the Two-Row Wampum, the terms of the spoken and woven agreement provided that the nations would live alongside each other—like two vessels running parallel on the same river. As such, that wampum bound the parties in a community of meaning, solemnified by an act of agreement materialized in the belt whose substance was as much about limiting the future interferences of one party in the self-governing of the other as about cooperating and collaborating when it suited both sides to do so. This perhaps explains why the Two-Row Wampum continues to be brought out and read, most recently in 2013 by Onondaga faithkeeper Oren Lyons. Lyons's reading came at a United Nations gathering called to "renew" the Two-Row Wampum, and the community it inaugurated, on the occasion of its four hundredth anniversary between the Onondaga, other members of the Haudenosaunee Confederacy, and the various colonial states with which it had originally been forged.[41]

At first glance, the emphasis that Native Nations placed on face-to-face engagement and the performative enactment of agreement as the meaningful site for understanding the terms of a treaty is rather different from the emphasis that Euro-American legal traditions place on the authority of textual records, treaties or otherwise. For many US officials, the text of a treaty became the operative form of the agreement, its terms constituting the final statement of all the provisions agreed to by both parties, and that which, by the terms of the US Constitution itself, once ratified by US Congress, became law.

Notwithstanding the fact that material records like wampum and ceremonial canes, as shown above, also serve as effective devices for materializing and memorializing agreements, especially for the parties who know themselves to have been bound by them, this emphasis on the text record plays into a lot of presumptions about the truth value of written documents, their ostensive neutrality, and the comparative unreliability of other modes of transmission. The general idea is that because written texts are, at least by comparison to speech, relatively durable forms of communication, they can carry the meaning their authors give to them across expanses of space and time. This seemingly commonsensical assumption of Euro-American communicative cultures can be found resting behind a variety of theories and rules of evidence and interpretation in common law traditions. These range from the rules of valid will formation, which strongly favor written wills over oral ones; to the parole evidence rule, which prohibits the introduction of evidence contrary to the terms of a written contract; to any of the prevailing theories of constitutional interpretation championed by different political factions on the Supreme Court.

---

41. Katsitsionni Fox, "Two Row Wampum Renewal Campaign Completes Journey to United Nations," *Indian Time Haudenosaunee News*, August 22, 2013, http://www.indiantime.net/story /2013/08/22/news/two-row-wampum-renewal-campaign-completes-journey-to-united-na tions/11091.html. (Accessed June 25, 2020.)

In the context of Native-US relations, the presumptive stability of meaning of written texts versus other modes of textual and oral communication,
especially with regard to treaty interpretation, runs up against some compli-
cating factors. First is that treaty agreements memorialized in texts that were
approved by Congress were all written in English, and in ways that could
not be parsed easily by the Native signatories, even when Native leaders, like
those in the meetings of the Jerome Commission, frequently had interpreters
capable of the tricky work of translation.

Even beyond this roadblock, we can ask whether the meanings of legal
texts are as "stable" or so transparently "speak for themselves" as prevailing
theories would have us believe. It is expected that treaties, like all material
records, are circulated through chains of reading and interpreting, sometimes
aloud, sometimes in public, but always in ways that inevitably de- and recon-
textualized the document in this or that later moment of text interpretation.
How different then is the practice of reading treaties from the practices of
reading wampum? Indeed, it was required that the document be sent back to
Washington before being ratified as law. This meant that the US parties to the
original meeting were rarely the ones who had final authority to accept or re-
ject the treaty terms. And yet, somehow, the extent to which treaty texts were
always embedded in subsequent performative acts of reading and interpreting appears to have been lost on settler colonial actors. As Cary Miller (2002)
writes of negotiations with the Anishinaabeg of the Great Lakes region, "The
Americans did not understand that as gift givers [in treaty ceremonies] the
Anishinaabeg expected them to stand by the promise made when they first
were presented, not just by the agreements that ended up in the text of American treaties" (240).

The implication of this insight is instructive for thinking about how making the form and content of treaty-making practices unrecognizable would
affect how these specific engagements were made meaningful. It would have
not taken Tribal leaders long to realize, just as Quanah Parker realized in
the Jerome Commission hearings, that US officials empowered to meet with
them face-to-face were seldom the ones actually empowered to approve the
final terms of their agreements. They would have to have known—as so many
Tribal leaders know now—that while they themselves acted with the intent
and expectation that these meetings were between the heads of sovereign nations, it was rarely the case that the US acted with this intent or sent the requisite levels of leadership consonant with such an intent. Thus, while Tribal
leaders placed greater emphasis on the relationships enshrined in the actual
face-to-face engagement, and the spirit with which those engagements were
undertaken, they likely did so with the knowledge that the specifics of these

agreements would be subject to revision, as the written texts would be sent back to Congress for approval, appropriation, and execution. Indeed, this seems to be what Parker was implying in his goading of Jerome about the lack of congressional appropriations to underwrite their offers to the KCA, and also why Jerome took such umbrage to those comments.

Nevertheless, this does not explain why US representatives would think that revisions could be made unilaterally and then foisted on Tribes as if the document perfectly and transparently enshrined the relationship created earlier. This would not be a benign difference between two cultures of interpretation of Tribal-US engagements; it would be an act of bad faith voiding the relationship entirely. Yet this and other acts of duplicity would be exactly what the KCA Tribes and their advocates would accuse the Jerome Commission of having done, and for which they sought redress in Congress and then the Supreme Court.

Setting this aside for now, one can see why Tribal leaders would be suspicious of any engagement with US officials who spoke of the "good intentions" of their government that later produced a text that diverged from their agreement in material ways. These and other issues related to the complex but ambiguous relations between Tribal Nations and the United States were not lost on US officials in the earliest days of the American Republic. But as the country transitioned from its fragile early years into a full-blown settler nation-state, treaty provisions with Indian Tribes increasingly showed an uneven bargaining power between the two and an increased willingness by US agents to take advantage of that unevenness (Deloria and Lytle 1983).

From the end of the eighteenth century and into the middle of the nineteenth century, treaty-making between Tribal Nations and the United States continued, but not in the same way for those whose Aboriginal territories abutted growing settler population centers. For those Nations, the tenor of the arrangements began to shift. Early treaties were amended or ignored and replaced by ones that removed Native populations to places far afield from their homelands. This period of federal policy toward Native Nations, roughly compassing the first half of the nineteenth century, is known as the era of Reservation and Removal. It is infamous for brutal policies toward Native Nations, most especially those enshrined in the Indian Removal Act of 1830, which authorized President Andrew Jackson to set aside swaths of recently acquired territory with an eye toward impelling Tribes to swap their Aboriginal homelands for lands west of the Mississippi River. This spawned the Cherokee Trail of Tears, in which approximately 16,500 Cherokee citizens were forced to march from their homelands in Georgia and Tennessee to the Indian Territory west of the Mississippi River, a trip of around two thousand miles, along which it is estimated that from one-quarter to one-half lost their lives. Between the years 1820 and 1850, they would be joined by other Tribes who were relocated to reservations in Indian Territory (present-day Oklahoma), including the Choctaw, Chickasaw, Creek, Seminole, Kiowa, Comanche, Apache, Citizen-Potawatomi, Shawnee, Cheyenne, Arapaho, and sixteen other Tribes.

It is against this backdrop, and specifically in two matters involving the Cherokee Nation, that the US Supreme Court would be asked to adjudicate, for the first time, the rights and relations between the federal government and a Native Nation with whom it had signed treaties, and whose terms it was being asked to enforce. It is to these cases that I now turn.

The Cherokee Cases and the Foundational Principles of Federal Indian Law

At the time the two Cherokee cases came before the Supreme Court, Chief Justice John Marshall was still on the bench. Marshall was the first, and by many accounts the greatest, chief justice, having authored the landmark opinion in *Marbury v. Madison*,[42] which enshrined the Court's power of judicial review, giving it the final authority to interpret the US Constitution.

But cases involving US relations with Native Nations would not come until decades later. The first case didn't involve the Cherokee, but it did set an important precedent about the nature of the rights that Native Nations held to lands they occupied within the boundaries of the still young US Republic. In that case, *Johnson v. M'Intosh*,[43] the Court held that the United States, as victor in the American Revolutionary War, succeeded to the title in lands claimed by England via the so-called "doctrine of discovery" and the rights that accrued to the "discovering" Nation by virtue of its supposed imperial conquests. The parties to the matter had competing claims to the same parcel of land in the former Virginia territory; Johnson claimed having purchased title directly from the Piankeshaw Indian Nation that occupied the territory; M'Intosh had purchased a federal fee patent title to it from the United States, many years later. In finding for M'Intosh, the fee patent holder, Marshall sounded what should have been a deeply alarming note for Native Nations expecting their legal rights to be upheld in the US judiciary. As he writes, in some of the earliest hints at the fundamental absolutism of US policies

---

42. Marbury v. Madison 5 U.S. (1 Cranch) 137 (1803).

43. Johnson and Graham's Lessee v. M'Intosh, 21 U.S. 8 Wheat. 543 (1823).

toward Tribal Nations, "Conquest gives a title which the courts of the conqueror cannot deny."[44]

If the alarm was dampened at all, it would have been at least partly because Marshall himself seems uneasy with the way his words suggest "might makes right" in the colonial encounter. This is revealed by how Marshall's opinion quickly pivots to argue that even though "title by conquest is acquired and maintained by force. . . . humanity demands, and a wise policy requires, that the rights of the conquered to property should remain unimpaired,"[45] until the conquered are fully assimilated into the larger domineering society. He then finds that while absolute title is held by the US, it is conditioned on an enduring Indigenous "right of occupancy" to those lands they possess, and in which they are to be protected by the US government so long as they hold them peaceably.[46] Even in this very first case, then, we see the ambiguous character of US orientation to its relations with Native Nations, one that teeters between a belligerence and beneficence that bears a striking homophony—one might even say a prefatory note—to the Jerome Commission's approach to the KCA some sixty years later.

But before then, the ambiguity emergent in *Johnson* finds even starker resonance in the so-called Cherokee cases that came a decade later. By this time, Marshall was seventy-seven years of age and in failing health. The United States was under the leadership of President Jackson, who had run and won the office in part on his exploits as a general in the country's wars against Indian Nations. It is not surprising then that his administration took a much more aggressive posture toward Native Nations within and abutting US borders than that of previous administrations. Nor is it surprising that many states hostile to Native interests felt that they too could exercise a greater degree of aggression toward Native Nations than had been attempted before.

Marshall's position seemed to reflect a longer view of Native-US relations, one that not only reflected the less overtly aggressive stance of the earlier administrations under which he served but also looked beyond the founding of the United States for its inspiration. His opinions in both cases involved elaborate analyses of historical and legal records. They also made sweeping claims about the ways in which European colonizers engaged with Native Nations, and how they came to give meaning to their relations vis-à-vis those engagements. The arguments he makes in them reflect on how these engagements must have seemed to the representatives of Native Nations, and even

44. *Johnson*, 21 U.S. at 588.
45. *Johnson*, 21 U.S. at 589.
46. *Johnson*, 21 U.S. at 585.

acknowledge the sociohistoric and linguistic differences that inevitably made communication and mutual understanding difficult across the negotiation table. Finally, Marshall's opinions queried whether and how these historic patterns of engagement between colonizer and Indigenous Nations, and the relations produced through them, have been carried on by the US settler state since its founding, and what those relations should look like going forward.

In the first case, *Cherokee Nation v. Georgia*,[47] the Cherokee Nation sought an injunction to stop the state of Georgia from implementing laws that it had passed in 1828 specifically to prohibit the Tribal Nation from exercising its self-governing authority over its land and citizens. Hoping to speed the process, particularly because Georgia had already begun encroaching on Cherokee lands to arrest, try, and convict Cherokee citizens, the Tribe petitioned directly to the Supreme Court seeking preliminary and permanent injunctive relief. The Cherokee relied on the language of Article III, Section 2, clause 1, of the US Constitution, which provides that the power of the Supreme Court extends "to controversies . . . between a state, or citizens thereof, and foreign states" and that in those cases "in which a state shall be party, the Supreme Court shall have original jurisdiction."

At issue was whether the Cherokee Nation was a "foreign state" such that it could sue in the Supreme Court in a manner over which the Court could take original jurisdiction. In delivering the Court's answer to this question, Marshall turned for guidance both to the text of the US Constitution and to the history of relations between Tribes and European nations and then the United States, including, notably, the negotiation of treaties.

It turns out that the Constitution makes mention of "Indian tribes" and "Indians" in two places, both in Article I, which details the powers of the federal legislature. First, in Section 2, otherwise known as the apportionment clause, the Constitution provides that "Indians not taxed" shall not be counted when determining the number of representatives a state will have in the House of Representatives. Second, and more important for Marshall's purposes in the case before the Court, Article I, Section 8, clause 3, reads: "The Congress shall have the power . . . to regulate Commerce with Foreign Nations, and among the several states, and with the Indian Tribes." By enumerating Indian Tribes as a third entity in a series that includes "foreign nations" and "several states," Marshall turned to the language of this clause (also known as the Indian commerce clause) and the principles of legal interpretation, such as the "presumption of consistent usage" rule, to determine whether or not the distinction of Tribes in the Indian commerce clause meant

47. Cherokee Nation v. Georgia, 30 U.S. (5 Pet) 1 (1831).

that they should also be distinguished from the term "foreign states" in the jurisdictional clause. In ultimately concluding that Indian Tribes were not in fact "foreign states" whose petitions the Supreme Court could hear in its original jurisdiction, Marshall could have simply relied on these practices of legal interpretation and meaning-making to rationalize his judgment on sound legal reasoning. But he did not. And, in fact, the question of the status of Indian Tribes, and particularly what their status meant for their relationship with the federal government generally, and the Supreme Court particularly, was a matter of serious contention and disputation among the justices on the Court. This may have compelled Marshall to go further in his reasoning to consider the history and contemporaneous state of relations between Tribes and the US government. It is in this effort that Marshall spent a considerable amount of time and ink in the opinion evaluating the meaning of practices of treaty-making between the executive branch of the US government and the many Tribes with which it had so engaged. He writes:

> The numerous treaties made with them by the United States recognize them as a people capable of maintaining the relations of peace and war, of being responsible in their political character for any violation of their engagements, or for any aggression committed on the citizens of the United States by any individual of their community. Laws have been enacted in the spirit of these treaties. The acts of our government plainly recognize the Cherokee nation as a state, and the courts are bound by those acts.[48]

Marshall nonetheless goes on to find that while the United States recognized the Cherokee Nation as a state, they were not "foreign states," as defined by Article III. Nor were the Cherokee "a state of the union. . . . [I]ndividually [the Cherokee] are aliens, not owing allegiance to the United States."[49] At the time of this opinion, Indians did not enjoy birthright citizenship in the United States, and would not for another ninety-three years. As a result, Marshall went on to conclude that the Supreme Court had no jurisdiction to hear their petition to its original jurisdiction, insofar as they do not meet the language of Article III, Section 2 granting that jurisdiction over petitions by states of the union or foreign states.

Note that Marshall here is primarily concerned with how US officials perceived treaty-making and other modes of engagement with the Cherokee, and what these perceptions might say about US law and policy regarding the Cherokee's status as a state. This is a far cry from asking how the Cherokee

---

48. *Cherokee Nation*, 30 U.S. at 16.
49. *Cherokee Nation*, 30 U.S. at 16.

themselves understood the engagements that resulted in treaties. It perhaps foreshadows the problems of "recognition" politics in settler colonial-Indigenous relations described by Coulthard (2014), Povinelli (2002), and others insofar as it suggests the ways in which the consideration of Native self-governance (and the norms, knowledge, and relations that constitute it) are relevant only to the extent that they are legible as objects of settler evaluation.

At this point, again, Marshall could have concluded his opinion. But he doesn't. Instead, he delves into the tricky matter of determining exactly what kind of state Indian Nations are and how their relation to the United States is to be understood legally. In so doing, he argues himself into a dilemma: while individually they are "aliens," they somehow cannot collectively be considered a "foreign state." Though he admits the persuasiveness of such logics of scale[50]—the argument that "each individual being foreign, the whole must be foreign . . . is imposing"[51]—he instead settles on creating a thoroughly novel (and thus particularly un-legal, at least in the Euro-American sense of deference to precedent) legal construction. And while it is here that questions of Cherokee views of their relations to the US and their modes of engagement do come under consideration, once again it is not as the presumptive stuff of Cherokee self-governance, to be understood as the Cherokee understood them, but rather as subject to the rather sweeping interpretive generalizations that Marshall himself seems willing to attribute to them. He writes, "They acknowledge themselves in their treaties to be under the protection of the United States . . . rely upon its kindness and its power; appeal to it for relief to their wants; and address the president as their great father."[52] While the language of the Treaty of Hopewell is susceptible to these interpretations if read in the English of the day, failing to appreciate that, for the Cherokee as for many other Native Nations, discourses of kinship and appeals to protection in these treaties imply reciprocal, mutual obligation and partnership between

---

50. Questioning logics of scale to characterize the status of Native Nations is discussed in chapter 5, including the ambiguous and even evasive ways in which US officials in the Bureau of Indian Affairs, Office of Federal Acknowledgment answer questions from the leaders of a Tribal Nation petitioning the United States to be recognized as an Indian Nation with whom it should have government-to-government relations. The US officials acknowledge that their determinations *could* turn on a representative sample of individual member data, but then they fail to clarify what would constitute a "representative sample." This is indicative, I argue, of the ongoing unevenness of power and rendering unrecognizable of CWS that rests at the heart of all Native Nations–US relations.

51. *Cherokee Nation* 30 U.S. at 16.

52. *Cherokee Nation*, 30 U.S. at 17–18.

the two nations so bound. By failing to appreciate this, one also fails to fully understand the extent to which the Cherokee may have always intended these treaties as expressions of their Indigenous juris-dictions of cooperation without submission.

Instead, Marshall concludes, in what is some of the most important language from his opinion,

> The condition of the Indians in relation to the United States is perhaps unlike that of any other two people in existence . . . They may, more correctly, perhaps be denominated domestic dependent nations. They occupy a territory to which we assert a title independent of their will, which must take effect in point of possession when their right of possession ceases. Meanwhile they are in a state of pupilage. Their relation to the United States resembles that of a ward to his guardian.[53]

For the purposes of this case, Marshall's novel analysis of Cherokee political status vis-à-vis the United States meant that the Cherokee was not a foreign nation for the purposes of Article III of the US Constitution. As a result, the Cherokee could not petition the US Supreme Court directly and so lost their case for lack of the Supreme Court's jurisdiction to hear it. Importantly, and perhaps anticipating this outcome, the Cherokee had a second case pending, this time involving a US citizen—a missionary ally named Samuel Worcester—who volunteered to challenge Georgia's authority over Cherokee territory by entering it without a state permit, in violation of Georgia law. In this second Cherokee case, *Worcester v. Georgia*,[54] the Court would find for Worcester. In his opinion, Marshall, once again writing for the majority, held that the Constitution gave exclusive authority to the US Congress to commerce with Indian Tribes, an authority that supersedes any and all state authority exercised to the contrary. In a telling passage, Marshall writes:

> It will scarcely be doubted by any one, that, so far as the Indians, as distinct communities, have formed a connexion with the federal government by treaties; and that such connexion is political, and is equally binding on both parties . . . so long as treaties and laws remain in full force, and apply to Indian nations, exercising the right of self-government . . . the judicial power can exercise no discretion in refusing to give effect to those laws, unless they shall be deemed unconstitutional.[55]

53. *Cherokee Nation* 30 U.S. at 17.
54. Worcester v. Georgia, 31 U.S. 515 (1832).
55. *Worcester*, 31 U.S. at 593.

He then finds that the treaties with the Cherokee violated by Georgia's acts were still in force, that they were enacted in a manner consonant with Congress's authority under the Indian commerce clause, and that the Cherokee were still exercising their rights of self-governance. As a result, and in short, Marshall concluded that the state of Georgia had no legitimate jurisdiction over actions taking place within Cherokee territory, and thus had illegally detained Worcester.

However, even here the question of the status of Native Nations, their relations with the United States, and what federal law demands remains rather fuzzy around the edges. Marshall is quick to note that for all their rights to it, "the exercise of the power of self-government by the Indians . . . is undoubtedly contemplated to be temporary . . . a sound national policy does require that the Indian tribes within our states should exchange their territories . . or, eventually, consent to become amalgamated in our political communities."[56]

It is instructive, I think, to note the way matters of the meaning of treaty-making, Tribal sovereignty, and Native-US relations converge in multiple ways in these two landmark decisions. In *Cherokee Nation*, after walking through the ways in which Tribes were *like* a state (but not a domestic one) made up of noncitizens, but were not a foreign state, the effect of the internal relations of Tribal membership and its scalar logics are read against the constraints of US colonization, to determine a question of federal jurisdiction. This holding, for the purposes of petitioning the Supreme Court, meant Tribes like the Cherokee were not foreign nations. This view, premised as it is on what US perceived Cherokee political status to be, rather than on what the Cherokee themselves understood as their capacity for self-governance and strived to express in their engagements with the US, has come to be read back into the political status of Tribal Nations generally. Ironically, Marshall's concerns for the jurisdiction of the Supreme Court becomes the bedrock for determining how Tribal authority is to determine the scope and content of their own jurisdictions—that is, their sovereignty—and to be acknowledged by the settler colonial state—that is, as "domestic dependent nations" in a state of "pupilage" to their guardian, the United States.

Marshall's opinion in *Worcester* appears to stand on firmer ground when excluding the power of Georgia to assert its jurisdiction over Cherokee territory. But it too contemplates circumstances when, perhaps at a later time, and even given a valid treaty with the United States, a state government might assert its jurisdictional authority over Native Nations within its borders.

56. *Worcester*, 31 U.S. at 593.

Backing much of the convergence between treaty-making, Tribal self-governance, and Native-US relations is, I argue, a certain kind of disruption—a cacophonous haksuba (Byrd 2011). Having to engage with Native Nations disrupts the smooth veneer of nascent American republicanism, a disruption whose mark is borne by the acts and effects of treaty-making. Consider again that treaties were almost always memorialized in written form, in English, and in ways that were relatively unfamiliar to Native Nations, at least as compared to their non-Native settler counterparts representing European and US governments. As we saw above, in Marshall's Cherokee case opinions, this relative difference, and the advantage that the US may have gained in it, was either ignored by him or taken as evidence of Native Nation submission to US domination. However, in subsequent Supreme Court jurisprudence, the question of how Native Nations would have given meaning to these treaties at the time of their enactment are matters treated less as objects of settler evaluation and more as the normative, epistemological, and relational elements of Indigenous juris-dictions that Native Nation actors brought to those agreements and by which they were enshrined and given force. To this day, federal courts are required to answer through special principles of judicial interpretation—the legal term of art is "canons of construction"—that apply uniquely to treaties, statutes, and regulatory texts articulating the relations between Tribal Nations and the United States.

Ironically, even the arguments made in US law for these special canons of construction (Wilkinson and Volkman 1975) involve an admixture of recognition of the fundamental sociocultural and linguistic differences between Tribes and the United States and a familiar ethnocentric chauvinism that even sympathetic non-Natives, seeing Tribes as "domestic dependent nations," rarely failed to express. An example comes from the majority opinion of *Jones v. Meehan*, authored by Justice Horace Gray.[57] That case involved a dispute between two US citizens, who each claimed a right to a plot of land that was the subject of an 1863 treaty between the United States and the Red Lake and Pembina bands of Ojibwe Indians. Gray writes that, in addition to noting the power discrepancies between the United States and Indian Tribes, there were also problems of communication.

> [It must always] be borne in mind that the negotiations for the treaty are conducted, on the part of the United States, an enlightened and powerful nation, ... masters of a written language, ... that the treaty is drawn up by them and in their own language; that the Indians, on the other hand are a weak and dependent people, who have no written language and are wholly unfamiliar

57. Jones v. Meehan, 175 U.S. 1 (1899).

with all the forms of legal expression, and whose only knowledge of the terms in which the treaty is framed is that imparted to them by the interpreter employed by the United States. . . . [58]

As such, Gray continues, "the treaty must therefore be construed not according to the technical meaning of its words to learned lawyers, but in the sense in which they would naturally be understood by the Indians."[59]

When read together, the foundational analyses of the Cherokee cases, and the import given to the making and interpreting of treaties between Tribes and the United States, signal the extent to which matters of meaning, relationality, and engagement have been called up when shaping US law and policy regarding Native Nations. In Marshall's view, the very idea of "domestic dependent nation" status of Tribal Nations, as pejorative as it sounds, also acknowledges the undeniable fact that Tribes were dealt with as nations with treaty-making capacity. This is suggestive of just how powerful moments of government-to-government engagement were (and still are) in determining the duties and obligations owed under US law to Tribal Nations. At the same time, treaty-making alone does not overcome, for Marshall, the brute consequence of colonial domination of Native Nations or the ambiguity it creates for a democratic republic that imagines itself as founded on novel political theories of social contract when dealing with those Nations that chose to remain outside the fold of its federation. Indeed, if anything, Marshall's formulation of the act of colonization as an act of conquest, first explicitly in his opinion in *Johnson*, and then by allusion in various places in the two opinions in the Cherokee cases, seems to want to treat it exactly as the kind of one-off event, over and done with, that the nascent American republic should cleanse itself of as quickly as possible. But as Wolfe (2006) has reminded us, settler colonialism is an enduring structure of social relations between Indigenous and settler nations, one that is never past, and the enduring *insistence* of Indigenous presence in the form of self-determining Native Nations that, however "diminished," do not vanish, or become assimilated remains the uncomfortable truth of the US's settler stain.

Marshall's opinions and the founding principles of federal Indian law reflect this discomfit and the enduring ambiguity of US law and policy toward Native nations. And while they are often couched in the language of beneficence, they too—much like the discourses of the Jerome Commission toward the KCA leaders—mix in a fair share of belligerence. Marshall's novel conclusion

58. *Meehan*, 175 U.S. at 11.
59. *Meehan*, 175 U.S. at 11.

is that insofar as Native Nations are necessarily curtailed in certain aspects of their sovereign authority, they have been made dependent on the US, even by their own admission (though I question this). But where they haven't been constrained, they retain powers of self-governance, while at the same time being owed a duty (again demonstrably pejorative in its framing) by the US, much as a guardian would to its ward. As much as this both acknowledges and preserves a measure of rights to self-governance in Tribes, and inaugurates what later will be called the federal Indian trust relationship, which must always be enacted in the best interest of Tribal Nations, it also quite patently lays out the patronizing, infantilizing image of Native Nations as somehow not quite equal to the US.

Treaty-making and interpreting again play a role here, because it is through treaties that the US secures the terms of the necessary and specific cooperation of Tribal Nations, who nonetheless retain their sovereign authority except and only where their powers have been explicitly curtailed by the treaty agreement they have signed. Moreover, says Justice Gray in the *Meehan* case, given that such treaties—at least as can be adjudged by US courts—were always finalized in a mode and form consistent with US legal textual practices and processes, and not in the modes with which the Tribal signatories were most familiar, their meaning and significance, and how they were to be understood to bind the Native Nations that were signatories to them, required special consideration. That is, and consistent with the requirements that the US owed a trust responsibility to the very same Native Nations whose sovereign powers were being constrained by the treaty language in question, it was imperative that US courts interpret the language of those treaties in a manner that would have been understood by them. Thus, at least since *Meehan*, the norms, knowledge, and relations that are to inform how the provisions of treaties are to be interpreted must incorporate how they were understood by the Native Nations that were signatories to them.

But even here, right at the surface of Gray's acknowledgment in *Meehan* of the communication barriers between the US ("an enlightened and powerful nation") and Tribes (a "weak and dependent people"),[60] and the need of courts to interpret treaties in Tribes' favor, is a judgment about Tribal Nations' capacities to adjust to US dominion, a tacit implication that it is their own backwardness and inferiority that makes their ongoing separation from the US, and the concomitant dependency of the former on the latter, necessary, if for now. Persistent in all of these foundational opinions of federal Indian law

---

60. *Meehan*, 175 U.S. at 11.

is the twinning of settler colonial beneficence and belligerence, an inexorable ambiguity that arguably endures in Tribal-US relations to this very day.

Indeed, almost two centuries later, the jurisprudence called federal Indian law still hews closely to these principles and their forked-tongue implications. I earlier described the ways in which US law today addresses the rights of Tribes as self-determining Nations that enjoy government-to-government relationships with the United States. One need only review the terms of the Indian Education and Self-Determination Act of 1976, or the executive order calling for consultation and coordination with Tribal governments, or any number of Supreme Court opinions in recent years, to see how, at least in word if not always in deed, the United States has an explicit policy of recognizing its relationship with Tribal Nations as one between sovereign, self-determining governments.

Likewise, federal Indian law is shot through with jurisprudence that recognizes that both treaty-making and interpretation (in a manner presumptively favorable to Tribes) play roles in working out contemporary rights of Tribal Nations. For example, in 1999, Justice Sandra Day O'Connor penned the majority opinion in a case before the US Supreme Court, relying on much the same logic as Justice Gray did in his *Meehan* opinion. In *Minnesota v. Milles Lacs Band of Chippewa Indians*,[61] the question of how to interpret an 1837 treaty with several Ojibwe Nations arose when the state of Minnesota argued that Ojibwe off-reservation hunting and fishing rights had been extinguished by subsequent treaties in 1850 and 1855 and when Minnesota was admitted to the union in 1858. As Justice O'Connor wrote:

> To determine whether [the 1855 treaty] language abrogates [earlier, 1837] Chippewa Treaty rights, we look beyond the written words to the larger context that frames the Treaty, including "the history of the treaty, the negotiations, and the practical construction adopted by the parties."[62]

By examining this context in this way, O'Connor finds that, despite so-called plain meaning theories of statutory interpretation in other areas of US law, "Indian treaties are to be interpreted liberally in favor of the Indians, [with] any ambiguities . . . to be resolved in their favor."[63] As such, the Court upheld the decision of the lower court, finding that the proper interpretation of the text of the 1855 treaty, as well as the acts admitting Minnesota to the

---

61. Minnesota v. Milles Lacs Band of Chippewa Indians, 562 U.S. 172 (1999).

62. *Milles Lacs Band of Chippewa Indians*, 562 U.S. at 196, quoting Choctaw Nation v. Oklahoma, 318 U.S. 423, 432 (1943).

63. *Milles Lacs Band of Chippewa Indians*, 562 U.S. at 200.

union, do not countenance finding that the Mille Lacs Band of Chippewa Indians lost their hunting, fishing, and gathering rights.

But this all raises two questions. What about the deference that should have been paid to Indigenous understanding of the terms of the 1867 Medicine Lodge Treaty in *Lone Wolf v. Hitchcock*?[64] Why was it so easy for that treaty to be set aside by a subsequent agreement that both leaders from the KCA Tribes and a number of relevant US officials agreed was fraudulently executed to intentionally mislead Native signatories? Even further, how can we account for the innumerable acts of deprivation that Tribes have repeatedly suffered at the hands of a US settler colonial nation that nonetheless claimed to be acting toward them as governments with whom they bore a trust responsibility? The answers reveal how, despite the promise of government-to-government relations and trust responsibilities enshrined in US law, the inherent ambiguity of Tribal Nations as both inside and outside the United States—as "domestic dependent nations"—also put them in states of peril. This is a peril in which they inevitably remain to this day.

The Disregard for Treaty-Making and the Undermining of Native Nation–US Relations at the Turn of the Twentieth Century: *Lone Wolf v. Hitchcock*

By the late nineteenth century, even the removal policies championed by Andrew Jackson's administration and other officials would not go far enough for many in Washington, DC. First came the rise of political forces promoting US imperialist expansion across the continent, sometimes called Manifest Destiny, and the 1840s acquisition (through US military action or threat of action) of territories extending over much of the Pacific Northwest, California, and the southwest (Prucha 1984). Second, the flow of Euro-American settlers west increased as news of the discovery of gold and the promise of a transcontinental railroad encouraged their migration. In 1849, perhaps signaling things to come, the United States reassigned the Office of Indian Affairs from the Department of War (precursor to the Department of Defense) to the Department of the Interior, which all but declared that its relations with Tribal Nations would no longer be approached as one of relations between nations but rather matters of US domestic policy. Notwithstanding this shift, treaty-making persisted, although, as described earlier, the practice was increasingly one of US imposition of terms on Native Nations.

64. *Lone Wolf v. Hitchcock*, 187 U.S. 553 (1903).

Unsurprisingly, Native Nations resisted. Violence repeatedly broke out during this period, resulting in some of the most infamous events in Tribal-US relations. These include the US-Dakota War of 1862, resulting in President Lincoln's ordering of the execution of thirty-eight Santee Sioux men (the largest mass execution in US history), and the Sand Creek Massacre of 1864, in which hundreds of unarmed Cheyenne and Arapaho women, children, and elderly men were murdered in their camp by US forces. Finally, in 1871, Congress passed the Indian Appropriations Act, which declared "hereafter no Indian nation or tribe" shall be recognized "as an independent power with whom the United States can treaty."[65]

Passage of the 1871 act inaugurated a new era of US relations and policies toward Native Nations, one that is sometimes referred to as the Assimilation and Allotment Era. While a number of US legislative and executive actions contributed to unprecedented intrusions into Tribal self-governance during this period, it was the Dawes Severalty Act of 1887[66] that would create the worst deprivations for Tribal Nations. It was the alternate name—the General Allotment Act—that would give the ensuing forty-five years of federal Indian policy its name. Official US actions toward Native Nations during this "Allotment Era" would effectuate the largest transfer of land possession out of the hands of Native Peoples. Over these decades, lands that previously had been reserved for Native Nations through treaties, statutes, or executive orders would be reduced by 65 percent, from about 138 million acres to less than 48 million acres. This profound record of systematic deprivation, and the assimilative principles that champions of allotment and other laws and policies (like the forced removal of Native children to residential schools across the United States) advocated, mark it as unequivocally the darkest period of Native Nations relations with the federal government (Deloria and Lytle 1983; Hoxie 1984; Prucha 1984).

It was these policies and their justifications that informed the laws that created the Jerome Commission and the actions it took in dealing with Lone Wolf, Quanah Parker, Whiteman, and the other representatives of the Kiowa, Comanche, and Apache Tribes at Fort Sill in September and October 1892. It was what shaped the opinions and orders of the US Supreme Court when it took up Lone Wolf's case on appeal from the Circuit Court of District

65. Indian Appropriations Act of 1871, ch. 120, §1, 16 Stat. 566, 25 U.S.C. ch. 3 § 71 (Mar. 3, 1871).

66. Dawes Severalty Act of 1887, Pub. L. 49-105, 24 Stat. 388, 25 U.S.C. ch 9 § 331 et seq. (Feb. 8, 1887).

Columbia, heard oral arguments in October 1902, and issued its opinion in January 1903.

Both Quanah Parker and Whiteman abandoned the effort to overturn the agreement after Congress ratified it in 1900. However, Lone Wolf filed a lawsuit in federal court in 1901, joined by non-Native advocacy groups and ranchers with business interests connected to the Kiowa. The complaint was drafted with the assistance of his lawyer, former judge and congressman William M. Springer. It claimed that the Jerome Agreement was an unlawful violation of Article 12 of the Medicine Lodge Treaty of 1867, inasmuch as the 456 signatories did not constitute the requisite three-quarters of the eligible adult male voting population of the KCA Tribes. Moreover, those who did sign, the complaint alleged, did so under false and fraudulent pretenses, having been misled by the commission and its officers. The agreement and Congress's decision to ratify it, therefore, were unconstitutional takings of the Tribes' property interests without due process. Lone Wolf's lawsuit sought to nullify the agreement, thereby stopping the KCA reservation from being allotted and opened for sale and settlement by the United States to non-Natives.[67]

Lone Wolf was correct in pointing out that the number of signatories did not meet the voting threshold of adult male members, but the opinion does not even adjudge that issue. Writing the majority opinion for the court, Justice Edward White begins his analysis by refuting Lone Wolf's claim that the agreement was a violation of Article 12 of the treaty. White argues that whatever rights might accrue to Lone Wolf and his fellow KCA citizens under these circumstances, they are not legal rights that can be adjudicated by the Supreme Court. The opinion explains this is because of the unique relation that the KCA Tribes, like all Tribal Nations, bear to the United States—"a relation of dependency they bore and continue to bear toward the government of the United States."[68]

The opinion earns its ignominy when White draws the unprecedented conclusion that this dependency is met by the "controlling authority of Congress in respect to the care and protection of the Indians."[69] Things only get worse from there for Lone Wolf, the KCA, and Tribes in general. White then explains that the source of Congress's authority is not to be found in the language of the Constitution, such as Marshall finds it in the landmark Cherokee cases described above, but rather in the nebulous theory of congressional

67. *Lone Wolf*, 187 U.S. at 568.
68. *Lone Wolf*, 187 U.S. at 564.
69. *Lone Wolf*, 187 U.S. at 564.

"plenary power."[70] White's argument does not establish where Congress's plenary power over Tribes comes from. There is no mention anywhere in the Constitution of Congress having such absolute, unqualified sovereign dominion over them. While the Indian Commerce Clause, and Marshall's reading of it in *Worcester v. Georgia*, affirms the supremacy of congressional power to deal with Tribal nations over exercises of state power that contravene it, this does not thereby mean Congress thereby has unchecked authority over Tribal Nations themselves. Instead, to conjure this dominion, White's opinion simply declares, "Plenary authority over tribal relations of the Indians has been exercised by Congress from the beginning."[71] It then continues, with similar hand waving, that this plenary power of Congress "has always been deemed a political one, not subject to be controlled by the judicial department of the government."[72] As such, White thus argues, whether Congress chooses to exercise that authority by adhering to the terms of its treaties with the KCA or abrogating those terms is not a matter for judicial review. Even questions as to the fraudulent and deceptive dealings alleged by Lone Wolf and the KCA are beyond the scope of judicial review, "since all these matters, in any event, were solely within the domain of the legislative authority, and its action is conclusive upon the courts."[73]

The opinion ends fatuously, saying that the Court can only conclude that where Congress held "full administrative power" over the KCA lands in question, its decision to unilaterally violate the terms of the Medicine Lodge Treaty's Article 12, or any other part of it, is not an action whose constitutionality can be questioned by the Court. Indeed, the Court "must presume that Congress acted in perfect good faith in the dealings with the Indians. . . . In any event, the judiciary cannot question or inquire into the motives which prompted the enactment of this legislation."[74] Thus, Lone Wolf lost the case not because the Court determined his claim was invalid but rather because it determined that it was not a legal claim over which the federal courts had jurisdiction.

There are many ways one can account for the bald hypocrisy exhibited in the KCA allotment debacle, not just by the Jerome Commission but also by a Supreme Court unwilling to question the propriety of Congress's acceptance

70. *Lone Wolf*, 187 U.S. at 565.
71. *Lone Wolf*, 187 U.S. at 566.
72. *Lone Wolf*, 187 U.S. at 566.
73. *Lone Wolf*, 187 U.S. at 567.
74. *Lone Wolf*, 187 U.S. at 568.

of the commission's agreement, despite patent evidence of bad dealings. One could chalk it up to avarice and mean-spirited manipulation, or perhaps even callous indifference. All of these elements certainly appear to be operating in this case. But then why go through all the trouble of having a Jerome Commission in the first place, and then allowing Congress's approval of it to be challenged all the way to the Supreme Court? Instead, I think a more persuasive account is that it was a US settler desire to maintain what Patrick Wolfe calls the "indigenous aura" (Wolfe 2006, 389)—necessary for the sense of its own Republic-based sovereign independence, but accomplished at the expense of Indigenous Peoples—that led to the horrific outcome in the *Lone Wolf* case.

It was, in fact, a recognition that US republicanism, in contradistinction to the English monarchism it threw off, demands maintaining the impression that the United States is consulting with and acting out of interest for Native Nations and their welfare, even when doing so seems to counter those interests. To accomplish this, US actors must express and enact an interest in Indigenous norms, knowledge, and relations, but only as objects of their judgment and control—that is, as objects of US sovereign power—rather than as foundational components of Indigenous self-governance. Thus, even when engaging with Native Nations and their leaders, as evidenced in the actions of the Jerome Commission, the point was never to treat Tribes like the KCA as genuinely sovereign nations, domestic dependent or otherwise. Nor was the Supreme Court's opinion in the *Lone Wolf* case ever concerned with the possibility that the commission failed in its duties to account for the possibility that KCA leaders were expressing their uniquely Indigenous juris-dictions when they were refusing to proceed with the negotiations at the pace set by the commission, or after they objected to the fraud and deceit they allege was perpetrated against them. Instead, the only questions for the Court were the scope of the United States' power to assert its will over Native Nations—a power that it found to be absolute given that "these Indian tribes *are* the ward of the Nation"[75]—and to what extent the exercise of this pure political power was even reviewable by the Supreme Court.[76] This explanation speaks directly to the most infamous line in White's opinion in the *Lone Wolf* case, where he blithely explains why the Court would not question the presumptive good faith used by Congress in deciding to accept the Jerome Commission's agreement. The opinion reads:

75. *Lone Wolf*, 187 U.S. at 567, quoting *U.S. v. Kagama*, 118 U.S. 375 (1886) at 382.
76. *Lone Wolf*, 187 U.S. at 568.

[F]ull administrative power was possessed by Congress over Indian tribal property. In effect, the action of Congress now complained of was but an exercise of such power, a mere change in the form of investment of Indian tribal property, the property of those who, as we have held, were in substantial effect the wards of the government.[77]

That is, inasmuch as Congress' authority is complete and Native Nations had no legal recourse to independently challenge acts of Congress ostensibly taken on their behalf—being not just subject to them but also being their "wards"—the Court could do nothing but presume that Congress asserted its plenary authority in good faith when it approved the KCA allotment agreement. It did not matter that there were objections from the very people who had signed it, and substantial evidence of underhanded behavior to accomplish it (B. Clark 1994; Singer 2002). Callous indifference certainly played a role. But I think this indifference was facilitated by other sentiments as well, namely: (1) assumptions about Native Nations and their capacities and (2) a fundamental inability or unwillingness on the part of the US government to appreciate that Native Nations made and interpreted treaties in ways that were enacted with (or, as Lone Wolf says "in the sight of") the spirit of their Indigenous sovereignty. And while that spirit, as it was invoked in the signing of the Treaty of Medicine Lodge, was hailed by Lone Wolf and other KCA leaders to remind the Jerome commissioners of the possibilities of their Peoples negotiating a path forward in cooperation with the US's interests and demands, it was, even then, a sovereignty that had not been submitted to the unqualified power of the US settler state. If the meeting interactions in the late summer of 1892 at Fort Sill reveal anything, it is that whatever the US officials may have thought, Quanah Parker, Whiteman, Lone Wolf, and the others were not coming to the engagement with the view that their Peoples would simply have the future of their lives, lands, and resources dictated to them, like the passive recipients of a sovereign US's promises of largesse or (as Commissioner White threatened) failing that, the brunt of its unyielding progress westward. The presumptions of the Supreme Court, Congress, and the Jerome Commission in this case thus involved not just ignorance of Native ways of knowing, relating, and norming but, perhaps even more damning, an orientation to Native ways solely as objects for their evaluation, judgment, and intervention, a with these Native Nations' own Indigenous juris-dictions when so doing.

77. *Lone Wolf,* 187 U.S. at 568.

Analyzing a similar act of Euro-American chauvinism, this time directed at the Hopi Tribe by a non-Native lawyer who served as their counsel (more on this in the next chapter), Vine Deloria Jr. discusses these juris-dictional inequities and their consequences. It was precisely the presumptions among Euro-Americans that they knew better than Native Nations what was in their best interest that often led to the worst outcomes of federal Indian law and policy. Deloria is quoted as saying, "Look, . . . you've got to understand the historical context. Nobody really believed the Indians had any rights. Nobody thought they would be around very long. 'We'll just try to help that little band of survivors as best we can'" (quoted in Wilkinson 2005, 311).

The same complaint was raised almost a century earlier, in an 1880 minority report by the House of Representatives' Indian Affairs Committee, in the debates on approval of the Dawes Act. It states that if the plan to break up Tribal reservations "were done in the name of Greed, it would be bad enough; but to do it in the name of Humanity, and under the cloak of an ardent desire to promote the Indian's welfare . . . is infinitely worse" (H. Rept. No. 1576, May 28 1880, 46th Cong. 2d sess., 10, quoted in Otis 1973, 18–19).

Engagements of Native Nations with their US counterparts are engagements of ongoing practices of Indigenous self-determination and sovereignty. Whatever the sincerity of US actors' intentions, I suggest that the failures evident in the experiences of the KCA leaders with the Jerome Commission, and then later in the *Lone Wolf* outcome, speak as much to the inability by US actors and agents to account for and understand Indigenous juris-dictions as to specific acts of duplicity and indifference. Indeed, these acts are arguably all the more egregious to Native Nations because it gives cover to legal principles that speak of Tribes as "domestic dependent nations," to which the US government owes a trust responsibility, and to which courts have held that the language of treaties be interpreted in a light most favorable to Native Peoples. For all the talk of acknowledging the inherent, enduring sovereignty of Tribal Nations, the US government's ongoing failure to appreciate this is in fact what, ironically, requires Native Nations' continued insistence on a right to engage with the United States, if only to hold on to the aspiration that at some point they may yet understand the true meaning of government-to-government relations. Of course, with this promise comes too the peril—the Indigenous perspectival counterpoint to the twinning of settler beneficence and belligerence—that by premising their engagement on an Indigenous juris-diction of cooperation without submission, Tribal Nations invariably create the conditions by which US agencies can claim the moral high ground in their dealings with Tribal Nations, even while heaping yet more injustice and indignity on them. This, anyway, seems to be the hard, enduring lesson from the Supreme Court's decision in *Lone Wolf.*

Conclusion

By 1928 the decimation that the Allotment and Assimilation Era had wreaked on Tribal Nations was evident. The secretary of the Interior commissioned a survey, and its findings were published in an extensive report titled *The Problem of Indian Administration* (sometimes called *The Meriam Report* after the survey's director and publication's author, Lewis Meriam). It found that despite the claims of champions of Allotment and Assimilation, "[a]n overwhelming majority of Indians are poor, even extremely poor" (Meriam 1928, 87). It found "disastrous" the "attempt to force individual Indians or groups of Indians to be what they do not want to be, to break their pride in themselves . . . or to deprive them of their Indian culture" (87). It also found, however, that "Indians are face to face with the predominating civilization of the whites," which has "as a rule largely destroyed the economic foundation upon which the Indian culture rested" and which "cannot be restored as it was" (87). The report concluded:

> [US policy toward Native Nations and their citizens] must give consideration to the desires of . . . the Indians. He who wishes to merge into the social and economic life [of the US] . . . should be given all practicable aid and advice. . . . He who wants to remain an Indian and live according to his old culture should be aided in doing so. (88)

But given what came before, is it any surprise that Native Nations would be skeptical of any policy the United States would put forward, even after allotment and assimilation was repudiated and reorganization instituted?

I opened this chapter with a description of a 2012 report published by the National Congress of American Indians on its review of US federal agencies' progress in implementing Executive Order 13,175 and the processes of "meaningful tribal consultation" it required them to have in place. I described how that report demanded that US federal agencies meet their obligations under the order and fully implement their consultation processes and procedures. However, it also explained that consultation alone would be insufficient to meet goals and that the United States had to go "beyond dialogue" in enacting real reform in its policies and procedures for relating to Tribal Nations. I suggested that this push-pull, or maybe more accurately this-and-still-more approach, is consistent with and suggestive of a longer arc of Tribal Nations' orientations of engaging with the United States. What would it mean to describe

NCAI's position as both calling for consultation and a move beyond it? This can only be understood when read against the long history of both the promise and peril that have befallen Tribal Nations when they have engaged the United States over the past two and a half centuries.

I then showed how, when looking at that history (and in particular at the way in which engagement, meaning, and relating have remained unanswered and unanswerable matters in federal Indian law), the long-standing twinning of US settler colonial beneficence and belligerence in working out their relations with Native Nations points to the promise and the peril Tribes will likely always face in those relations. Tribal actors representing their Nations nonetheless continue to engage their US counterparts through an orientation of cooperation without submission, but this reveals the high stakes such meetings continue to have for Tribal leaders engaged in the everyday work of Tribal governance.

What exactly is meant by "cooperation without submission"? Which notions of political authority and responsibility should Tribal actors advocate for in their stance with US counterparts? In the next chapter I explore cooperation without submission in relation to Hopi modes of political action.

PART TWO

Hopi Juris-diction

3

CWS: A Hopi Sociopolitical Theory of Knowing, Relating, and Norming

Introduction

In this chapter, I consider in greater detail the particular Hopi contexts within which to understand Emory Sekaquaptewa's insight that "in Hopi, culture teaches us cooperation without submission" (in Ferrero 1984). I explore how CWS can be understood as Sekaquaptewa's expression of a theory of Hopi sociopolitical order that is achieved without coercion through open-ended collaboration among Hopi villages, clans, and ceremonial societies, each of which is understood as possessing unique norms, knowledge, and relational practices. Insofar as CWS expresses the underlying principle of a sociality premised on the articulation of groups with coordinated spheres of normative authority, not on a centralized coercive power, it bears all the hallmarks of an Indigenous Hopi juris-diction that enacts Hopi sovereignty in the everyday workings of Hopi community life. I also suggest that CWS is discernible in the practices and discourses that Hopi have expressed about their interclan relations as well as in their dealings with later-arriving Hopi political forms, including the Hopi Constitution and Hopi Tribal government (both adopted in 1936). This includes their relations with non-Hopi and non-Natives with whom they have engaged both in the past and in the present.

How might CWS illuminate acts by Hopi that confound Euro-American legal and social-scientific efforts (including my own) to represent their culture and society? Why do Hopi invite modes of engagement with those same Euro-American actors and institutions, even when they do not understand or account for the knowledge practices, relations, and norms that undergird Hopi social relations and commitments? I argue that this requires reflecting on Hopi norms of *wiwta* (relationality, connections) and Hopi understandings of navoti (defined in chapter 1 as traditional, sacred knowledge or knowledge gained through hearing) and how these intersect in the decentralized distribution of social power and authority in Hopi society both historically and in the present. This chapter explains how this decentralization is shored up by Hopis' strict rules of ritual secrecy—for example, the accepted norm that one clan's sacred knowledge (and the power that comes with it) cannot be shared with non-Hopi or even Hopi who are members of other clans. These rules of secrecy, and their staunch enforcement, constitute the necessary conditions of Hopi CWS. The result is a Hopi social order in which no one segment of Hopi society can legitimately claim authority over any other. Rather, Hopi order is ideologically premised on the mutual recognition and respect of the lines and limits of authority possessed by the many different clans and religious societies across Hopi's twelve historically autonomous villages. This includes the role that each clan plays, in its own way and in relation to the others, in the ongoing history of the Hopi Nation. I also argue that only through a better (albeit always incomplete) understanding of Hopi theories of CWS as juris-diction can we appreciate how the seemingly paradoxical stances that Hopi Tribal actors take in these engagements—in which they appear simultaneously to refuse and invite relations with their non-Native counterparts—might actually constitute the details of these Hopi actors' everyday accomplishments of their Nation's sovereignty and self-determination.

To that end, I first turn to an interaction that took place between Hopi leaders who were called as witnesses in a hearing before the Indian Claims Commission in 1961.

✦

INTERLUDE: KNOWLEDGE AND RELATIONS IN A HOPI CLAIMS HEARING

The Indian Claims Commission (ICC) was an administrative tribunal created by congressional statute in 1946 that authorized the body to "hear and determine . . . claims against the United States on behalf of any Indian tribe, band or other identifiable group of American Indians residing within . . . the United States or Alaska."[1] Of the 370 petitions submitted to the ICC between 1951 and 1978, which represented over 850 separate claims (Indian Claims Commission 1978; Le Duc 1957; Lurie 1978), the majority were brought by Tribes pursuant to the commission's jurisdiction to hear, among other things, "claims arising from the taking by the United States . . . of lands owned or occupied by the claimant without the payment for such lands"[2] (see Indian Claims Commission 1978).

---

1. Indian Claims Commission Act of 1946, 60 Stat. 1050, 25 U.S.C. 70(a) et seq.
2. Indian Claims Commission Act of 1946.

Though the ICC was to have completed its work by 1957, the sheer volume of petitions and complexity of cases made it necessary for Congress to grant five extensions of time to the panel to continue their work until 1978. Even then, other accommodations would also be necessary, including several procedural and personnel amendments passed in 1967, among them the expansion of the number commissioners hearing cases from three to five and a fast-tracking of the provision of expert testimony. Still, nearly all the Tribal petitions filed before the 1951 deadline would take many years to be heard and closed, with some running beyond the 1978 date of the ICCs official expiration.

The Hopi Nation's case was no exception to this long process. They filed their first petitions in August 1951, two months before the original October deadline, with representatives filing two separate petitions just days apart. The first was filed on behalf of the Hopi Tribal government by its counsel, John S. Boyden, a lawyer from Salt Lake City. The other petition, filed three days later, was submitted by a smaller group calling itself the Leaders of the Hopi Village of Shungopavi, one of the twelve historically autonomous villages federated in 1936 into a single Hopi Tribe.[3] In 1951 there were many Hopi who challenged the legitimacy of the federation that created the Hopi Tribe, seeing it and those who served in Tribal government as compromised by US and other non-Hopi interests. These second petitioners refused to sign onto the Tribe's first petition, choosing instead to file their own (Clemmer 1995; Geertz 1994; Wilkinson 1999).

The Shungopavi petition is interesting for how it presents Hopi claims against the US government. Typed in English, the petition opens with the leaders explaining that they "now meet our traditional obligations and present to you, the Indian Claims Commission, the traditional claim of the Hopi Indian People."[4]

They then elaborate their claim, reciting Hopi tradition and explaining how their history and their current way of life are related to the land they seek to have returned to them, notwithstanding that the ICC was only authorized to award monetary restitution to Tribes, and not the land that they and so many other Native petitioners sought. This makes the thirteen-page petition all the more heartrending to read, especially when they explain:

> [We] humbly and with deepest thought and sincerity present our claim to the
> Hopi land (Tusqua) as it is fixed by our traditional life and which we must use

3. Hopi Village of Shungopavi v. United States of America, Docket No. 196, 210, Indian Claims Commission Records, RG 33494-23-054, National Archives, Washington, DC.

4. Petition of the Hopi Leaders of the Village of Shungopavi, Indian Claims Commission Docket No. 210, Aug. 8, 1951 at 1.

in our traditional way in carrying out our traditional practices and regulations. . . . The Hopi Tusqua (land) is our love and will always be. . . . Our land,
our religion and our life are one.[5]

The ICC dismissed the Shungopavi petition without ever answering it.
They might have done so for reasons of format: the Shungopavi filing was
not a formal legal petition because it was lacking citations to US law and
statements of points, authorities, and relevant facts. Perhaps it was dismissed
because it requested a return of land taken from it by the United States rather
than a monetary award, which was a remedy that the ICC was not empowered to grant. Finally, the Shungopavi petition might have been dismissed
because the leaders of that village, as the claimants identified themselves, did
not represent a government of the Hopi Tribe that the United States acknowledged as sharing a government-to-government relationship. The ICC could
be justified for any of these reasons in dismissing this claim. Because there
was no response from the ICC at all, it is impossible to know on what grounds
it denied the petition.

By contrast, the ICC responded to the petition filed by the Hopi Tribal
government, accepted jurisdiction over it, and set it for a hearing. This is
perhaps not so surprising. Boyden was a well-known figure in the region as
a leader in Mormon Church, as a booster of water and energy development
projects, and as a leading figure in revitalizing a Hopi Tribal representative
government that had gone dormant in the years during and immediately after
World War II. In all those efforts, he had made a name for himself not only in
Utah and Arizona state politics but also in the circles of the federal administration as it related to Native Nations and natural resource exploitation in the
American Southwest.

It turns out that Boyden also had a personal interest in seeing the Hopi
Tribal government revitalized. At the same time when he was working with
select Hopi leadership (notably including my mentor's father, also named
Emory Sekaquaptewa, among others), he was informing executives at Peabody Coal Company in confidential meetings about the large coal deposits
found on the Hopi reservation (Wilkinson 1999). He was actively speaking
with Peabody and other interested parties to sell them on the possibility that
the coal on the Hopi reservation would be commercially exploitable once
a viable Hopi Tribal government was in place to approve any agreement to
lease the Tribe's mineral rights. Such approvals could happen only after the
resolution of a generations-long land dispute between the Hopi and Navajo

5. Indian Claims Commission Docket No. 210, Aug. 8, 1951 at 2–3.

Nations, including over the lands with the richest seams of coal. It was a dispute, moreover, that the Hopi long felt had been exacerbated by the United States by either actively encouraging or turning a blind eye to Navajo encroachment and violent exclusion of Hopi on lands with important ceremonial locales and which the Hopi viewed as their Aboriginal homeland.

Boyden was always open about the fact that his unpaid position as the Hopi Tribe's general counsel was premised on the possibility that in the future, if he "could do something with [Hopi] resources, I will get paid" (quoted in Wilkinson 1999, 287). Nevertheless, he categorically denied ever representing Peabody Coal on matters related to its dealings with Hopi. Many suggest that Boyden's own papers, as well as the rather bad lease agreement that the Hopi Tribe approved with Peabody Coal and the settlement for an amount far below the market value of the claims that it extinguished, prove otherwise (Wilkinson 1999). Subsequent agreements and lawsuits against Peabody Coal by the Tribe rectified the more egregious terms of their original lease agreement, but the settlement monies remain a hotly contested issue among Hopi, with many saying that money should have never been accepted as compensation for lost territory that constitutes the very core of who they are as a Nation.

It is understandable that the Hopi Tribal government was susceptible to accusations of complicity, witting or unwitting, in the unscrupulous machinations of the non-Native actors with whom it engaged, even those ostensibly claiming to work on its behalf. I also think it is possible to see at least some Hopi leaders choosing to engage with their non-Native counterparts in ways that reflect Hopi Indigenous theories of CWS. This is evident, for example, in the Shungopavi petition, which came from Hopi leaders in an autonomous village, and not as part of the Tribal government that was to be its representative voice to the United States (Wilkinson 1999). The Shungopavi petition sought restitution of land rights, with petitioners engaging US agencies on terms proffered by the same federal system that had dispossessed them. Their mode of argumentation was not to capitulate to US forms and theories of legal claiming but to press their claims based on their traditional knowledge and their obligations to care for the land they call *Hopitutskwa*, their homelands. Their form of engagement, refusal to accept others' representations of their position, and insistence on stating their complaints to an ICC commission that was (perhaps not unsurprisingly) unwilling or unable to hear it all bear the hallmark of Hopi cooperation without submission.

These Hopi norms, knowledge, relations, and theories and practices of cooperation without submission reveal themselves even more fully in the hours of oral testimony that Hopi witnesses provided in ICC evidentiary hearings from 1961 to 1976. It is here that we get a better sense of the everyday work of Hopi-US engagement as the site for Hopi self-determination in the making.

Consider the following interaction at the Hopi Tribe's ICC hearing that took place in October 1961 between a Hopi traditional leader named Duke Pahona and Boyden, the lawyer for the Hopi Tribe. It occurs after Boyden establishes that Pahona is his village's *tsaakmongwi*, or crier chief, a position of considerable authority. He assumed this role partly because of his membership in the Tsu'ngyam (Snake Clan) and partly because his maternal uncle, the tsaakmongwi before him, tapped him to receive the traditional knowledge and responsibilities that went with that role. For the Hopi in the room, the recitation of these credentials alone would mark Pahona as a *navoti'ytaqa*, a man of knowledge and respect, someone who would be understood as having the requisite gravitas to lend legitimacy to his testimony.

But this is not the only reason he was called as a witness to testify. Pahona's ceremonial position gave him access to certain traditional sacred knowledge and paraphernalia that directly bore on some of the land claims that the Hopi were making before the commission. In particular, he was the possessor of, and had brought with him, an object the Hopi call a *tiiponi*, which are emblems of Hopi ceremonial office held and passed from one officeholder to the next. Pahona's tiiponi was particularly relevant to these proceedings not only because it represented his position but also it had been given to Snake Clan leaders a century earlier by Navajo leaders to memorialize a mutually agreed upon territorial border between their two nations.

Pahona testifies to this history, sharing the location where the border agreement took place, to which his tiiponi pointed, but claiming the Navajo had since violated the agreement. Interestingly, despite being the sole authority charged with possessing the tiiponi, and even being in possession of it that day, Pahona refuses to publicly share what it is made of, at least at first. After Boyden asks Pahona to describe the contents of the tiiponi, Pahona responds:

006   Pahona   It is a secret that I just can't expose here.
007   Boyden   But it is something that is handed to you is it not?
008   Pahona   Yes, sir.

The issue is that despite his ceremonial authority, Hopi norms about the transmission of ceremonial knowledge prevent the display of the tiiponi to anyone who is not a member of Pahona's ceremonial society or his clan. All that he is willing to share is that it was indeed "handed" to him by his *taha* (maternal uncle).

But then, after some discussion about the location of the border in question, and the history of the agreement, Pahona seems to have a change of heart. This happens after Boyden asking the following:

020	Boyden	Now, do you have that [tiiponi]?
021	Pahona	Yes, sir.
022	Boyden	Have you shown that to anyone?
023	Pahona	I haven't shown it to anybody excepting down at Prescott at the time the hearing was going on.
		I thought it was the right time to show it but I didn't show it.
024	Boyden	Now, why didn't you show it when you came to Prescott?
025	Pahona	Well, it wasn't the right time, it wasn't right for me to show it until this claim proposition come up, then my lawyer told me to bring it up and show it.
026	Boyden	So your lawyer was me at that time, was it not?
027	Pahona	Yes, sir.
028	Boyden	And I told you it was not the proper case to bring it in, the claims case?
029	Pahona	Yes, sir.
030	Boyden	So now, you have brought it with you?
031	Pahona	Yes, sir.
032	Boyden	Now, you don't want this to leave your possession do you?
033	Pahona	No, sir.
034	Boyden	Do you have any objection to showing it at this time, then?
035	Pahona	No, sir.

What to make of this interaction? Why is Pahona initially unwilling to share the makeup of the Snake Clan tiiponi, though he is willing to describe how it had been given to him by his uncle, and moreover that it signifies an important agreement between the Hopi and Navajo Tribes relevant to the case at hand? Recall that Pahona is testifying in Washington, DC, some two thousand miles from his home on the Hopi reservation. It is all the more curious that he would refuse to describe an object of such import that he brought so far with him, an object that he explains had never "been shown to anybody." And then, what to make of the (seemingly preplanned decision) to reveal it to the commissioners and the rest of the hearing participants (including notably, other Hopi representatives from different clans), after Boyden requests him to do so? How should we understand Pahona's assent not only to reveal this sacred ceremonial object he is unwilling to even describe just moments before but also the claim, as Boyden asserts, that it is the non-Hopi attorney's idea that Pahona not show his tiiponi at a previous hearing, but instead to do it here.

Without being present at the hearing, it is impossible to know what the sentiment in the room was at the singular moment when Pahona reveals his tiiponi, and in so doing arguably establishing ceremonial authority and violating the obligations that come with it at the very same time. Given such a charged event, for Hopi, it is perhaps a bit of a blessing that the reporter's transcript memorializes the event in typical laconic fashion in which nonverbal acts are represented, with a simple parenthetical:

039   (The witness produced the Tiponi under discussion.)

I suggest that Pahona's testimony, and the ways in which the lines and limits of traditional sacred knowledge, its transmission, and the norms and social relations it presupposes and produces—with all the people in the room, Hopi and non-Hopi, advocate, adversary, and administrator alike—all resonate with Hopi theories of CWS. Indeed, and famously, virtually every effort by Euro-Americans to engage with Hopi via two dominant modes of modern knowledge production (or epistemology)—that is, law and science—have regularly and repeatedly confronted both limits and lines of engagement from Hopi Peoples insisting on their rights to regulate how their stories will and will not unfold. I argue that the limits that Hopi actors present to those non-Natives seeking to engage them and their norms, knowledge, and relations resonate with how such matters are conveyed and policed by and between Hopi themselves.

✶

Hopis have always been deeply engaged in diagnosing the epistemological and relational lines and limits among each other, relying on complexities of navoti and wiwta to do so in ways that enact performances and transmissions of Hopi knowledge with key Hopi normative authority. In so doing, Hopi concerns about who possesses navoti, how they came to have it, and with whom they choose to share it animate questions of authority and relationality that constitute the everyday enactment of Hopi sociopolitical practices.

I argue that these Hopi theories of knowledge production, and the dispersed, decentralized, and diffused ways in which knowledge is transmitted to some and withheld from others, are at the heart of Hopi theories of social

ordering, self-determination, and sovereignty that give specific meaning to
Hopi notions of CWS. I argue that Hopi notions of navoti and wiwta make
texts and interactions in which Hopi knowledge is a topic sites for Hopi to
enact their normative authority and relationships to those with whom they
are engaged. This is true not only for interactions between Hopi but also between Hopi and non-Hopi. It is this idea that is understood by Hopi notions
of cooperation without submission, and that I believe operates in Hopi Tribal
engagements with US officials and agencies. This explains why Hopi regularly
take exception to the Euro-American modes of knowledge that non-Native
actors deploy, and the legal and scientific authority they seek to generate. It
also explains why they invite other modes of relating that foreground the required respect and mutuality when Hopi are informing the legal and political
decisions under deliberation. This is true for Hopi Tribal actors engaging in
the everyday work of Tribal engagements with non-Natives, even when those
non-Natives engage them, as Boyden seems to have done, with duplicity,
complicity, and self-dealing. As one Hopi said to an author who investigated
Boyden's work with the Hopi:

> The Hopi way is that you trust everybody. If a stranger asks you for some-
> thing, you give it to him. If he betrays that trust, that's his problem, not the
> Hopi's problem. The Hopi aren't the victims, other people are the victims. But
> many people have violated our trust. (quoted in Wilkinson 1999, 288–289)

I thus suggest that the Hopi, like many Native Nations caught up with settler colonial relations, claim an enduring sovereign authority in which normative knowledge and the relations forged by its transmission play animating
roles. This is true not just for working out a legal or political claim specifically
but also for negotiating the whole of Native-US relations more generally. Indeed, for subjects who describe themselves as Indigenous, and thereby mark
their anterior positionality vis-à-vis contemporary nation-states, one might
say that this mode of engagement constitutes a kind of cooperation without
submission that has always defined the everyday operations of their governance as self-determining nations.

But as with any theory, Indigenous or otherwise, an anthropological and
critical approach to unpacking its operations requires some consideration
of the sociohistorical and communicative contexts from which it originally
emerged. I now turn to that context, albeit in a manner that reveals the very
problems of legal and scientific knowledge practices that the Hopi have strug-
gled against. I will first review the ways in which Euro-American legal and
social-scientific knowledge has described Hopi society and culture over the

years, and the problems—for Hopi and non-Hopi alike—these descriptions have raised. I then turn to the ways in which Hopi understandings of their philosophies, histories, institutions, and practices have started shifting from being the object of Euro-American inquiry to at least partly informing their guiding theories, and how. In so doing, I hope this chapter clarifies, as much as it describes, the ways in which the Hopi have continued to assert, despite ongoing "unrecognition" on the part of their non-Native counterparts, their sovereign authority and self-determining right to dictate the terms of their representation by, and relationships to, Euro-American agencies and institutions. This chapter lays the foundation of Indigenous Hopi theories that inform the other chapters in this book and of proper relations respecting Hopi commitments to CWS.

What Euro-American Law and Science "Know" about the Hopi

According to the 2010 US Census, of the approximate 13,000 Hopi Tribal members, around 5,300 call the Hopi reservation their primary residence.[6] This reservation, demarcated by executive order of President Chester Arthur in 1882, compasses 1.5 million acres of Aboriginal Hopi lands, a fraction of the much larger territorial expanse that Hopis claim as their Hopitutskwa (figure 3.1).[7]

Tribal members living on the reservation occupy twelve villages located either on or around three mesas called, since the arrival of Euro-Americans in the early 1800s, First, Second and Third Mesa (running east to west). Before the 1930s, nine of these villages operated under autonomous village leadership without a Tribal organization or Tribal governance structure. After 1936, and pursuant to the Indian Reorganization Act, these autonomous Hopi villages were federated into a Hopi Tribe. At that time, a convention of Hopi leaders and federal officials drafted the constitution and by-laws of the Hopi Tribe, which passed into force via election by adult Hopi members. This vote was not without controversy given that less than one-third of the eligible Hopi population cast a ballot.

6. US Census 2010, "Table 1. American Indian and Alaska Native Population by Tribe for the United States: 2010," and "TableID PCT3. American Indian And Alaska Native Alone or in Combination With One or More Other Races and with One or More Tribes Reported for Selected Tribes, Hopi Reservation and Off-Reservation Trust Lands," 2010 Census CPH-T-6, American Indian and Alaska Native Tribes in the United States and Puerto Rico (Washington, DC: US Census Bureau)

7. Executive Order of President Chester A. Arthur, December 16,1882; Moqui (or Hopi) Reserve. In *Executive Orders Relating to Indian Reserves From May 14, 1855 to July 1, 1902.* Compiled by the Indian Office Under Authority of Act of Congress Approved May 17, 1882 22 Stat. p. 88. (Washington, DC: Government Printing Office, 1902), p. 9.

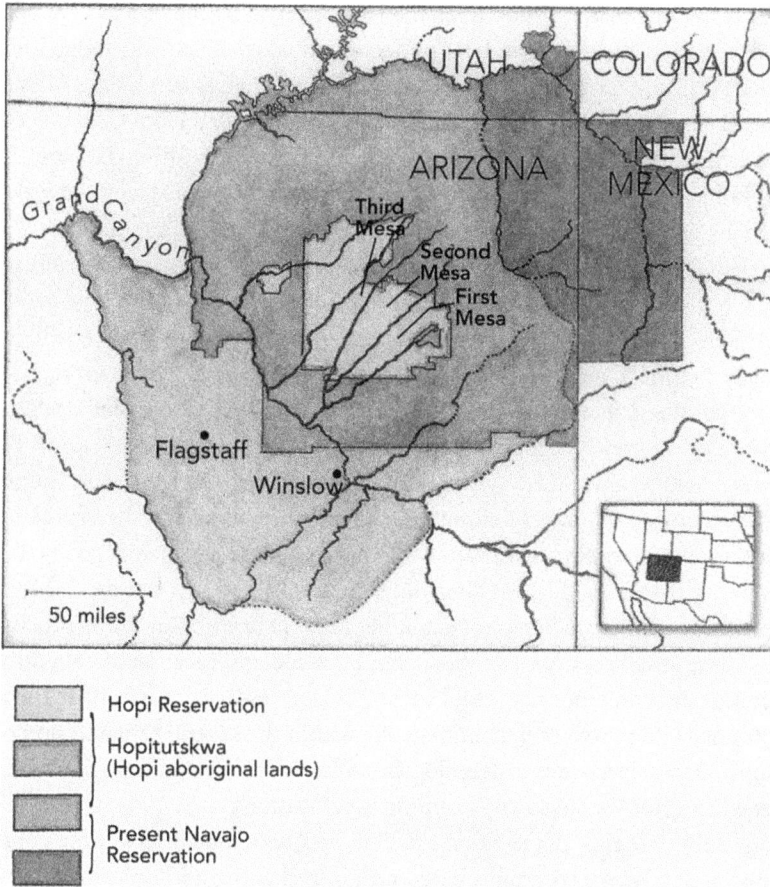

FIGURE 3.1. Hopitutskwa: Hopi Aboriginal homelands. Used with permission from Peter Whiteley.

Significantly, this nonparticipation may have been an expression of opposition. Even the federal agent from the Bureau of Indian Affairs (BIA) charged with overseeing the drafting and election process recognized that "those [Hopi] who are against something stay away from meetings at which it is to be discussed and generally refuse to vote on it" (La Farge 1937, 8). Nonetheless, on December 19, 1936, the Hopi Constitution was deemed by the US secretary of the interior to have been ratified by popular election, even though only 755 of the 2,538 Hopis eligible to vote did so—and of those, 104 voted against it.

The Hopi Constitution called for the creation of a Hopi Tribal Council, constituted of representatives elected by members of each Hopi village. They were expected to exercise legislative and executive powers over intervillage matters as well as matters between the Hopi Tribe and other US federal, state, and Tribal entities. The judicial power of the Hopi Tribe was lodged with the BIA, in the form of a Hopi Court of Indian Offenses run by the BIA's assigned Hopi agent. But in 1972, the Tribal Council passed Hopi Ordinance 21, abolishing the BIA's Courts of Indian Offenses and establishing the Hopi Tribal Judiciary, which includes both a trial and appellate court staffed by Hopi Tribal officials acting as judges, prosecutors, bailiffs, and court clerks.

Though the Tribal institutions established by the 1936 Hopi Constitution have become "the de facto political form for the majority of Hopi people" (Whiteley 1988, 230), the legitimacy questions surrounding Hopi Tribal governance more generally remain "a dominant issue in Hopi politics" (223). It is these politics that are refracted through a lens that divides so-called traditionalist from progressive Hopi (Clemmer 1995; Geertz 1994; Whiteley 1988). This divisiveness was not unanticipated by the drafters of the Hopi Constitution. With an objective of ameliorating the traditionalist objections, the 1936 constitution included explicit reservation of power to village leadership, giving them authority over intravillage matters, including disputes over family, child custody, and adoption; assignment and inheritance of farming land; and property.

Thus, in telling what is known about the sociopolitical practices and institutions of contemporary Hopi society, it is necessary to investigate the institutions and practices that animate life within the several semiautonomous Hopi villages. Here the epistemological authority of law and legal scholarship generally gives way to social-scientific investigations.

Anthropologists suggest that even before 1936, Hopi villages were constituted of several social groups based on kin reckoning and descent, which is measured matrilineally. These groups are known as phratries, clans, lineages, and sublineages, which move from broader to narrower groupings in which each category tends to include at least one of the categories that follow it. They also agree that Hopi residence is matrilocal and marriage exogamous at the phratry level (Clemmer 1978; Eggan 1950; Levy 1992; Nagata 1970; Titiev 1944).

Anthropologists also found that Hopi village life is governed through duties and obligations generated among village members in an elaborate ceremonial cycle that occupies the entire Hopi year. These ceremonies are based on the navoti of each individual clan gained during its originary migrations before settling at the village it now occupies. Hopi ceremonies are typically overseen by the heads of the clans, but they are performed by members of larger ceremonial societies whose initiates transect clan lines across the village (R. Brandt 1954; Geertz 1994; Titiev 1944).

These ceremonies instantiate the origins of clans, enacting the same central narrative that informs Hopi prophecies (discussed below). In this narrative, each clan emerged from the Third World into this, the Fourth World, and migrated to its current village site. The first clan to arrive met Maasaw, the spirit owner of the land, and in exchange for agreeing to live in proper relationship to the land—namely, the perpetuation of a ritually ordained dry-farming process in which corn was the central crop—the clan was allowed to use the land for its own well-being. Each clan that arrived after the first was required to perform a ceremony based on the knowledge it had learned from some spirit ancestor (which would later become its totem, an animal such as a bear, snake, badger, or spider but also elements such as fire and natural substances such as reed and sand). In exchange for that performance, and if it was efficacious to advancing community well-being (i.e., bringing rain), the clan was given a parcel of farming land and allowed to build its central home and thereafter be a part of the village community. Each clan has its own version of this narrative that serves as the charter of that clan's place in the village community. As such, the yearly ceremonial performance that enacts that charter and the cycle constituted by each of these clan-owned ceremonies is, as anthropologists have argued, the enactment and instantiation of the village community charter as a whole (e.g., Titiev 1944).

As Whiteley (1988) aptly put it, "[C]lanship continues to give the [Hopi] individual a primary identity that supersedes village or mesa membership or more general 'Hopi' identity" (177). Moreover, an anthropological truism is that Hopi clans are the corporate holders of land, ceremonial homes, and offices of ritual authority that correspond to each clan's original contribution to the village. And the ritual embodiment of these origins via the ceremony controlled by each clan thus constitutes, over the course of the cycle, the yearly reassertion of the charter by which the village itself is constituted (Geertz 1994).

This, at least, is the story that Euro-American law and science generally tell about Hopi culture, society, and the juridico-political institutions that animate Hopi life today. Hopefully, readers of this book discern an alarmingly pat story that moves from the familiar terrain of Euro-American juridical and political actions regarding the Hopi to Hopi Tribal governance modalities that resemble European institutions, back to the seemingly autochthonic modes of Hopi social norms, structures, and practices. But, as readers should also expect, the picture of contemporary Hopi sovereignty is far more complex, despite a leading anthropologist of the Hopi writing: "Anthropology practically begins at Hopi and Hopi is substantially represented . . . in every theoretical paradigm [of the discipline]" (Whiteley 1998, 7). To account for the complexities attending an understanding of Hopi sociality, one must consider the ways in which, at least for Hopi, the knowledge of their ways is itself diffuse and dispersed, and necessitates the ostensibly contradictory commitment to a social order grounded in an Indigenous juris-diction of CWS.

Returning to the internal debates on the creation and operation of the Hopi Tribal government, many members emphasize that the traditionalist-versus-progressive distinction often bears no real relationship to Hopi Peoples' actual commitment to ceremonial life. Some point to those who have worked for years in Tribal government and are known to be deeply involved in village ceremonies and hold clan leadership positions. Others suggest that those who call themselves traditionalist often find greater audiences for their message among non-Hopi than among fellow Tribal members.

The latter point to the extent to which these traditionalists often avail themselves of political activity outside of the Hopi community, including trips to Washington, DC, and the United Nations, or joining in alliances with counterculture and Pan-Indian activists (Geertz 1994). By doing so, they alienate themselves from the very village, clan, and ceremonial relations of which they claim leadership, insofar as it is decidedly *qahopi* (morally wrong, literally "not Hopi") to claim a position of traditional authority and offer sacred clan knowledge that is not to be shared with noninitiates.

The complexities of the politics of Hopi tradition thus raise questions about competing claims to ceremonial authority, clan identity, and the transmission of Hopi knowledge. Anthropological efforts to answer these questions have been the source of some entrenched confusion in Euro-American efforts to "know" Hopi. At the heart of that confusion are questions of traditional knowledge as a closely held source and marker of social power and authority.

Received wisdom is to view the clan as a "corporate" possessor of land, clan homes, and the sacred knowledge and authority from which these material rights emanate, but many suggest that actual Hopi practices of transmission of these resources reveals something quite different (e.g., Eggan 1950; Levy 1992; Titiev 1944; Whiteley 1986, 1987). For example, Titiev describes his own confusion about Hopi, that "whenever the statement is made that a certain office of ceremonial privilege belongs to a clan, concrete data always shows that the transmission is above all, within the narrow circle of actual blood-kin [lineage] and only secondarily to unrelated clansmen" (Titiev 1944, 46). Eggan (1950) highlights the same contradiction when he writes that the "clan is the outstanding unit of social organization. . . . The Hopi have utilized the clan as a primitive 'corporation'" (110), but also argues that it is "the lineage [that] is of primary importance to the Hopi because it contains the *mechanism* for transmitting rights, duties, land, houses, and ceremonial knowledge" (109).

What quickly emerges in compassing the extant ethnography of Hopi clanship is an apparent conflict between analysts' descriptions of Hopi clans as "corporate" *possessors* of cultural, epistemological, and material resources and the vision of lineage and descent as the "mechanism" of *transmission*, privileging access to those resources for some clan members over others.

Whiteley explains that this conflict gives a central role to Hopi considerations of navoti. As mentioned earlier, navoti refers ideally to "valued knowledge" that "concerns the ability to influence, create or transform events in the world," most importantly to bring rain (Whiteley 1998, 94). Navoti is precisely that sacred, efficacious knowledge originally transmitted to each clan by the totemic ancestor it encountered during migrations, and then passed down through the generations during secret ritual interactions between initiates to the same ceremonial society, or among (certain) members of the same clan (Whiteley 1998; see also Kroskrity 1993; Whiteley 1985, 1986, 1988).

Whiteley argues that the apparent contradictions between property possession and transmission among the Hopi have to do with a social-scientific rendering of Hopi society as revolving around the egalitarian distribution of material resources within clan corporations unrecognizable. In fact, he writes, "from a Hopi perspective, the valued resource lies not in material conditions, but in the ability to transform these through supernatural skills" (Whiteley 1998, 92): skills gained through navoti. Thus it is differential access to navoti that explains the contradiction between the supposedly corporate character of Hopi clanship and the transmission of property (in practice at least) along more narrow lines of direct descent.

Instead, Whiteley suggests that Hopi make something akin to a "class" distinction between *pavansinom* (important/ruling people) and *sukavungsinom* (common/ordinary people) in which "*pavansinom* are primarily those . . . who hold principal offices in the ritual order. Non-members of apical segments and members of clans which own no ceremonies, important offices, or highly valued ritual knowledge generally lack control over significant supernatural power are thus *sukavungsinom*" (Whiteley 1986, 70).[8]

This access to navoti is also tightly guarded (Whiteley 1986). The central role that secrecy plays in Pueblo ceremonialism and social stratification has been well documented in the ethnographic and archaeological records (E. Brandt 1980, 1994; Debenport 2015; Ortiz 1969; Whiteley 1988, 1998). As Whiteley writes:

> Hopi ritual practice is highly secretive. . . . Secrecy is strictly enjoined on all initiates and breaches meet with severe social and supernatural sanctions. . . .

---

8. For evidence of knowledge-based social stratification in the archaeological record related to Hopi, see E. Brandt 1980, 1994.

> Secrecy serves to keep valued knowledge, in this oral culture, exclusively in
> the hands of an elite group of ritual specialists. (Whiteley 1998, 92).

This strict regime of secrecy around navoti and its ritual transmission imposes limits on access to knowledge of tradition in ways that make it a scarce resource, held by some to the exclusion of others. It is in light of this "paradigm of secrecy" that ritual knowledge "serves as the scheme of value, the 'currency,' perhaps, of power" (Whiteley 1986, 74).

But even Whiteley's efforts to reconcile the differences between Hopi possession and inheritance through the lens of navoti has received critical reconsideration. The research of Jerrold Levy (1992) shows how the historical politico-religious position of lineages within Hopi clans have, in fact, shifted over time. He writes that within multilineage clans, "the actual function of lineages—as prime, alternate, or marginal—works to rearrange the status of the lineages and lineage segments within a single generation. In effect, lineage composition is almost constantly in a state of flux" (48). Levy argues that a particular head lineage can fail to reproduce in the next generation, so other lineages within these clans assume the positions of clan leadership and ceremonial authority available to them. Thus, even though some lineages seem excluded from inheriting these resources at a particular moment in time, and therefore appear as sukavungsinom, there nonetheless exists the potential that at a later point they will gain access via inheritance. Levy describes a certain fluidity with which Whiteley's "class" distinctions play out for Hopi Peoples. Even in the largest multilineage clans, there always remains a chance, however slight, that any individual woman and her descendants might succeed to prime positions within the clan. Thus, succession alone (or lack thereof) makes it possible for any sukavungsinom to become pavansinom, and vice versa.

An even more dynamic vision of this distinction was offered by Emory Sekaquaptewa. From his perspective, the difference between pavansinom and sukavungsinom has never constituted a universally recognized hierarchy within clans, but rather is a subjective distinction by which some Hopi individuals describe others (Sekaquaptewa, personal communication, August 10, 2000). That is, they are politically motivated monikers, by which Hopi selectively label their allies as important/ruling people or their ideological enemies as common/ordinary people. Or vice versa. Given the abiding Hopi ethic of humility and disavowals of social power and authority, Hopi regularly describe themselves as "no one special," while looking askance at rivals whose pride leads them to think of themselves as some self-appointed "fathers to all of us." Sometimes, a Hopi person's explicit disavowals of social power would be quickly followed up with allusions to their participation in this or that secret ceremony that would have been accessible only to an initiate of considerable ritual authority. Nonetheless, those who got described as claiming the authority of "traditional leaders" would regularly be described by Emory as being all too willing to recite their supposed navoti to all who would listen, and do so "like a song"—that is, *sounding* beautiful but signifying nothing (Richland 2010). Either way, it should be recognized that describing someone as pavansinom or sukavungsinom carries implications that say more about the speaker's own relation to the person being described than any inherent authority or deep knowledge held by that person.

All of this leads to the argument that ceremonial knowledge and social relations are deeply intertwined in the interactional accomplishment of Hopi social power and authority, and they may be significant in actual categories of relation. That is, given that the distinction between pavansinom and sukavungsinom seems rather porous, one can imagine the significant symbolic and even political advantage that accrues to those Hopi actors who, through the practices and performances of their authoritative engagements, identify themselves (albeit often only by inference) as being pavansinom. This can generate significant leverage from which to press their claims to cultural and material resources. Moreover, given that the distinction turns fundamentally on the possession of navoti, including deep understanding of the clan origin narratives, one can also recognize the significant legitimacy Hopi actors gain if they can both properly situate claims to resources in a framework that marks theirs as an informed understanding of navoti and themselves as being the pavansinom capable of such deep, inscrutable understanding. This is corroborated by Whiteley: "Ritual knowledge is a 'strategic resource.' . . . The structure of ritual leadership is simultaneously the structure of political leadership" (Whiteley 1986, 71).

Hopi Knowing, Norming, and Relating to Euro-American Appropriations

I have often wondered how this ethic, which is deeply interwoven in Hopi intrasocietal relations within clans and villages, might also explain the ways in which the Hopi Tribal government today orients to and enacts its relations with traditional seats of Hopi village and clan authority and with the Hopi People generally. Recently, the Hopi Tribe adopted the *Hopit Potskwaniat*, (Hopi plan for the future, or a way forward for living the Hopi life) as an expression of its constitutive commitments and goals. The document references two concepts: *nami'nangwa* and *sumi'nangwa*. These might be thought to capture some of what Emory Sekaquaptewa was translating as cooperation without submission. The first term, "nami'nangwa," is glossed as a "mutual concern for others' welfare" (Bureau of Applied Research in Anthropology 1997). It combines the reciprocal destinative/dative prefix *naami*- (mutually toward/for each other) with the noun *unangwa*, which Hopi translate as heart, chest, or breast, and, as importantly, the center of one's being and identity as it relates to their wants, wishes, and desires. "Sumi'nangwa" combines *unangwa* with the adverbial nonsingular prefix *suumi*-, which is glossed as denoting a coming together "in one place, as a whole, collectively" (Bureau of Applied Research in Anthropology 1997).

Though the two terms seem to indicate the notions of collaboration and cooperation that have been well described in the literature about and by Hopi, I think their co-occurrence suggests that, in the context of the Hopit Potskwaniat, they may signify to Hopi a subtle but important difference. Indeed, in the first term, the prefix *naami*- is used to index not only the reciprocal (mutually toward each other) but also the reflexive (toward oneself). One can perhaps see how this term also captures the sense of a noncoercive, nonsubmission quality of mutual concern, care, and cooperation that rests at the heart of Hopi social norms and practices. As captured by "nami'nangwa," one might also say that, for Hopi, a regard for others is also a regard for oneself, and to care for others is to care for oneself.

In the Hopit Potskwaniat, is it expected one would read the concept of nami'nangwa alongside, yet distinct from, the holism of the "togetherness" captured by the adverbial *suumi*- of the notion of sumi'nangwa (a heart toward the whole)? Their co-occurrence would seem to foreground the idea that the goal of striving to orient one's wants, wishes, desires, and prayers toward the benefit of the Hopi collective—to have a heart toward the whole—one must do so willingly, voluntarily, seeing one's own individual benefit from such an effort. In short, reading these two notions side by side as the guiding principles of Hopi governance under the Hopit Potskwaniat suggests just the kind of irreducibly complex combination of simultaneous mutuality and autonomy captured so eloquently by the phrase "cooperation without submission." Moreover, doing so offers a different perspective on what might, at first, seem like contradictory stances taken by Hopi leaders, past and present, in their engagements with non-Native agencies and organizations, including the United States.

Cooperation without Submission, the *Tsu'tsikive*, and the Hopi Cultural Preservation Office

Whether it was coincidence, a subtle aspect of their advocacy, or some Hopi providence, the significance that Duke Pahona—the Hopi witness in the ICC claims case described earlier—was also a chief of the Snake Clan would likely not have been lost on the ICC commissioners. The Snake Clan, after all, controls and enacts the *tsu'tsikive*, the snake ceremony and what non-Natives often refer to as the Hopi snake dance. By the late nineteenth century, that ritual had become a prime interest of Euro-American visitors to the three remote, high-desert mesas (Fewkes [1900] 1977; Voth [1903] 1967).

Heinrich R. Voth was a Mennonite missionary and early researcher among the Hopi; he lived with them in the village of Kykotsmovi for nearly a decade at the end of the nineteenth century. He explained that by the 1890s, "of the many rites and performances in the Hopi ceremonial calendar, none is perhaps better known—in a general way—than the snake ceremony . . . it has been witnessed by far more white people than any other Hopi ceremony" (Voth [1903] 1967, 271). As Voth notes, this supposed "knowledge" has always been one of familiarity, not comprehension. Visitors' fascination is the undoubtedly spectacular display of ceremonial participants dancing in their village plazas with live rattlesnakes dangling from their mouths and hands, but that is the final public element of what is a much more elaborate sixteen-day ceremony, the bulk of which occurs in the kivas. As Voth explains, before 1896, "no white person had ever been permitted to witness the secret part of the Snake ceremony until the writer of this paper gained admittance" (271).

Even at the time of Voth's observations, many Hopi were rather ambivalent about the Euro-American attention their ceremony received. Voth notes on more than one occasion Hopi participants objecting to him being among them in the kiva, "fearing . . . that my presence might interfere with the efficacy of the ceremony" (Voth [1903] 1967, 292). Despite these objections, Voth stayed to observe and document the bulk of the snake ceremony, as well as other aspects of Hopi ceremonial and everyday life, all of which would later be published by Chicago's Field Columbian Museum as some of the first—and still most—comprehensive ethnographic research on Hopi culture and society. The Field Columbian Museum is now known as the Field Museum, and it is some of the cultural patrimony originally collected by Voth that today sits on shroud-covered shelves in the depths of its collections center, right alongside the un-accessioned Hopi prayer feather hung by Hopi officials during a recent consultation concerning their repatriation. Their obligations to these beings never ceased, however dormant the relations may have been after a century-long disruption.

But if the Hopi thought that Voth's access and appropriations might satisfy American appetites for "exotica," they were wrong. Less than two decades later, Americans desired to perform Hopi culture themselves. Starting in 1921, in the northern Arizona town of Prescott, American businessmen would burlesque the Hopi snake dance with their own public "Smoki" performances, dressing in red-face and dancing in front of plywood kivas with bull snakes in their mouths. Though the Smokis would later become something of a "public service" fraternal order, boasting membership that included some of Arizona's most influential men (including Barry Goldwater), they would continue their "snake dances" into the early 1990s, when protests led by Hopi Tribal members generated sufficient public pressure to force them to desist (Whiteley 1998).

Between these and other incidents of disruption, dispossession, and appropriation by Americans, including those made in the name of social science, many Hopi had had enough. By the end of the twentieth century, several Hopi villages had officially closed the public parts of their snake ceremonies, as well as other ceremonial events held throughout the year, and members considered whether further anthropological and archaeological research as a whole should come to an end (Whiteley 1998).

These unwanted intrusions, as well as a particularly egregious act by a linguist to publish esoteric Hopi ceremonial knowledge against their objections, led Hopi Tribal chairman Vernon Masayesva to create a new position in his cabinet in 1990, to which he appointed Leigh Kuwanwisiwma, who had played a key role protesting both the Smoki dances and the scholarly publication by the linguist. A few years later, the Hopi Tribal Council passed legislation to formalize the Hopi Cultural Preservation Office as a part of the Hopi Tribe's Department of Natural Resources, and Kuwanwisiwma was named its first director. He would serve in that capacity for nearly thirty years, retiring only in 2018.

Over that period of time, Kuwanwisiwma was a towering presence in the field of Indigenous cultural heritage protection and preservation, and not just in the southwest of the United States but also around the world. This was a product both of his unwavering advocacy for Hopi cultural property rights and his willingness to partner with those non-Native researchers and their institutions that were ready to rethink their own commitments to the very Hopi norms and practices they claimed to take an interest in. In a 2008 interview with archaeologist T. J. Ferguson, one of his longtime non-Native partners, Kuwanwisiwma specifically references notions of jurisdiction when talking about how he envisions his office's collaborations with non-Native researchers:

> We know the reality of archaeology—where, for example, I think locally archaeology and maybe the jurisdictions have had to compromise. . . . They still proceed with the project or the field schools or the excavations, and it also accommodates the [Hopi] cultural concerns. . . . So I think that's an example

of where—maybe not everybody is satisfied—but certainly [compromise is] there. (Kuwanwisiwma 2008, 161)

And indeed, Kuwanwisiwma remained an active and engaged partner with non-Native archaeologists and other scholars in the publication of research that devolves some benefit to the claims and interests of the Hopi Tribe, whether directly or indirectly (Ferguson, Dongoske, and Kuwanwisiwma 2001; Kuwanwisiwma 2002; Ferguson and Colwell 2008; Ferguson, Koyiyumptewa, and Hopkins 2015; Kuwanwisiwma, Ferguson, and Colwell 2018). Indeed, after working tirelessly to shut down the Smokis' "snake dance"—what he once described as both a "serious and hilarious . . . romanticizing of Hopi culture, looking at about fifty white guys trying to dance"—Kuwanwisiwma would later become a longtime volunteer member of the Native American Board of Advisors of the Smoki Museum, an institution in Prescott that houses the Smokis' world-class collection of ancient pottery from the Hopi and other Pueblo Nations, displaying some of them right alongside a history of the Smoki organization and images from its public performances.

While a large measure of the mission that the HCPO sees itself as fulfilling involves protecting Hopis "rights to privacy and to Hopi Intellectual Property"[9] it is also the case that this protection sometimes means collaboration and engagement with non-Natives, so long as it is accomplished in ways that respect and promote Hopi interests. As is explained on the HCPO's official website:[10]

In this information age, we are concerned with protecting our own ideas. . . . After non-Hopis saw ceremonial dances, tape recorded copies of music were sold to outside sources. . . . Choreography from ceremonial dances has been copied and performed in non-sacred settings. Even the pictures of the ceremonies have been included in books without written permission. . . . All of these actions are breaches of Hopi intellectual property rights, used by non-Hopi for personal and commercial benefit without Hopi permission.

For the HCPO under Kuwanwisiwma's management, the problem was not only a violation of the Hopi knowledge practices, relations, and norms but also that those violations were perpetrated for non-Hopi benefit and without consulting with or gaining permission of the Hopi Tribe. This has been a consistent theme of the HCPO in its pursuit of its mission. Through its efforts,

9. Hopi Cultural Preservation Office, Protocol for Research, Publication and Recordings: Motion, Visual, Sound, Multimedia and other Mechanical Devices, p. 1 (document on file with author).

10. jan.ucc.nau.edu/hcpo-p/intellectPropRights.html (accessed June 27, 2020).

the HCPO has played a central role in monitoring the uses of Hopi cultural patrimony. Its agents have engaged in the protection of Hopi cultural and intellectual property on numerous fronts, including consulting on the housing and/or repatriation of Hopi materials kept in various public museums and private collections (see chapter 1); testifying as expert witnesses in federal, state, and Tribal litigation in which Hopi culture was implicated; and supervising the regulation of social-scientific research on the Hopi reservation.

At first glance, the notions and practices by which Hopi assert limits on who can know what about their ceremonies and the traditions they embody appear to be part of a broader scheme of Indigenous identity politics that has emerged in the last quarter of the twentieth century. Significantly, those politics have been at the center of an ongoing, often bitter, debate between Indigenous leaders and non-Native social scientists. The latter are critical of the notions of tradition and culture insofar as they embody, they say, inauthentic representations of essentialized Tribal pasts and cultural differences designed primarily for political gain by drawing strict borders of inclusion and exclusion and claiming authority against others based on those limits (Dombrowski 2001; Povinelli 2002).

It is undoubtedly true that Hopi social actors regularly invoke discourses of tradition in pursuing a contemporary politics of cultural difference, upon which they laminate claims to sovereignty and rights to self-determination. Moreover, they do so in ways that often produce conflicting statements about what "is" Hopi traditional knowledge and who has access to it, and in ways that suggest something of a rhetorical "invention" of what are claimed to be "timeless" Hopi norms and practices.

For example, Armin Geertz (1994), in his work on Hopi prophecy, views Hopi traditional practices and tradition as constantly reworked to fit the political and social contexts in which they are articulated. Based on a central core narrative shared by all Hopi as the story of their beginnings—Geertz calls it the emergence story—all prophetic narratives performed by different Hopi social actors at different times diverge from the core story with regard to certain details. It is the addition of such details, Geertz argues, that Hopis articulate in order to rationalize their political stances as they relate to the sociopolitical contexts in which these narratives are given.

An illuminating example is his description of a series of prophecies given in 1955 in hearings before the Bureau of Indian Affairs. Set up by a Hopi political coalition that called itself traditionalist—by virtue of their opposition to Hopi Tribal governance and its cooperation with Euro-Americans—these meetings were nonetheless open to those Hopi who supported the Tribal government and its policies.

Having both sides at this hearing, says Geertz, reveals interesting ways in which tradition is employed to generate and justify competing political stances. Geertz writes:

> Reading the minutes of the Hearings, one cannot avoid noticing the obvious disagreement evident in statements from the opposing factions on the Reservation. The terminology and details of supposedly age-old prophecies were no exceptions to this. On the one hand, we read statements describing the coming White Man in messianic terms . . . , and on the other hand, statements describing him as the great deceiver. (Geertz 1994, 204–5)

At first blush, Geertz's model of tradition seems no different than the models offered by critics of so-called inventions of Indigenous traditions (Clifton 1989; Hanson 1997; but see Clifford 2013). Indeed, at several points Geertz points out that many of these prophetic statements were articulated only after the occurrence of the events they claimed to predict, implicitly suggesting his own doubts on their truly prophetic character (Geertz 1994, 204–5).

But Geertz makes a critical adjustment that sets his model apart from other social-scientific analyses of "invented" Indigenous traditions. He suggests that it is problematic to view Hopi prophecies as making claims to "truth" or "fact," at least as Euro-American legal and scientific knowledge practices understand such claims. Instead, he calls for reliance on an "ethno-hermeneutic approach" to analyzing these discourses, suggesting that "there is no need . . . for us to account for . . . truth value. . . . But there is a need to explain [their] use, function, and meaning by and for the people who believe in it " (Geertz 1994, 147).

Importantly, Geertz's ethnohermeneutic approach has parallels in the more recent work of Hopi historian Lomayumtewa Ishii (2001), who dedicates his critical historiography to combating what he calls the "scientific historicide" perpetrated by Euro-American research that has "alienated and virtually silenced the Hopi voice" (3). In bringing to light the ways in which Hopi Peoples give meaning to their own pasts, Ishii reveals "the phenomenological principles of Hopi epistemology" (3), particularly as they are expressed through Hopi tradition and prophecy. Representations of the past in Hopi discourses of tradition and prophecy are significant not first and foremost as expressions of "fact" about events that have come and gone, but rather as admonitions for how Hopis ought to live in the present and future. As he writes:

> There is a Hopi memory consistent with Hopi epistemology that is qualitatively different than Anglophone views. . . . This Hopi view sees historical events as cyclical and prophetic in nature . . . and has become the logos of Hopi survival and cultural persistence. (Ishii 2001, 6)

Following this, I approach the complex rhetorics of traditional knowledge employed by Hopi political actors as having a particular valence for them. It is grounded in their own understanding of this knowledge—this navoti as a resource for claiming normative authority and the social relations both assumed and produced by that authority, through acts and understandings of the lines and limits of knowledge transmission, under what circumstances, and how.

This Hopi-specific understanding of the limits of knowledge is even suggested by the cautionary language on the HCPO's website. As a result of the non-Hopi "expropriations" of Hopi intellectual property, the website explains, "sacred rituals have been exposed to others out of context and without Hopi permission. . . . Information has reached individuals for whom it was not intended (e.g., Hopi youth, members of other clans, or non-Hopi)." The HCPO views its mission as much about protecting against the improper distribution of knowledge among Hopi Tribal members (i.e., Hopi youth and members of other clans), as from non-Hopis. This suggests that the politics of knowledge production and transmission informing Hopi practices is particular and does not easily map onto the politics of "invented tradition" more generally.

Pursuing the ways in which Hopi normative authority is enacted in navoti limits the legal and social-scientific epistemologies used to diagnose it; thus it has been necessary to briefly review what law and science actually claim to know about Hopi culture and society. While this may seem counterintuitive in a chapter about limits, it is often the case that the most reliable path to the unknown starts from the seemingly most secure epistemological purchase. But now we have to ask, if navoti and its significance in Hopi life are not things that map easily onto what scholars and officials have claimed to know about Hopi culture and society, what then can be said about them and the Hopi epistemologies, normativities, and relationalities that they produce and presuppose? And what does any of this have to do with Hopi Indigenous juris-dictions of cooperation without submission?

Knowing, Relating, Norming, and Hopi Juris-dictions

As noted above, the distinction between pavansinom and sukavungsinom when understood discursively is revealed as a practice by which Hopi individuals describe their social power and that of others in different ways, under different circumstances, and to different ends. This leads to the argument that distinctions between pavansinom and sukavungsinom may be as significant as rhetorical strategies as they are as actual categories of relation. That is, since the distinction between pavansinom and sukavungsinom is not set, there are symbolic and political advantages for those Hopi actors who can deftly navigate the interactional contexts where it is appropriate to allude to one's legitimate access to secret, sacred knowledge (and thus performing their status as pavansinom) while at the same time being sure to point up that whatever authority might accrue to them because of this access, they are still "not really anybody"; that is, sukavungsinom. Indeed, threading this rhetorical needle is particularly important for Hopi who find themselves in politically charged interactional contexts where they are speaking with or before Hopi from other clans. That is, while a Hopi speaker might be well served alluding to their own position as authoritative in their own clan's ceremonies and traditions, it is still the case that, vis-à-vis other clans and their ways of knowing, norming, and relating, they remain "not really anybody" and would do well to acknowledge that.

Bringing these complexities of Hopi relationality and epistemology into dialogue with what I earlier described as the role of discourse in contemporary Hopi politics creates an opening to understand the social significance of Hopi knowledge, its transmission, and the limits of that transmission with regard to Hopi juris-dictions of CWS, and Tribal sovereignty in action. As I contend below, the decision to maintain or break limits on this transmission of navoti figures centrally in both Hopi ideologies about traditional knowledge and the ways traditional discourse is actually performed in contemporary Tribal governance. In so doing, I once again follow the perspectives of Lomayumtewa Ishii, who argues that the particularities of Hopi epistemology are fundamentally informed by how knowledge is transmitted via oral communication. As he writes, "In order to articulate a Hopi perspective . . . it is imperative to critically examine the cultural contexts that are involved with orality and how orality links cultural structures with historical events" (Ishii 2001, 11).

I opened this chapter with a scene from a land claims hearing before the US Indian Claims Commission, convened to hear the Hopi Tribal Nation's claims against the United States and the Navajo Nation for takings of lands reserved to the Hopi Tribe, but which were encroached upon by Navajo settlers with the approval of the United States. I focused on a moment in the testimony when Duke Pahona, a Hopi ceremonial and clan leader, demurs to a request by his lawyer to publicly describe the contents of his tiiponi, the emblem of his ceremonial office. By doing this, he seems to thwart the value of his own testimony, insofar as he just explained that the tiiponi and its content memorialized a centuries-old agreement between the Hopi and Navajo Peoples about their respective land rights, rights he and his fellow Hopis claimed were now violated. I argue that his change of action is premised on Hopi theories of navoti (knowledge), wiwta (relations), and the norms that govern the lines and limits of how ceremonial information can pass and to whom. But then Pahona reverses course again, and at the bidding of his non-Hopi lawyer, produces the tiiponi, having planned at least enough in advance to travel with it to the hearing. He unwraps it and allows the commissioners to see it and even handle its contents. What to make of this?

This and other "reversals" that have characterized Hopi engagements with non-Native agencies and organizations are perhaps more understandable to non-Hopis if read in light of the larger context of Hopi theories and practices of knowledge, relations, and norms, laid out above, that together inform the Hopi principle of cooperation without submission. Pahona's initial refusal to describe the contents of his tiiponi and then his producing of it reset the conditions of the hearing interaction in ways that comport with Hopi theories and practices of traditional knowledge transmission and the relations it produces. Pahona's refusal, for example, makes explicit the extent to which Hopi traditional knowledge operates as a limiting resource in the context of contemporary Hopi governance practices, in which only members of his ceremonial society or his clan are privy to that knowledge, and all others are on notice that they do not share the insights and perspectives it affords. But by then reversing course, and displaying the tiiponi to the commissioners, Pahona enacts his authority as holder of the ceremonial office to which it attaches, and which gives Hopi-specific relational and normative sanction of his traditional right to determine when and where such lines of knowledge transmission should be extended to others, including non-Hopis. He thus marks his traditional authority and stakes his juris-dictional claim by first showing his unwillingness to submit to ICC hearing protocols but then cooperating enough to articulate Hopi actions and authority in response to the commission's calls for his knowledge about the land disputes under consideration before it. Pahona is affirmatively asserting, through his juris-diction, the scope of Hopi normative and relational authority over the matter at hand. Much like the placing of a Hopi prayer feather in the basement storage facility at the Field Museum, alongside the shrouded collections of Hopi material culture housed there, the generative limits of Pahona's act of refusing to show and then sharing his tiiponi is an assertion of his traditional authority, and an invitation to the commissioners to engage him and the Hopi he represents in the relations inaugurated by his act of knowledge transmission—a transmission, you'll recall, that in in being called as a witness, was requested of him by his lawyer and the commission itself. And all of this is true whether or not the non-Hopi commissioners and lawyers, including Boyden, understood the breadth of these epistemological, normative and relational implications or

not. Either way, what Pahona was enacting in that critical moment of his testimony was a Hopi juris-diction of cooperation without submission.

In this regard, Pahona's actions put me in mind of something Ishii argues:

> There is a long recognition that a total understanding of the entire Hopi
> scheme of things is never attainable. In one sense, this lack of centralized
> knowledge ensures that different clans and societies must carry their weight
> in order for Hopi life to exist. (Ishii 2001, 145)

Ishii explains that this orientation to the normative and relational limits imposed by Hopi traditional epistemologies "presents a problem to Anglophones
who want to know everything" (145). Nevertheless, it is key to Hopi understandings of their own place in the world. Ishii notes that it is acknowledging
the limits of their own knowledge that, ironically, provides Hopi with a kind
of certitude. He writes, in a way that sounds almost paradoxical to non-Hopis,
that "the certainty associated with not-knowing is a form of Hopi knowledge
in which we know the limitations of ourselves within our society" (145).

In this chapter I have attempted to unpack the juris-dictional elements of
Hopi notions of cooperation without submission by showing how they enact
Hopi norms, relations, and ways of knowing. In particular I have endeavored to show in it the extent to which Hopi traditional knowledge operates
as both a limited and limiting resource, confounding Euro-American efforts
to "know" the Hopi, and generating a kind of Hopi certainty with which they
claim their rights to sovereignty and political self-determination.

As I have shown, the wrangling with epistemological limits resides at
the heart of many of the complex and competing discourses of Hopi tradition through which Hopi engage in the everyday practices of their kin relations, ceremonial practices, and even Tribal governance. Hopi Peoples view
tradition as navoti, that "knowledge gained through hearing" (Malotki and
Lomatuway'ma 1987, 58). The concept implicitly invokes the esoteric interactions in which such knowledge is transmitted among initiates in the same
ceremonial society or among (certain) members of the same clan, and, most
significantly, around which a regime of secrecy endures to this day. I have
thus argued for reading this Hopi understanding of navoti back into the confrontations that Hopis have had with Euro-American law and science since
the late eighteenth century. In the face of intrusions perpetrated by those who
would endeavor to "know" the Hopi, and the actual instances of appropriation and dispossession of their knowledge that have been accomplished in
the name of Euro-American law and science, is it any surprise that the Hopi
have regularly balked at such efforts to take the measure of their culture and

society? It is against this history that we can understand the insistence by Hopi leaders like Duke Pahona and Leigh Kuwanwisiwma that the Hopi People shall decide for themselves the lines and limits of what can be known about them, and how that knowledge can and cannot be transmitted. It is these enactments, and the knowing, norming, and relating that they presuppose and enact—"the realms of not knowing" that, Lomayumtewa Ishii writes, "gives us comfort and certainty" (Ishii 2001,145)—that I argue underpin the Hopi sociopolitical theories my mentor Emory Sekaquaptewa was referring to when he explained that "in Hopi, culture teaches us 'cooperation without submission'" (in Ferrero 1984). It is also the animating principle that I argue informs Hopi leaders' decisions to engage with their non-Native counterparts and the various US agencies they represent, a principle that is revealed in the juris-dictions they bring to bear in the details of those interactions. And it is in the next chapter that I turn a series of those interactions that I observed in a recent visit Hopi leaders made to representatives of the US Forest Service for the Tonto National Forest in Payson, Arizona.

4

Juris-dictions of Significance: CWS in a Hopi-US Engagement

Introduction

In the previous chapter, I situated the Hopi theory of CWS within the macro-sociological structures of Hopi social order and theories of knowing, relating, and norming that inform that order, both historically and in the present. I suggested how, when understood in that light, Hopi leaders' engagements with Euro-American actors, instructions, and agencies—usually through scientific inquiry or political and legal interventions—are characterized, at least initially, by refusals to non-Hopi efforts to know more about, or to offer (normative) order to Hopi life. These initial refusals, however, are often followed by offers of a different kind of relation that see possibilities for mutual benefit between coequal, self-governing partners who respect the different ways Hopi and non-Hopi know about and make sense of their worlds, and do their best to align their actions accordingly to not interfere with each other, and, where interference is unavoidable, to genuinely engage in a collaborative and mutual decision-making effort to figure out how to move forward. Hopi society is based on different clans and villages coming together, each with their respective traditions and ceremonial practices, yet they voluntarily coordinate activities and values for the mutual benefit of the whole. So too do Hopi leaders and representatives engaging with non-Natives seek opportunities to cooperate in ways that do not demand that they yield their own interests and obligations, which undergird Hopi cooperation without submission.

In starting to understand these Hopi contexts, one can perhaps see how the notion of CWS bears certain analogies to notions of jurisdiction. That each Hopi clan, ceremonial society, village, and even the Tribe at large ideally has its own authoritative domain, held in relation to but distinct from the authoritative domains of others, bears some of the hallmarks of conventional notions of jurisdiction in Euro-American legal tradition. For example, each

Hopi clan, village, and ceremonial society exercises its influence and authority over the activities of certain Hopi individuals in light of their kinship ties and ritual obligations, relations that shift across dimensions of social space and time in the everyday unfolding of Hopi lives, as they mature, become initiated, gain knowledge, move, have children, and so on. And each clan's shifting influence over Hopi Peoples' lives and actions have to be coordinated with the influence of the other Hopi clans and societies. This requires ongoing, complex negotiations that are understood as either contributing to the vital functioning of the larger Hopi social order or threatening it when in conflict. In this complex dance of normativity, knowledge, and relations, the lines and limits of each clan's authoritative domain are constantly being adjusted, tested, and reworked as they edge up against the lines and limits of other clans, and often not without friction. Under these conditions, a theory of Hopi sociopolitical order like cooperation without submission can look much like the push-pull refusals of and invitations to relations described in the last chapter. The examples offered there of Hopi representatives in their back-and-forth with US officials from the Indian Claims Commission suggest how these same jurisdictional commitments might be extended in and through Hopi engagements with non-Native officials, agencies, and organizations.

Too often, however, Hopi orientations to these engagements and the extent to which they are grounded in CWS have been ignored, misunderstood, or knowingly disregarded by their non-Native counterparts. I believe this is true for many of the reasons I describe in chapter 2 as the regular failures of engagement that mark the 250-year history of US–Native Nation relations and the federal laws and policies that shape that history. As I argue there, among the underappreciated casualties of ending treaty-making between Native Nations and the United States has been the transformation of the dealings between the two away from negotiating obligations and rights to be enjoyed by and between two sovereign nations into evaluative assessments by which US agents feel emboldened to adjudge whether or not Tribal Nations and their claims qualify for this or that federal program. There are plenty of examples between 1871 to today of Tribes petitioning the US government to consider their interests and develop or take policy actions that will, they believe, set a course for improving the lives of Tribal Nations and their citizens. The fact remains, however, that in nearly every instance, the presumption was that, as the request of a "ward to its guardian,"[1] every Tribal petition—whether to the legislative or executive branch—was treated (at best) as an argument over the

---

1. Cherokee Nation v. Georgia, 30 U.S. (5 Pet.) 1, 17 (1831).

interpretation of terms dictated to it by the settler state or (perhaps at their worst) as almost a pitiful prayer for special dispensation from settler dictates.

What remains unclear is how Hopi commitments to CWS are enacted in the face of this persistent misrecognition by settler US officials and scholars, and why. That is, insofar as I have argued that Hopi CWS is not just an expression of jurisdiction but also of juris-diction (law-speech that both presumes and enacts the normative authority on which it is grounded), it is necessary to consider Indigenous Hopi sovereignty at play even in the most routine details of its legal interactions with US officials.

I argue in this chapter that to do this requires delving deeper into the particular ways in which Hopi representatives enact, through discourse, their authoritative spheres of knowledge, relations, and norms that are distinct from those of their non-Native counterparts. Hopi invite their counterparts into relations of mutuality and coordination of their respective interests when making decisions about policies or regulations. And they do so whether or not US officials appreciate and recognize their acts as such. In what follows I suggest that without observing Hopi concepts of knowledge production and its transmission, efficacies, and limits, non-Natives who simply arrange meetings in which the goal is exchanges of information premised on their non-Native epistemologies ignore the fact that engagement first requires laying a foundation for baseline mutuality. Such mutuality does not require agreement or a parity of knowledge but rather a respect for the relative knowledge each possesses, and an expectation of and appreciation for the ongoing normative and relational entanglement between the two that partial, relative knowledge affords and demands between Hopi and non-Hopi for the foreseeable future. I argue that the extension of Hopi notions of CWS to non-Native actors, agencies, and institution preserves the right of refusal even as it allows opportunities for engagement. And it may just be the preservation of this refusal—this *insistence* on their enduring Indigenous sovereignty—that motivates Hopi leaders to continue to engage with US actors, even when they are all but certain to be disappointed with the outcomes.

To understand these stakes of Hopi juris-diction, I turn to a specific engagement I observed in June 2013, between representatives of the Hopi Cultural Preservation Office (HCPO) and non-Native archaeologists from the US Forest Service (USFS). The latter had asked the former for a consultation on both the handling of several historic Hopi sites under their management and a proposed sale of forest land to a private entity. I first describe the scene and the importance of the consultation for the parties to it before I turn to a discussion of Hopi theories of norming, knowing, and relating that I argue informed the meaning that the Hopi actors assigned to the consultation but which, alas, the USFS did not understand. I then return to the details of the interaction, making a case that a juris-dictional analysis affords an appreciation of the significance of the sites, the negotiations, and the regulatory processes to which this interaction was ostensibly directed. The chapter ends with reflections on how and why Tribal consultations with non-Natives does and does not work, and what can be expected from engagements in which Hopi endeavor to enact a juris-diction of CWS.

⋆

INTERLUDE: A CONSULTATION IN THE TONTO NATIONAL FOREST

We had just crossed an unmarked chaparral trail across the Payson Ranger District of the Tonto National Forest in north-central Arizona. In the higher elevations of what locals call Rim Country, at the southern edge of the Colorado Plateau, it was hot and dusty at 8:30 a.m. Being July, the heat was to be expected. I was excited to be there as part of a study on the history and practices of the HCPO, a project Leigh Kuwanwisiwma, HCPO's director (see chapters 1 and 3 on his work) had invited me to join. Though he was not with us that day, I am quite sure that his concerns and commitments were present through members of the Office's Cultural Resource Advisory Task Team: six men and one woman from two of the twelve villages that constitute the Hopi Tribe. They had been asked by the HCPO to share what they could with the USFS archaeologists and to represent the Hopi clans and villages that, in Kuwanwisiwma's opinion, had the most immediate cultural interests and commitments relevant to the USFS.

We hiked to our first destination—a ridge with a commanding view of the spruce pine fields in the valley below, interspersed with roughhewn sandstone blocks and red, rocky outcrops reminiscent of the more spectacular mesas of nearby Sedona, Arizona. My Hopi friends, who had been joking with each other just moments earlier, grew quiet. The silence revealed itself as a kind of reverence, followed by whispers in Hopi of *kwaakwhá* and *askwali* (thanks) and punctuated with an occasional *Is uti!* (Oh my!).

The USFS had contacted the Hopi as part of a traditional cultural properties (TCP) investigation on the lands of the Tonto National Forest (Parker and King 1990). In this case, the USFS had recently proposed selling a 253-acre parcel of the forest to a private developer and Arizona State University. Before doing so, and under various federal laws, executive orders, and regulations, the USFS was required to consult with Tribal Nations. The Hopi are (as of today) one of the 574 Tribes recognized by federal law as having a government-to-government relationship with the United States (see chapter 2). The USFS was seeking information and input from them about the potential impacts such a sale would have on their cultural resources.[2]

The Hopi exclamations took me by surprise because we arrived at what to me looked like a pile of sandstone rocks. It was explained that we were standing on what was likely a site of historic human occupation, and what the archaeologists had labeled AR-03-12-04-2046 (fig. 4.1). The USFS had surmised from their own and others' investigations conducted in the mid-1980s that the mostly buried site was likely from the Formative Period, dating from AD 1600 to AD 1875, accompanied as it was by artifact scatters that bore characteristics of what the archaeologists called Tonto plain ware or Tonto red ware ceramics (J. Clark 2001). In truth, it was only after an archaeologist held out his hand to show me a potsherd he had picked up as we approached the area that I had any inkling of what might count, at least to archaeologists, as evidence of a prior human presence on the ridge.

But these ceramic fragments were also significant for the Hopi team members, and carried a different meaning for them than for the archaeologists. These differences in meaning would be consequential for how this particular consultation would unfold. The meaning Hopi attributed to these rocks and ceramics is consonant with their concepts of the sacred more generally. For Hopi, their meaning is drawn equally from the long histories of deprivation and domination by both colonial and other Indigenous forces, on ideologies of Pueblo ceremonial secrecy, and the staunch refusals that Hopi have always put up against access to their ceremonial knowledge by noninitiates, especially non-Hopi (Whiteley 1998). It is for all these reasons that Hopi Peoples have told me that sacred sites like their shrines and boundary markers often get violated unwittingly. As one Hopi member explained to me that day, "Some will just dismiss it as a pile of rocks." A second member added, "They have significance, you know, and they're not supposed to be disturbed."

Hopi often call individual potsherds and other archaeological materials such as masonry, middens, and postholes *itaakuku*, and collectively the term is *itaakukveni*. These terms are telling. The former combines the Hopi first-person plural possessive pronoun *itaa-* (our) with the combinational form of the noun *kúuku* (track). It is often glossed by Hopi with the English phrase

2. See 36 C.F.R. 60.4, Native American Graves Protection and Repatriation Act, Pub. L. No. 101-601, 25 U.S.C. 3001 et seq., 104 Stat. 3048 (1990); National Historic Preservation Act of 1966 (As Amended 1992), Publ. L. No. 89-665, 54 U.S.C. § 300101 et seq. (June 18, 1934). See also Parker and King 1990.

FIGURE 4.1. HCPO team and USFS archaeologists. Traditional cultural properties investigation, Site AR-03-12-04-2046, July 11, 2013. Photo courtesy of Saul Hedquist, used with permission.

"our footprints." The latter affixes –*veni*, or "markings," which foregrounds the sense in which such footprints serve as a demarcation. My Hopi colleagues explain that these terms, when used to reference the archaeological materials we saw that day in the Tonto, mark the site as a migratory passage used by the ancestors they call *Hoopoq'yaqam* (those who went to the Northeast), and which define the southeastern border of their homeland, what the Hopi call *Hopitutskwa*. I was told that itaakukveni mark not just the southern boundary but all of Hopitutskwa, an expanse that stretches from the confluence of the Verde and Salt Rivers in the southeast, the Puerco River to the east, the Colorado River in the west, and Lake Powell in the northwest, and arguably beyond (Ferguson, Jenkins, and Dongoske 1996; Hedquist et al. 2014; Hopkins et al. 2017; Jenkins, Ferguson, and Dongoske 1994).

As the Hopi tell it, Hopitutskwa is the land promised to them by the deity who first occupied this world, Maasaw, but only so long as they continued to move across it, learning from and caring for the many beings who crowd what Americans continue to see as an empty high-desert wilderness (fig. 4.2, and see fig. 4.1). Indeed, as I described in chapter 3, we would do well to remember that the very term *Hopi* only more recently signifies an ethnonational identity of the People who constitute members of the contemporary

Hopi Tribal Nation. More fundamentally, the term is an expression of ethical valuation, a marker of right behavior, used to describe those groups of people—today called *ngyam* (clans)—whose ancestors migrated across the region; and upon arrival to their current residences, showed that they had learned how to "behave well." They did so by performing ceremonies based on sacred, secret powerful knowledge they had acquired on their travels, in ways that brought rain and abundance to the village, thus warranting their admission to the community. This helps shed light on what at least some Hopi mean when they describe Hopitutskwa, and perhaps even the earth itself, as a space and place to which they owe ethical obligations that can be fulfilled only through the continued performance of the selfsame ceremonies their ancestors did so long ago, affirming annually their continued place in the social fabric of their villages (Koyiyumptewa and Colwell-Chanthaphonh 2011; Richland 2010, Whiteley 1998).

One can see how matters of jurisdiction are directly related in the consultation between the Hopi and the USFS. The analogies between Hopìtutskwa and territorial authority, and the roles that sites and itaakukveni play in defining the boundaries of time and space, bear more than a passing resemblance to the conventional sense of Euro-American concepts of jurisdiction as a reference to some aegis of authority over which the laws of a nation-state are understood to be in force. Indeed, this sense did seem part of what my Hopi colleagues were explaining. A day earlier, in their introductory meeting with the USFS archaeologists, one of the Hopi team members, HT2, volunteered just how important he believed these itaakukveni to be for Hopi. Speaking in English, he explained:

> We all know, on Hopi, that, you know, there was a great migration, in the beginning. You know, when we first got here. We've all known that—we were instructed that when we go, to "leave your footprints." Meaning that, ah, if you build houses there, you know, leave them there. If you put marks on the rock walls, you know, it—that's, you know—indicating that this clan or that clan has been here. So its many clans and many tribal peoples that pass through here, so.

As with most traditional Hopi narratives, the migration stories that HT2 was indexing are always backed by pointed ethical lessons. But, in much the same way that Keith Basso (1996) describes San Carlos Apache storytelling, the lessons of Hopi stories, grounded as they are in the specificities of place where significant events are said to have occurred, are nonetheless only obliquely delivered, cognizable to those who are attuned to them from past experience, guilty conscience, or perhaps both. Thus, it may well have

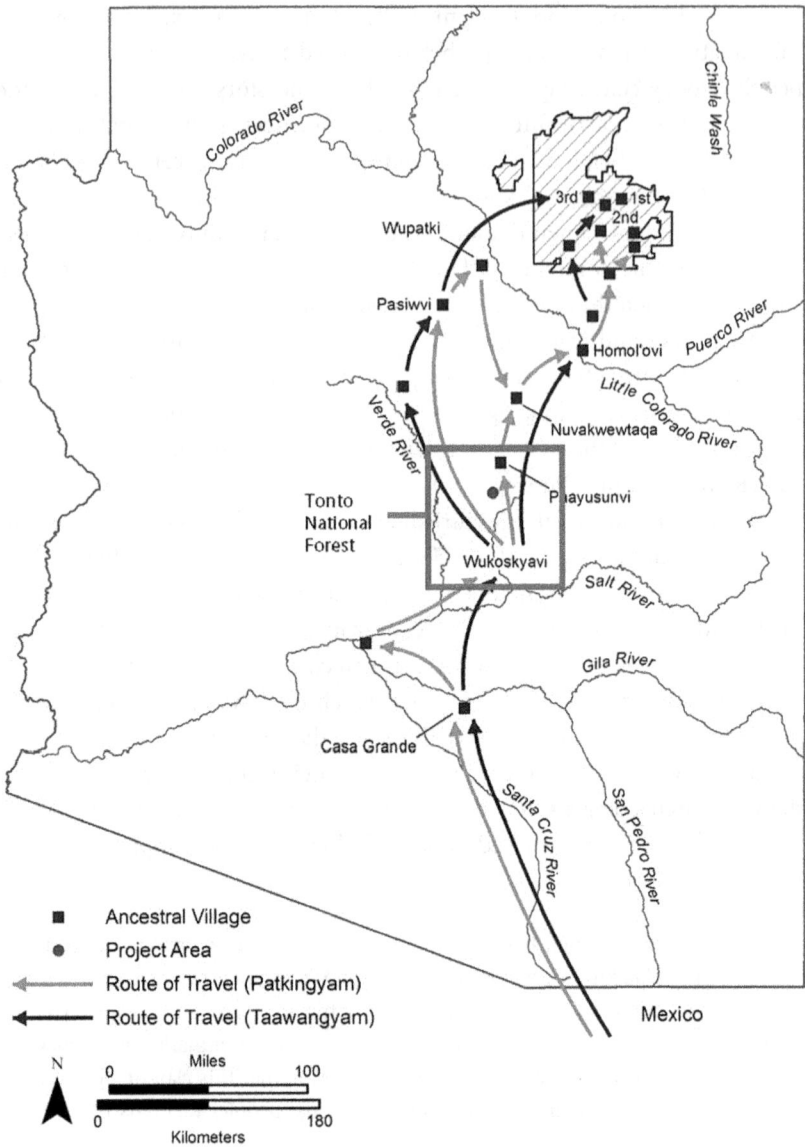

FIGURE 4.2. Ancestral migrations of Hopi Patkingyam (Water Clan) and Taawangyam (Sun Clan) from the south. Migrations land in Tonto National Forest, including proposed land sale areas. Map courtesy of Hopi Cultural Preservation Office, August 2013, used with permission.

been that the archaeologists missed the significance of sites and itaakukveni as marks of jurisdiction in this telling of the Hopi migration story and the demands it makes on the present occupants of the region.[3]

Later, another Hopi team member puts a finer point on the problem after the archaeologists inform them, for the first time, that leaving the sites and itaakukveni as they were would not be possible, given that if the sale of land goes through, the property and all materials on it would leave Forest Service hands. That seemed the first time the Hopi team realized that their consultation was sought not to weigh in on how to continue management and maintenance of their cultural patrimony but rather for input on the significance of the site to aid the USFS in justifying the expenditure of federal funds to excavate them for the archaeological record. This galled them, and reflected what HT5 had told me earlier on this trip—when it comes to these consultations, "some people listen, some people don't," but "it seems like it's always at the last minute that they want things done, you know. Out of time to give [a] response."

In retrospect, the USFS asking the Hopi down to the Tonto ostensibly to seek their consultation, but really only to justify their preconceived plans to excavate the sites, smacks of just the same kinds of bait-and-switch observed in the Jerome Commission's dealings with the KCA Tribal leaders around the allotment of their reservation, recounted in chapter 2. Recall David Jerome's misleading representations to Quanah Parker and others that the 1867 Treaty of Medicine Lodge was not going to expire, and anything agreed upon in their negotiations on that day wouldn't result in the KCA being removed from their lands. While technically true, what was left unsaid, and what was so misleading as to almost seem willful, was that agreeing to allotment would have so dramatically changed the way individual KCA members held their lands, and so reduced the overall size of the KCA reservation, as to make it virtually unrecognizable. Likewise here, albeit on a seemingly smaller scale, while it was technically true that the USFS was interested in consulting with the Hopi Tribe about the significance of the sites in question to them, the norms, knowledge, and relations they were going to share about their itaakukveni was being solicited not to protect them, but rather to harm them irreparably.

It is this point that HT1 tries to explain to the USFS, describing the trouble that disturbing itaakukveni poses:

3. For a good discussion generally on the legal protections available to Native Nations seeking to protect sacred sites that are not within their reservation or otherwise on lands they control, see . Carpenter 2005.

> There's, there's ceremonies at Hopi that still recount the path, ah, to Hopi. Which is—is still very much alive. And these places that, that they have left, you know, people are—we believe that people are still there. Their spirits are still there. So we dis—we disturb that, or somehow allow for it to be disturbed, it's a form of, ah, taboo, I guess. It's something that we highly respect.

Nevertheless, and perhaps feeling that the prospects of leaving the sites undisturbed were not good, HT2 concedes that going along with the consultation, if it aids in at least preserving the information in the archaeological record, is the lesser evil. Turning to his fellow Hopi team members, but notably speaking in English for the benefit of the non-Hopis in the room, he says "We can collect the data, and then put it in the records for—for future generations to learn from is probably something. I don't know, consolation." Thus the Hopi team decided to continue with this particular TCP investigation. The entire next day was spent much the way I described in the opening of this chapter: Hopi team members and USFS archaeologists hiking the hot dusty trails of the Tonto. Two USFS archaeologists guided everyone to the sites and oversaw the consultation progress while a third archaeologist discussed how to document the significance of different sites. I kept a recorder running all day, collecting six hours of interactions that were supplemented with five hours of recorded interviews with Leigh Kuwanwisiwma and Hopi team members before, during, and after this trip.

The following day, the Hopi team and I made the return trip to the Hopi mesas while the archaeologists returned to Tucson to write a report on the consultation findings. Less than a month later, the Hopi Cultural Preservation Office submitted its final report to the Tonto National Forest supervisor, signed by Leigh.[4] In it, the HCPO concluded: "The Hopi tribe considers all . . . sites in the area to be Hopi ancestral sites and traditional cultural properties eligible for inclusion in the National Register of Historic Places." The report recommends "avoidance of adverse effects," but acknowledges that "if avoidance . . . is not feasible, the Hopi Cultural Preservation Office should be consulted about the mitigation . . . including treatment plans involving archaeological data recovery."[5]

Ten days later, on August 12, 2013, the USFS announced its decision, which included a consideration of the HCPO report. The Finding of No Significant Impact (FONSI) made on that day allowed the sale of the proposed lands to

---

4. Hedquist and Koyiyumptewa 2013.
5. Hedquist and Koyiyumptewa 2013, ii.

FIGURE 4.3. Site AR-03-12-04-2046. From "Sale Gets Go-Ahead. Archaeologists Clear Way for University Site," by Peter Aleshire, *Payson Roundup*, August 28, 2015. Photo courtesy of Alexis Bechman, used with permission.

go forward as originally planned. Interestingly, however, the Hopi sites and itaakuku still got excavated (fig. 4.3), albeit with funds secured from Arizona State University, not the US government. Because of the FONSI declaration, the HCPO could not have any involvement in the subsequent excavation and still have not been informed as to the disposition of the cultural patrimony—their itaakukveni—recovered there.

What can account for this decision by the USFS? Why did the Hopi persist in working on this TCP investigation even after they learned that it would only further federal actions contrary to Hopi norms of avoidance and nondisturbance of itaakukveni? And why do they persist, time and again, in even responding to these invitations when it seems they are always confirmed in their suspicions that consultations are more of a rubber stamp than a real opportunity for Tribal input and comanagement? As one of the USFS archaeologists working with the HCPO in 2013 told me, the Hopi office "is really the gold standard" for responsiveness and professionalism. Yet just as Kuwanwisiwma told me, too often federal agencies ignore Tribal consultation contributions, and sometimes even "end up using our intel against us!" A legal researcher for the HCPO put it in a manner reminiscent of the critiques of consultation described in chapter 2 that call for Native Nation–US engagements to go "beyond dialogue." He said that while the letter of the law requires agents of the USFS and other federal bodies "to consult . . . there's no law that requires them to even listen."

*

Consultation as Juris-diction

Notwithstanding these legitimate frustrations, I suggest that something else is afoot here. I believe much needed perspective is gained in analyzing the details of Hopi participation in the TCP investigation through the respective orientations to Hopi norming, knowing, relating that emerged over the course of the consultation interactions produced that day.

More specifically, insofar as both the US and Hopi evaluations of the "significance" of these sites turn on their quality as evidence of the ancestral migrations of Hopi forebears across Hopi homelands—a movement across space and time—the discursive narration of knowledge about the significance of itaakukveni and sites can be productively analyzed through the lens of what the literary critic Mikhail Bakhtin (1981) called the "chronotope." Chronotope is a neologism that combines the Greek roots for time (*kronos*) and place (*topos*) to highlight the ways in which both are figured in different genres of literary narrative. As he famously explained, the concept of chronotope describes "the intrinsic connectedness of temporal and spatial relationships that are artistically expressed in literature . . . [and] it expresses the inseparability of space and time"; it can "even be said that it . . . defines genre and generic distinctions" across different literary forms (84–85). It is a time-space envelope within which the actions and events of a narrative take place, and what gives the story the sense of its internal coherence.

I think Bakhtin's chronotope offers some useful analytic specificity to the ways in which the role of language and interactional storytelling can be applied to law and legal practices. Valverde has recently redeployed Bahktin's concept to very good effect in her analysis of the ways "different legal processes are shaped and given meaning by particular spacetimes" (Valverde 2015, 11). My related interest in bringing the concept of chronotope to bear on Hopi interactions is to ask how the time-space of Hopi juris-dictional authority is constituted by narratives that Hopi team members relate regarding their engagements with USFS archaeologists on that ridge in the Tonto. There is not enough space here to survey contributions to the analysis of legal language that take legal narrative and storytelling as their focus (see, e.g., Baron 1999; Brooks 2006; Brooks and Gerwitz 1996; Mertz 1994; Richland 2013), but suffice it to say that this scholarship coheres around an insight of Robert Cover: "The very imposition of a normative force upon a state of affairs, real or imagined, is the act of creating narrative" (Cover 1993, 102).

One way to understand the fecundity of legal narrative research is to ask how narrative figures in generating both legal power and legitimizing the claims to authority that undergird that power. In particular, I am interested in the perspective gained when a focus on narrative can lead to an understanding of specific instances of social action as parts of broader arcs of social meaning. How do they link up with prior moments of social action and point toward current unfolding activities and events? Ochs and Capps (2001) write that "narrative is a way of using language or another symbolic system to imbue life events with a temporal and logical order, to demystify them and establish coherence across past, present, and as yet unrealized experience" (2).

Understanding the spatiotemporalities that legal language as narrative generates offers important insights into how, again as a kind of juris-diction, micro-details of discourse and text in law contribute directly to the macro-sociological structure of law as a mode of authority and power. This is where Bakhtin's notion of chronotope becomes so useful. He suggests that in pursuing the discursive devices through which such chronotopic moves are accomplished, we come to understand the dimensions of fictional "worlds"— the narrated experience of passage of time and traversals of space that the characters undergo, and readers live through along with them. There is also something of the extra-novelistic real world in which those stories were written and read—the births, deaths, triumphs, and tragedies that mark the author's and readers' lives "outside the book"—that constitute the generative limits that demarcate a narrative's "dominion," the bounds of its juris-diction.

Returning to the Hopi consultation with the USFS, it is possible to see the construction of narrative time-space playing out in the ways Hopi team members tell the story of the significance of the sites under consideration. I focus here on how different team members engage with two key interlocutors in the course of their telling the stories of the significance of the itaakukveni in the Tonto. One was a trusted non-Hopi archaeologist who regularly works with the HCPO on consultations like these and frequently copublishes reports and peer-reviewed publications with HCPO staff; the other was a revered ancestor arriving in the form of a gray hawk, whose intervention—while unplanned— was not unexpected, at least by the Hopi. Each played a key role in the unfolding shape and character of the Hopi team members' narrative, the time-space of these sites and itaakukveni, and the kind of "significance" they claim they make on Hopi, not only by virtue of the Hopi pasts that were lived in and through them, but of the Hopi (and non-Hopi) present and future that was still unfolding and for which the itaakukveni still had import.

Indeed, that these sites were significant not just for the pasts they represented, but the present and future with which they were still entangled, was a
truism evidenced for the Hopi by the very fact that we had all gathered there, on
that ridge in the Tonto, for a consultation about them. As such, the boundaries
between the spatiotemporal dimensions of the migration narrative—indexing
the site's significance—became mixed with those of the Tribal consultation.
For the Hopi, this was an opportunity to turn the interaction, ostensibly about
conveying their knowledge on the sites and their significance, into something
else—an invitation to the US archaeologists to engage juris-dictionally with the
Hopi normative relationships of comanagement and cultural preservation to
understand what ethically binds them to their itaakukveni, their Hopitutskwa
and the stewardship they owe to the People and places that occupy it.

Juris-dictions of "Significance"

Under US federal law, an archaeological site will be deemed "significant" and
in need of a plan for impact mitigation or avoidance if it is potentially eligible
for admission in the National Register of Historic Places. To qualify, a site
must meet the following definition:[6]

> The quality of significance in American history, architecture, archaeology, en-
> gineering, and culture is present in districts, sites, buildings, structures, and
> objects that possess integrity of location, design, setting, materials, workman-
> ship, feeling, and association and
>
> (a)   that are associated with events that have made a significant contribution
>   to the broad patterns of our history; or
> (b)   that are associated with the lives of persons significant in our past; or
> (c)   that embody the distinctive characteristics of a type, period, or method
>   of construction, or that represent the work of a master, or that possess
>   high artistic values, or that represent a significant and distinguishable
>   entity whose components may lack individual distinction; or
> (d)   that have yielded, or may be likely to yield, information important in
>   prehistory or history.

It was these criteria for which the archaeologists sought Hopi input. If the
Hopi could make this site meet this definition, then the US archaeologists

---

6. "National Register of Historic Places, Criteria of Evaluation." Title 36 Parks, Forests and
Public Property, Chapter 1 National Parks Service, Department of Interior, Code of Federal
Regulations §60.4.

could justify the use of federal funds to support excavation of the sites. As we stood on that ridge, I recorded the following interaction between two Hopi team members and the trusted non-Hopi archaeologist (A) just mentioned. He was knowledgeable on the federal regulatory criteria of "significance" of sites and thus could anticipate how the Hopi were likely to respond. Speaking first to Hopi Team Member 1 (HTI), the archaeologist says,

Eliciting "Significance"

[00:10:50.02]

026	A	So if we think about the– the– National Register criteria, The eligibility of traditional cultural properties, and that being, important events in the past,=
027	HT1	Mm hm
028	A	=and important ah– ah– people. Individuals.
029	HT1	Mm hm.
030	A	Ahhh the work of a master, unique construction. Things like that.=
031	HT1	[Mm hm.
032	A	[=And also ah providing ah information about the past. Those are the– the– four criteria for eligibility.
033	HT1	Mm hm.
034	A	What would this site– this location, ancestral place, what criteria would this meet of those.
035	HT1	It would meet all of them.
036	A	All of them.
037	HT1	All of them. Yeah.
038		(1.3 seconds)
039	HT1	I mean like in the– in the South, where these people migrated from, they built pyramids. From that pyramid they– they watched the solars, you know.
040	A	Mm hm.

041   HT1   Here they probably couldn't build a pyramid,
            you know,
            So they looked for the highest points
            They could do that.
042   A   [Ah–
043   HT1   [You know it's that kind of thing.
            And from having determined the year,
            Their destination.
            Because they're still on migration
            At this point, you know, so.
044   (2.0 Seconds)
045   HT1   So these things are– are good ahm– teaching
            areas for– for our ahm generations, you know.
            They come and, you know,
            "These are places where they did that."
046   (3.3 seconds)
            And they can see that– watch the rising sun.
047   A   Mm hm.
            So it could be a unique feature in that regard.
            Just because of its unique location.
            Ability to see the horizon.
048   HT1   Yeah.
049   A   And– and celestials.

Note that the archaeologist opens by elicitating a response from HT1 with the talk at turns 026–034 by paraphrasing the legal criteria outlined in the federal regulations for evaluating significance. HT1 replies at turn 035 with the rather minimalist response, "It would meet all of them." Though one cannot be sure, one suspects that A knows more is to come, given that Hopi stories of places like these, tied as they are to stories of migration, tend to always start "at the beginning" of the history of the Hopi People (Shaul 2002). Thus, while A lists the federal criteria as ostensibly the topic of talk, he seems to let the response go where it must. This is suggested by A's minimal uptake to HT1's initial response and the repetition of "all of them" at 036, and taking nearly a full second and a half of silence before he continues. Such pausing reflects A's familiarity with Hopi interactional style, in which speakers are generally recognized as holding the turn at talk—particularly in formal settings like these—even after substantial pauses. Someone less familiar might have jumped in immediately, presuming the turn had ended and thus potentially foreclosing the opportunity for the more elaborate story to present itself. Already matters of "meaningful consultation" hang in the interactional balance, and A's (apparent) forbearance of Euro-American inclinations to fill the silence left after turn 037 point to how he facilitated this conversation. Moreover, it created space for a Hopi story that should be taken as responsive to the ways in which "significance" is figured in US law and National Register criteria. This becomes a critical rubric for understanding what follows.

Thus, as A seemingly anticipates, HT1 initiates his narrative at turn 039, starting at the place "where these people"—that is, Hopi forebears— "migrated from." There is then a description of certain elements of the ceremonial-agronomical-astronomical practices that they would have undertaken at their place of origin, where they "built pyramids" and from which they "watched the solars." Deploying a method of analogic deduction not unlike what professional archaeologists do when interpreting an archaeological record, HT1 proffers the explanation, at turns 039, 041, and 043, that since they were migrating, they lacked the wherewithal to build pyramids, so instead "they looked for the highest points." This included the ridge on which we were standing, and where they continue their ceremonial-agronomical-astronomical practices. Note not only the radical compression of past time-space that such a proposition puts forward—as if the fifteen hundred miles from the structures of Central Mexico to where we were standing in the Tonto, and the centuries between those Mesoamerican civilizations and the Formative Period in the Tonto, could be compassed by the same group of people. Also note the presumptive teleology it ascribes to the imagined inhabitants. After all, the justification HT1 provides for why his ancestors did not build their own pyramids is that "they were on migration."

At face value these seem like factually questionable claims, but this would ignore Hopi concepts of *pasiwni* (designing) and *tiingnavi* (ceremonial planning), which are foundational in Hopi metaphysics (Sekaquaptewa 1972; Whiteley 1998 Whorf 1956) . It also ignores the fundamental conservatism of Pueblo cultural formations (Kroskrity 1993; Ortiz 1972; Whiteley 1998). Given these concepts, it is thus less surprising that they inform Hopi migration stories. The significance of the ridge is figured primarily in time-space calibration to the current location of Hopi villages as the always-intended destination of the migrations—130 miles north—which Maasaw laid out for them and where their forebears would have understood themselves to be headed even then (see chapter 3).

This compression of past-present-future is expanded in the very next turn, 045, when HT1 explains that sites and itaakukveni are "good teaching areas for our . . . generations" because they can learn "these are places where they did that." Thus, the chronotope of this narrative, the time-space of the past-to-now, is extended to encompass the socialization of generations to come of Hopi, about their Peoples' migrations from Central Mexico to their current homeland. The phrase "our generations" talks of an ongoing practice of instruction that shoots through the present and remains open the future generations of Hopi People who will learn of these migrations, and learn about them from places like the ones where we are standing, where Hopi ancestors stood millennia before us. In this way, the story offered by HT1 offers a time-space in which, as Bakhtin (1981) wrote, "time thickens . . . takes on flesh, becomes artistically visible, likewise, space becomes charged and responsive to the movements of time, plot, and history" (84)

It is clear how far this discussion moved from the regulatory criteria of significance, which focus on the contributions that sites might make to the historic record. Whether of events, persons, or cultural phenomena, the National Register's criteria of evaluation rest on an implicit presumption that significance includes an objectively recognizable and universally valorized "past." While the narrative proffered by HT1 certainly offers some evidence of historical significance, it compasses more than that by drawing a jurisdictional time-space that calibrates a thickening that flows between the then-there to the here-now and the onward-still.

This was not all that was happening. Insofar as HT1's narrative delivered a time-space encompassing the past to the present and possible futures, it also blurred the distinction between the story being told and the act of storytelling itself. This is most evident about two minutes later, when another participant enters the interaction, and draws the attention of HT1. After some discussion on the navigation techniques likely used by Hopi ancestors (following the sun and stars), the conversation seems to be winding down. After a long eight-second pause, HT1 turns to another Hopi team member to ask, "What was that?" Though it is not clear from the audio what he was responding to, soon after the screech of what sounds like a raptor is audible on the recording. This provokes him to turn to the other Hopi team members, drawing them into a different interaction.

An Intervention

[00:13:49.05]

097	HT1	So that's how they knew.
098		(7.7 seconds)
099	HT1	What was that?
100		(a bird screeches)

101	HT4	*Masap'ye?*
		The bird?
102	HT1	*Pas pay himu– ahm masikwayo aw himu pu' yanti?*
		That thing– ahm gray hawk came here for something?
103	HT2	*Owi. Pay hiitakw umungem sel– se'ela.*
		Yeah, it's been here for you since this– this morning.
		Masikwayo.
		That gray hawk.
104	HT3	Um hm.

After making note of the sound at turn 099, HT1 gets uptake from HT4, who says in Hopi, at turn 101, that it was a bird. HT1 then identifies it as a gray hawk, and asks after its intentions; that is, whether it "came here for something" (at 102). This is confirmed by another Hopi team member, HT2, who explains that the hawk has been around since earlier in the morning, and had come "for you." The Hopi term *umungem* combines the second-person plural prefix *umuu-* with the benefactive postposition *-ngem* (*umungem*), thereby suggesting that the bird's intentions are beneficial to and intended for HT1 and some unspecified others, perhaps the archaeologists and others (like me) who, given the shift to Hopi, might not know they are being referenced.

Here, the arrival of the *masikwayo* (gray hawk) is framed as a surprise intervention by HT1, and it comes at the end of his narrative about the significance of the site and itaakukveni, but not before the sound eruption arrests the narration itself. HT1, in collaboration with HT2 and the masikwayo, stages a key moment in the extension of the juris-dictional time-space that was already suggested by HT1. The story of the significance of this site and itaakukveni now sequentially coordinates the distant mythic past in an arc that connects to a possible future, and, robustly, through the present engagement. The implication is available, at least to these Hopi speakers, that if the masikwayo is here, it is because sites and itaakukveni like this one are significant not just for the past but for the immediate present as well.

This is made explicit a few minutes later by HT1, when he launches one more narrative just as the archaeologist begins to wrap up the elicitation.

A Final Reflection

[00:16:57.04]

| 141 | A | Anything else you want to discuss about this site? |
| 142 | | Before we move on? |

143   HT1   You know, so far we've seen some–
              what– what was that, eagle?
144   A   Mm.
145   HT1   (That bird).
              Remember we said, yesterday,
              that the– the spirits are very much alive, here.
              Well, they know that we're here.
              So they would come visit us in– tha– that kind [of form.
146   HT6   [In that form
147   HT1   Yeah. Animals or whatever, you know.
              They will– they will come around.
              (some turns at talk omitted)
159   It was interesting,
              when we were in ahm Teotihuacan,
              the people there told us that,
              "You know, when you go up to the sun pyramid,
              there will be a lot of monarch butterflies there.
              They're our people that come to see you."
              So when I went up there,
              Man. there was butterflies all over the place=
160   JR   [Hunh.
161   A   [Mm hm.
162   HT1   [Right on top of that.
163   A   Mm hm [Mm hm.
164   HT1   [At the very top
              Well, we believe the same thing, you know.
              When you come visit here,
              then they will come.
              In whatever animals that you see.

The significance of the time-space that HT1 assigns to this site and itaakukveni is made patently clear. The arcs of meaning, and the juris-dictional time-space that calibrates them, now move through the present being lived by those on that ridge. As explained at turns 145 and 147, in just the short trek up the ridge that morning, all of us saw several animals that embody the spirits of the ancestors. These are the selfsame spirits that, the day before, HT1 argued were still living at sites and itaakukveni, and whose presence must be respected.

Here, HT1 goes further still. Starting at turn 159, he describes an analogous experience during his recent trip to Mexico's Teotihuacan, where a chance meeting with some Indigenous People revealed that they believe their ancestors live on as butterflies at the top of a pyramid. Sure enough, he found after a climb to the top, "there was butterflies all over the place." Of course, one is to remember that the sun pyramid at Teotihuacan is precisely the kind of pyramid from which Hopi forebears, in HT1's prior narrative, would have originally used when living in Central Mexico, prior to the sacred migrations to the northeast, including where we were standing at that moment. Just as on that trip to Mexico HT1 had met People whose ancestors lived on as butterflies on that pyramid, so too had we just now encountered Hopi ancestors living here—the gray hawk screeching above, a hummingbird that zipped across our path, the fawn that bolted from the underbrush. The significance of this site and itaakukveni is thus not just one that he is telling us about; it is also one that is guided by his interpretation of the right signs that we are in fact already encompassed by and experiencing for ourselves. No wonder that he summarizes at 164 that "we believe the same thing. When you come visit here, they will come." Just as their ancestors did on that day in the Tonto, so have they done (regularly) in the past, and so would they presumably do in the future, should Hopi juris-diction and its markers remain undisturbed.

Stretching the narrative time-space to convey a sense of the significance of this and other itaakukveni it is indexing is why Koyiyumptewa and Colwell-Chanthaphonh write that "the past is now" (2011, 443). That is, of course, if these itaakukveni we were walking among on that day in the Tonto remain protected, in place, safe from excavation or other disturbance. After all, that was the point of this story and its telling. Namely, that the significance of that place to Hopi on that day was precisely as a place of instruction about events in the past, instructions that will be able to continue for future generations of Hopi, and perhaps even other non-Hopi who, like us, will get the chance to share in the traditional knowledge of the site's significance and thereby be cradled (to invoke Simpson's (2007) evocative notion) in the norms and relationships of cooperation without submission that this place now envelops all of us in. It is the narrative enactment of Hopi juris-diction and the scope of authority that HCPO officials were trying to exemplify as always already interpolating those of us—Hopi and non-Hopi alike—gathered there on that ridge. And while, like any noninitiate, our ignorance might have previously excused our inability to appreciate and act on the significance of this place, now that we have been given this glimpse of navoti, Hopi ethics hold that at a minimum, we must endeavor to avoid interfering in efforts to leave these places undisturbed.

I say "us" because I too was not exempt from this interpolation. As we were walking away from the site, about five minutes later, HT4 and HT2 reiterated the visitation and its significance to me.

Leaving an Offering

[00:21:05.04] (In this exchange, I am JR.)

195	HT4	That was probably one of the ancestors that [showed up.
196	JR	[Mm
197	HT4	And then that hawk came [all that way.
198	JR	[Mm
199		(2.3 seconds)
200	HT2	*It ura homʼoyi horokna atkyeʼvo angkw.*
		Let's remember to take our offerings down there.
		Qa ʼe paasa puʼ oovi
		Not too much though.
201	HT4	*Owi*
		Yes.
202	HT2	*Pangqw homa pitu.*
		Put the offering there.

When both men began to pull out their *hoomamoki* (sacred cornmeal bags) and slow their pace to find somewhere to place their offerings, I knew to walk on. Though I have some sense of the significance of this act, I also know that, as someone not initiated in any Hopi ceremonial society, it is not my place to know these things. This, at least, is something that I have learned: the ethics of not-knowing, as much as the ethics of being given knowledge, seem to me to figure centrally in what the HCPO and its team members expect when they engage in consultations. And in light of that, I thought, the right thing for me to do in that moment was to avoid disturbing them in their responsibilities.

Conclusion

Recall from previous chapters the role that knowledge—navoti—and its transmission and limits—plays in Hopi political theories of cooperation without submission. This offers insight into what the Hopi team may have been after when they participated in the Tribal consultation that day in the Tonto, and how the manner in which they did so could constitute a unique kind of Hopi juris-diction. On the one hand, the transmission of knowledge that HT1 narrated—the "significance" of sites and itaakukveni where their forebears came on their sacred migrations, and to know they now reside as hawks, deer, and birds—would seem to entail acts that are not only, or even primarily, about the sharing of information about Hopi history. Rather, they are freighted with the meaningfulness of the act of transmission itself. The import of the story HT1 told is, from this perspective, shot through with the norms of the act of storytelling. That the masikwayo intervened at a key moment in the narrating event only confirmed this fact to the Hopi and, I suggest, they hoped to the federal archaeologists as well. That is, masikwayo's arrival became a narrative resource that the Hopi team marshaled to draw the present moment into a shared jurisdictional time-space with both recent and distant past Hopi experiences with the pyramid in Central Mexico. It worked to strengthen the claims that they were making as to the "significance" of this place.

At the same time, HT1s telling blurred the boundary between the narrated events of Hopi migration and the narrating event of the TCP consultation, and it extended the ethics of Hopi navoti—the act of its transmission and the responsibilities that attend its reception—to the present, and ideally the future. By telling this story in this way, I suggest that HT1 and his fellow team members endeavored to bring their USFS counterparts into a jurisdictional relationship of comanagement and ethical obligation to care for these itaakukveni in whatever way possible, and with the burden of the decisions they take in relation to that information moving forward.

I also argue that the give-and-take between HCPO team members and their archaeological counterparts concerning the "significance" of these sites and itaakukveni in the Tonto involved a search for normative grounds for cooperation and mutuality, even when undertaken against the ostensibly "objective" criteria of federal regulations. Of course, the narratives of significance offered by the Hopi were explicitly oriented to the present normative valuations and ethical commitments that they owed to such sites and itaakukveni. The Hopi endeavored to extend through agreement and cooperation such norms to the archaeologists with whom they now shared (and with the visitation of the masikwayo, in fact, lived) their navoti and its demands.

In the end, it is unclear whether the USFS archaeologists and their superiors appreciated the full significance of this consultation, or of the itaakukveni around which it was organized. Nonetheless, this retelling of that day at the ridge is to help make clear why the Hopi persist in engaging in consultation processes even after knowing their calls will go unheeded. This is nothing new for Hopi. As an HCPO staff member bemoaned to me in the days before the trip:

> I'm not sure it's making any difference. I'm not supposed to be as dark and uh, negative as that. Leigh assures me that we have to keep teaching them. I argue or debate . . . violent revolution or peace? And I say, "Would you invite Cortes

in for dinner?" and he goes, "Yes." I guess even the ignorant have to be treated with respect.

The significance of engagement for the Hopi, like all Native Nations, is the extent to which it provides a site for them to enact their presupposed Indigenous jurisdiction, through the use of discursive and narrative devices that the Hopi team use to attempt to recruit the USFS archaeologists to collaboratively produce and find themselves normatively compelled by on that day, and in the future. As I showed, this significance may have been lost on their non-Native counterparts. But even in the face of US agency ignorance, the meaningful trajectory of Hopi ethical obligations to their homeland and the beings that live there were enacted anyway. Hopi jurisdiction over the Tonto was not described, it was inscribed; it was not just talked about, but markedly performed. Along the way, an Indigenous refusal was mounted to settler colonial legal and scientific logics. More than resistance, though, it was an enactment of Hopi *insistence*. It was an expression of Hopi self-determination performed in a perfectly unruly way that simultaneously made good on the obligations they owe to extant relations (to those that came before and buzzed among them still), while at the same time extending a similar opportunity to their USFS counterparts to also engage with them in ways that comported with Hopi ethics of cooperation without submission. In this sense, the consultation included Hopi jurisdiction—through juris-diction. This was true whether or not the US agents had the capacity to understand and embrace it.

PART THREE

Making Indigenous Juris-diction Unrecognizable

5

Perils of Engagement and Failures of Federal Acknowledgment

Introduction

In this chapter I relate the most difficult episode I experienced in my years as a scholar and advocate working with Tribal Nations. In bearing witness to this event, I felt in equal measure the honor of being asked to observe and the outrage, horror, and shame of what occurred. It is this chapter, more than any other, that has given me pause when writing, and has made me wonder about the utility of notions like cooperation without submission in Native-US engagements.

I do not doubt the abiding stance of CWS by Tribal leaders and advocates in their engagements with US agencies. Neither do I doubt that it is indeed a mode of enacting Indigenous juris-diction in engagements with the United States. Tribal Nations insist on their sovereign rights to self-determination and to enact them in ways that, first and foremost, refuse to accede to the either/or logics of complicity/resistance, and instead presuppose and entail their enduring *insistence*. Nonetheless, there are certain moments in which the full force of the failures of the United States' understanding of Tribal sovereignty reveals itself in the most egregious ways, and there is no amount of attention to the vitality of Indigenous acts of self-determination that can or should overwrite such settler colonial violence. It is this demonstrably painful and utterly coercive quality of Native-US engagement that gives Native engagement the quality of what Scott Lyons (2010) calls "x-marks"—"a sign of consent in a context of coercion" (2)—that I find most challenging to CWS as a mode of Indigenous juris-diction. The challenge comes not because this quality of Native-US engagement is so spectacularly violent— though it can be—but rather because it can be and is often accomplished in ways so mundane, so usual, and so predictable as to very nearly be expected. Native Nation leaders, advocates, and activists nonetheless still engage with non-Natives, even while continuing to insist that such engagements are their juris-dictional acts of self-determination. This insistence echoes Lyons's sense of x-marks as signifying "a decision one makes when something has already been decided for you," which, however compelled, "is still a decision" (3). Lyons assures us that these marks "can sometimes turn out all right and occasionally even good" (3).

The very need for such assurance means that the Native-US engagements Lyons might dub as x-marks often do not turn out all right and good. This chapter is about one of those engagements. Perhaps not surprisingly, following Coulthard (2014)—albeit in the United States and not in Canada—it took place during the processes of recognition and acknowledgment pursuant to US federal law, following procedures first developed in the 1970s, reformed in the 1980s and 1990s, and again in 2015, but which remain problematic to this day. If there ever is a site for understanding the perils Tribal Nations face when seeking a CWS-informed engagement and relations with a US government that claims to value engagement and relations with them, it is in the processes of federal acknowledgment. The peril, I argue, rests in the fact that US agents make unrecognizable what a CWS-informed engagement with Native Nations consists in. This unrecognizability of CWS happens most explicitly in and through the interactions governed by regulatory processes in which Tribes are required to prove their character as "Indian Tribes" according to criteria that speak more to Euro-American norms of law and science, and objectification, rather than as the knowledge, norms, and relations enacted in and through Indigenous juris-dictions.

This chapter tells about the Vernon's Ridge Tribal Nation—a pseudonym to protect the Tribe's anonymity—which has sought, and has for over forty years continuously pressed, its claim for legal recognition as a Tribal Nation and thus formal acknowledgment from the United States government as sharing with it a government-to-government relationship.

✶

INTERLUDE: A CALL

Some years ago,[1] I received a phone call from the Tribal chairman of the Vernon's Ridge Tribal Nation (hereafter, VRTN) telling me to quickly come to Tribal headquarters. An administrator from the Office of Federal Acknowl-

---

1. I am declining to specify the exact year of the events I am relating here because the number of federal acknowledgment petitions decided every year are so few, and readily searchable on the internet, that revealing the exact date of the event might inadvertently reveal the identity of the Native Nation.

edgment, which is located in Washington, DC, had called to tell him that the office had reached its final decision on the Tribe's petition for federal recognition, and that they were going to announce it publicly later that afternoon. "She said the solicitor is going to call at 1:00," he explained, excitedly. "And they never call if the news is bad." He had already activated the Tribal phone tree, called an emergency meeting of the VRTN leadership, and wanted me to come down to bear witness to this historical moment.

The Office of Federal Acknowledgment (OFA) is housed in the Bureau of Indian Affairs. Since 1994 it has been the main administrative office charged with overseeing federal acknowledgment, the lead regulatory process by which Tribal Nations petition the federal government for legal recognition as an entity with whom the US government shall have a government-to-government relationship. The process itself is outlined in Title 25, Part 83 of the Code of Federal Regulations.[2] Though it has been amended since,[3] at the time the VRTN filed its petition, it required among other things that Tribes prove via documentary evidence that their group has been "identified as an Indian entity continuously since 1900,"[4] is a distinct community from historical times to the present,[5] has political influence or authority over its members,[6] and its members are descendants of a "historical Indian tribe."[7]

Under these criteria, petitioning Tribal Nations like the VRTN must show that their individual members and their community as a whole can be traced to one or more historical Tribes. The language of the regulations and official guidelines—and of the OFA officers themselves—advise petitioners that the office relies on a variety of materials and phenomena—individual documents; public, religious, and private archives; digital ancestry databases; and even DNA evidence—to marshal proof of individual and group Indian-ness, both past and present, and most importantly to prove continuity between the two.

When I arrived at the VRTN headquarters, the normally staid office was buzzing with people of all ages, some of whom had spent four decades waiting for this news. They had responded to the call by dropping whatever they were doing, getting food from home or stopping by the store (food is a requirement at any gathering of Tribal members), and heading straight to the

2. Procedures for Establishing that an American Indian Group Exists as an Indian Tribe, 25 C.F.R. 83, 59 Fed. Reg. 9293 (Feb. 25, 1994).

3. See Federal Acknowledgment of American Indian Tribes, 25 C.F.R. 83, 80 Fed. Reg. 37861 (July 1, 2015).

4. 25 C.F.R. 83.7(a).

5. 25 C.F.R. 83.7(b).

6. 25 C.F.R. 83.7(c).

7. 25 C.F.R. 83.7(e).

office. After a group prayer, members filled up their paper plates with fried chicken, potato salad, chips, and cookies, grabbed a soft drink, and found a seat wherever they could among the desks, computer consoles, copying machines, and books. Surrounding them was the various ceremonial paraphernalia that covered the walls as well as photographs of elders and others who had contributed so much to the Tribe, but who had passed on before the arrival of this monumental day. They then waited for the call to come.

The call came an hour later. Despite the delay, people were still excited, as evidenced by the number of camera phones they immediately trained on the chairman. Despite promising to use the speaker phone, the chairman picked up the receiver instead. No one could hear what was being said on the other line, but it did not take long before we all sensed that something was very wrong. The smile on the chairman's face was gone, and he was shaking his head. Turning, I saw that the secretary of the Tribe, who just moments before had been kissing her teenage son on the face and squeezing him, had tears streaming down her cheeks. Her son, head down, refused to meet anyone's eye. Meanwhile, the chairman told the solicitor that he respectfully disagreed with their findings and ensured him that the Tribe would read the decision document closely. By the time the chairman hung up, the electric quiet of bated breath was now stunned silence. When he finally spoke to the gathered crowd, we could already sense what he had to report: that the OFA declined to acknowledge their petition and that the VRTN community—that is, the very people before him in their Tribal headquarters—were people who for federal purposes, did not exist as an Indian Tribe.

*

I argue in this chapter that the tragedies caused by US administrative wrongdoing—a most banal tyranny of settler bureaucracy—of the type that the VRTN was forced to suffer that day, reveal more than just the enduring problems attending the politics of recognition that have characterized Indigenous-settler relations more generally (Coulthard 2014; Eisenberg et al. 2015; Povinelli 2002; cf. Taylor 1994). There is rather something of the unrecognizable in these acknowledgment proceedings, by which I mean that in their ostensive interest in Indigenous norms, knowledge, and relations as the objects of their evaluations, US officials display an unwillingness or inability to give a firm answer on what kinds of evidence are sufficient to meet the regulatory criteria for federal acknowledgment. This reluctance to offer concrete evidentiary recommendations may be motivated by OFA officials' awareness of, and even appreciation for, the diversity of different Tribal Nations' pasts and presents. But in a context in which petitioners are asked to prove their norms, knowledge, and relations are sufficiently Indigenous *and* that the Tribe is sufficiently self-governing, and to do so according to settler colonial evidentiary criteria enshrined in US regulations, this reticence appears purposefully obstructive.

I thus say unrecognizable not because these processes are unfamiliar to anyone who is Indigenous or works with and for Indigenous Nations and their rights to self-governance. The scene that played out for the VRTN is all too familiar (Coulthard 2014; Povinelli 2002). The historical and contemporary landscapes of settler colonialism across the world are lousy with examples of Native Nations being told that they can and should expect a willing partner in their non-Native counterparts, only to find out from the settler state's final assessment that partnership is impossible because, somehow, it is the Indigenous Peoples themselves who do not measure up. Indeed, for some scholars, given the structural ambitions of settler colonial projects, these bait-and-switch politics are the key modality by which settlers claim to be able to take the measure of Native Nations, and inevitably take measures against them as well, while perpetuating their own existence and absolving themselves of their ethnocidal pasts (Wolfe 2006).

By unrecognizable, I suggest here instead that at the heart of the regimes of recognition that animate Native-Settler nation relations around the world there is something other than unfamiliarity in operation. The problem is not one of strangeness but of a kind of animosity to Tribal Nationhood, which is produced by the estrangement that comes from having for too long valued what Wolfe calls the "indigenous aura" (Wolfe 2006, 389). In the US, this adds to the national myth but at the expense of real relations with Native Peoples. The OFA is interested in Indigenous norms, knowledge, and relations, but not so interested in understanding how they are the foundation of Indigenous juris-dictions of CWS. By not sharing control of the evaluation and decision-making processes with those Native Nations under specific consideration, the federal government effectuates a regime in which those Tribal Nations are deemed unrecognizable and a genuine government-to-government relationship rendered impossible. This is true no matter the good intentions of any individual OFA official.

I show below how this played out in the interactions between OFA agents and VRTN leaders in a technical assistance meeting concerning how the VRTN might best develop the evidentiary record they needed to file in support of their petition. In particular, when the questions turned to the kinds of evidence necessary to establish VRTN's historical continuity with an Indigenous population that had self-governing authority, the OFA's slippery logics of scale (Blommaert 2007; Carr and Lempert 2016; Latour 2005; Lempert

2012) and scalability (Tsing 2012) cast a pall over the future of the VRTN's petition. These would ultimately bear out in the denial of their petition.

In the interaction between the parties to this meeting, the talk repeatedly faltered in those moments when OFA officials or VRTN leaders attempted to puzzle out when and how certain kinds of records—what the participants called "membership files" constituting primary historical records, birth certificates, marriage licenses, and individual genealogical records—count as evidence linking present individuals to present groups and when they count as evidence linking present individuals and groups to past individuals and groups.

It is precisely the ways in which the question of the scalability of these documents was left indeterminate—presumed by the OFA's organization, operation, and procedures but never clearly articulated in the discussion of the files—that reveal how the federal acknowledgment process is constituted of and by a kind of evidentiary double bind within which the VRTN was caught. Recently, scholars have suggested that nonscalability is as much an accomplishment of the situated representation of social phenomena as is any affirmative measure of scale (Carr and Lempert 2016). I argue that neither scalability nor nonscalability alone explains the promise and problems that the federal acknowledgment process posed for this petitioner. Instead, both were used by OFA agents—wittingly or unwittingly—in a closely held logic against which VRTN's norms, knowledge, and relations were framed as unrecognizable objects of settler evaluation. As a result, the VRTN failed to meet the regulatory criteria for US acknowledgment. Thus, the OFA, despite its avowed interest in VRTNs history and culture, denied the petition. In the calculations of the federal acknowledgment process, the VRTN's Indigenous juris-diction of CWS, the sovereignty they produce through it, and the relations they sought to forge with the US based on their insistence in it never had a chance.

The Cunning of (Un)Recognition

In her critique of the Australian settler state at the end of the twentieth century, anthropologist Elizabeth Povinelli (2002) reveals how political disavowals of the long-standing claim of Australia as *terra nullius* at the time of its colonization, and the concomitant acknowledgment (in principle) of the Native title of Aboriginal Nations, had the ironic effect of actually furthering Indigenous marginalization and abjection. She calls this effect the "cunning of recognition," arguing that the Australian Supreme Court's decision in the 1992 *Mabo and others vs. Queensland*, along with other legal decisions and statutes enshrining Australia's policy of national multiculturalism, only *seems* to advance Aboriginal rights to land while actually doing less for them and more for the Australian state. It does this, Povinelli explains, by requiring Aboriginal Peoples' petitioning for their Native title rights to prove they maintain continuity with their ancestral populations and cultural forms, a task made difficult given Australian settler history in which the official policy had long been to assimilate them and compel their abandonment of these ancestral ways.

To make matters worse, the Australian system not only required demonstration of a cultural continuity that was evaluated according to settler logics of evidence and proof, but then the state also disclaimed these enactments of identity if they seemed too much like a "performance" designed primarily for non-Indigenous audiences like the state that is deciding on their land claims. As she explains, the ironic double bind of Australian politics of recognition made impossible demands on Aboriginal Peoples that could not be met; namely, she writes, they are required to,

> orient their sensual, emotional, and corporeal identities toward the nation's and law's image of traditional cultural forms and national reconciliation and at the same time ghost this *being for* the nation so as not to have their desires for some economic certainty in their lives appear opportunistic. (Povinelli 2002, 7)

Scholars of Indigenous-settler colonial relations in other parts of the world have made similar critiques. In studies of Canadian and US settler state regimes, the claims these states make to engage Native Nations in government-to-government relationships are likewise premised on rationalist, bureaucratic logics that only claim to afford pathways for genuine Tribal self-determination. As with the cunning of recognition that Povinelli observes in Australian politics of multiculturalism, the regimes of recognition in Canada and the United States arguably work in fact to further marginalize Indigenous Peoples. Governments in North America use processes of recognition and various juridico-political channels (including treaty negotiation, congressional legislation, and administrative and legal processes) that place responsibility for not being "recognizably" Indigenous on the petitioning Nations themselves. They find themselves blamed for their own assimilation—often forced on them over generations—and that they no longer count as a Tribe because of their failures to maintain a distinct and continuous relationship to their ancestral populations and traditional cultural forms (Cramer 2005; B. Miller 2003; M. Miller 2004).

Finally, while Aboriginal Nations fail to meet impossible metrics of recognition, setter state representatives claim that these processes are evidence

of settler state's own reformation. As the argument goes, at least they are trying to remedy the errors of their colonialist ways and now show an interest in,
appreciation for, and willingness to support Indigenous norms, knowledge,
and relations. Povinelli (2002) suggests this may be the entire point of settler
regime recognition projects. The settler state is making a show of breaking
from its past to claim a renewed and reformed moral high ground.

The bitterness with which these double binds have played out in the North
American context have led more than one scholar to call for abandonment
of recognition regimes altogether. Glen Coulthard (2014) writes, "I argue that
the politics of recognition in its contemporary liberal form promises to reproduce the very configurations of colonialist, racist, patriarchal state power
that Indigenous Peoples' demands for recognition have historically sought
to transcend" (6). Despite the fact that the Canadian state has disavowed the
principles of Indigenous exclusion and (later) assimilation that characterized
official Canadian policy toward First Nations Peoples for well over a century until the 1970s, Coulthard has argued that procedures of negotiation,
consultation, and recognition are really designed to further effectuate the
dispossession of Native Peoples from their lands and their ways of life. The
official shifts in policies that exclude, assimilate, or recognize the "relationship between Indigenous Peoples and the state has remained colonial to its
foundation" (6).

However valid these criticisms—to the extent that they paint a picture of
Indigenous abjection in the face of settler state rule and a near impossibility
in the politics of recognition—they risk missing the critical vitality of Native
Nations, both "recognized" and "unrecognized." Povinelli (2002) argues that
for Indigenous subjects, the double bind of recognition logics "do not simply
produce good theater, rather they inspire impossible dreams *to be* this impossible object and to transport its ancient prenational meanings and practices
to the present" (6). Insofar as her argument focuses on Indigenous subjects
as caught in these vicious logics, it fails to attend to the ways in which Native
Nations today map out paths of life that, however much they may (out of necessity) touch on settler colonial demands, are not captured by them.

Critical theorist Gerald Vizenor (1999, 2008) has called this Indigenous
vitality "survivance." By it he means to convey the ways in which Native Nations are always charting the course of their lifeways beyond responsiveness
to colonial domination. As he writes, "Native survivance is an active sense of
presence, the continuance of Native stories, not a mere reaction, or a surviv-
able name. Native survivance stories are renunciations of dominance, tragedy and victimry" (1999, vii). Of course, the argument that Povinelli and
Coulthard each level against the politics of recognition is precisely its inability

to attend to and engage Tribes on the terms of their own self-governance and path making; in other words, their ongoing vitality as contemporaries. Recognition itself is an impossibility, and no matter who wields it or to what ends, the possibility of genuinely acknowledging the humanity, nationhood, and rights to self-governance of Indigenous Peoples cannot be compassed by non-Native political entities—settler or otherwise (Eisenberg et al. 2015).

In making this argument, Povinelli, Coulthard, and others are in very good company. Postcolonial Caribbean scholar and revolutionary Frantz Fanon (1967) grounded his pessimism about recognition politics in colonial contexts on a thorough rejection of their Hegelian, dialectical underpinnings and especially of the so-called master-bondsman relationship. In theorizing that relationship, Hegel argued it was the bondsman, not the master, who was the more liberated because his humanity was not dependent on the master's acknowledgment for his existence, whereas a master was only a master if the bondsman saw him as such. As a result, by denying the humanity of the bondsman, the master was in the end denying his own humanity insofar as it depended on the bondsman's recognition. Fanon would have none of this. "What he wants from the slave is not recognition but work" (Fanon 1967, 220). For Fanon, there was thus nothing to recommend an approach to postcolonial relations between colonizer and colonized that assumed that acknowledgment by an alter was a condition of human liberation, and he derided postcolonial political movements that relied on these dialectics of seeing and being seen in relation to their European counterparts.

Another way into the critique of contemporary politics of recognition in settler colonialism is to understand that recognition in the Hegelian sense is not the point. That is, the "impossibility" that Povinelli describes in the Australian settler context, and what I call the "unrecognizable" character is not just the absence of acknowledgment, but rather an active accomplishment of settler colonial agents. In the US context, it is observable in the ways OFA actors participate in recognition processes rather than something inherent in the relationships expressed in an abstract dialectic. By attending to the details of interaction between Native Nation officials and their settler state counterparts in the processes of recognition, we learn that determining Tribal Nations as unrecognizable is accomplished through the talk of settler regime actors doing the work of acknowledgment.

At the same time, there is a subtle difference between the impossibility of recognition and the active accomplishment of unrecognizability in the policies and procedures of acknowledgment proceedings, one that leaves a space for an Indigenous *insistence* via juris-dictions of cooperation without submission. It is discernable in the gap between the ways regulatory practices

of recognition are deployed by US agents and how the leaders of Tribal Nations, insistent on their rights to engage those officials, do so in ways that demand a mutuality grounded in their norms, knowledge, and relations. And
this is true whether US officials are able recognize these conditions of Tribal
engagement, conditions grounded in their Indigenous jurisdictions or not.
This mutuality is, importantly, something that Coulthard (2014) indirectly
suggests is available even in the Hegelian model of dialectic recognition. It is
this kind of mutuality through recognition, perhaps. that might explain why
Tribal Nations continue to engage their US counterparts through regulatory
schemes like "meaningful tribal consultation." It also explains why so many
seem unwilling to give up on the government-to-government relationship
espoused by US law and policy, even after such a long history of dispossession
and deceit, sometimes accomplished by settler actors claiming to act in the
name of Tribal welfare. Whether accurate or not, unfortunately, this mode
of genuine mutual recognition remains a long way off, no matter the good
intentions of some federal players. To understand how to move in the direction of real recognition, it is first necessary to reveal how the unrecognizable has been built into the processes and procedures of acknowledgment,
and how it is applied by federal actors working with Indigenous leaders. I
offer a close analysis of engagement between VRTN Tribal officials and OFA
researchers and solicitors, and specifically how unrecognizability emerged
from OFA actors who were unable or unwilling to answer VRTN questions
related to evidentiary requirements of relevant regulations. The interaction
reveals how VRTN norms, knowledge, and relations—the very stuff of VRTN
juris-dictions of CWS—were the topics of consideration in the meeting, but
only as objects of settler evaluation rather than as organizing principles of the
engagement itself. To begin, I first offer a brief description of the history and
contemporary operation of the federal acknowledgment process.

The Federal Acknowledgment Process

The federal acknowledgment process was initiated in response to recommendations for reforming how the United States was fulfilling its trust responsibility to Tribal Nations. Those recommendations came in the final report of
the American Indian Policy Review Commission in 1977.[8] The commission,
comprising leaders of seven federally recognized Tribal Nations and several

---

8. American Indian Policy Review Commission, *Final Report*, May 1977, vols. 1 and 2 (Washington, DC: US Government Printing Office). All following citations in this section marked only
by page number are to this report.

sitting and former US legislators, was convened pursuant to Public Law 93-580,[9] passed in 1975, which called for a comprehensive review of the history of laws and policies constituting the relationship between the United States and the Tribal Nations within its borders. After two years of data collection and analysis by eleven different task forces (composed of over fifty Tribal members representing twenty-three different Tribes), the commission produced a six-hundred-page report that included 206 specific recommendations for improving how the federal government executes government-to-government relationships with Tribal Nations.

In sum, the commission recommended that "Congress reaffirm and direct all executive agencies to administer the trust responsibility consistent with the following principles and procedures. . . . [That it] is an established legal obligation which requires the United States to protect and enhance Indian trust resources and tribal self-government" (17). Importantly, the commission acknowledged that this responsibility should extend not only to those Tribal Nations with whom the United States had a preexisting governing relationship but also to those Tribes that have been "terminated . . . overlooked, forgotten, or ignored . . . because of past policies which failed to recognize their status [as Tribal Nations] or sought to end it" (15).

Task Force 10 and chapter 13 of the report specifically address the problems around the failure to recognize Tribal Nations with which the federal government had no preexisting formal relationship, and the "accidents and vagaries of history" (461) that have led some Tribes to be recognized but not others. At the time of the report, the commission concluded that of the 400 Tribes existing within the boundaries of the United States, only 289 were recognized by the US government, leaving more than 100,000 Native individuals "excluded from the privileges and protections of the Federal-Indian relationship" (461). The problem, the commission concluded, has been the unilateral assumption of authority by federal executive branch offices to deny services and recognition to certain Tribes but not others. As they write, "there is no legal basis for withholding general services from Indians, with the sole exception of specific termination acts. There is no legitimate foundation for denying Indian identification to any tribe or community" (461). Most central, the commission contends, is the problem that "the process of identification has been inconsistent. . . . Trying to find a pattern for the administrative determination of a federally recognized tribe is an exercise in futility" (461–462).

9. Joint Resolution to Provide for the Establishment of the American Indian Policy Review Commission, Pub. L. No. 93-580, 25 U.S.C. § 174 (1975).

To address these problems, the commission recommended the creation of a special office for the establishment of Native Nations–federal relationships, whose purpose would be to contact and provide technical assistance to all "known so-called unrecognized tribes" (481) seeking to submit petitions for recognition as a Tribal Nation with a formal relationship with the federal government. In addition to assisting in this effort, the office would be responsible for determining whether or not a Tribe met the requirements for federal recognition. The commission then enumerated several criteria that the office would use to evaluate Tribal petitions for recognition:

   a. The tribe exhibits evidence of historic continuance as an Indian tribal group from the time of European contact or from a time predating European contact.

   b. The Indian group has had treaty relations with the United States, individual States, or preexisting colonial and/or territorial governments.

   c. The group has been denominated an Indian tribe or designated as "Indian" by an Act of Congress or executive order of State governments which provided for or otherwise affected or identified the governmental structure, jurisdiction, or property of the tribal groups in a special or unique relationship to the State government.

   d. The Indian group has held collective rights in tribal lands or funds whether or not it was expressly designated a tribe.

   e. The group has been treated as Indian by other Indian tribes or groups.

   f. The Indian group has exercised political authority over its members though a tribal council or other such governmental structures which the Indian group has determined and defined as its own form of government.

   g. The group has been officially designated as an Indian tribe, group, or community by the Federal government or by a State government, county (or parish) government, township, or local municipality. (482)

The commission did not fashion these criteria out of whole cloth but took inspiration for them from *The Handbook of Federal Indian Law* (477, quoting Cohen 1958, chapter 14, "The Legal Status of Indian Tribes," § 1, "Tribal Existence," 270–271), compiled by Felix Cohen, associate solicitor with the Department of Interior. Cohen, along with the commissioner of Indian affairs, John Collier, was the chief architect of the 1934 Wheeler-Howard Act, also known as the Indian Reorganization Act.[10] It ushered in a new period of federal support for Tribal sovereignty and self-governance after the long dark era

10. Wheeler-Howard Act of 1934 (Indian Reorganization Act), Pub. L. No. 73-383, 25 U.S.C. ch. 14, subch. V. § 461 et seq.

of forced cultural assimilation and Tribal land dissolution that had preceded it. The commission valued Cohen's handbook because it was considered by many to be not only the leading authority on federal Indian law but also one that was sympathetic to the rights of Native Nations generally.

This fact, coupled with the idea that the proposed office would both assist petitioning Tribal Nations seeking recognition and evaluate the petitions they helped prepare, meant that the commission's recommendation was to create a federal recognition process that heavily favored the approvals, rather than denials, of petitions for recognition of Tribal Nations. Indeed, the commission was explicit in its preference and offered a general requirement for any office in charge of processing Tribal Nations' petitions for federal recognition: "Every Indian tribal group which seeks recognition must be recognized: every determination that a group is not an Indian tribal group must be justified soundly on the failure of that group" to meet the relevant evidentiary criteria (479).

Equally striking is how the commission intended its criteria to be used by federal officials reviewing petitions for Tribal recognition. Rather than making it mandatory that Tribal petitioners meet *all* the criteria described in the report (and shown above), the commission was explicit in providing, in much the same way Cohen himself provided in his handbook (Cohen 1958, 270–271) announcing the criteria, that Tribal Nations need only show that they meet *one* of the seven criteria to be eligible for and presumptively entitled to recognition. Thus, the commission was explicit in recommending that any federal process for recognition be consistent with the trust responsibility the United States owes to Tribes, the presumption being that a petitioning Tribe was to be recognized. When the office overseeing this process determines that it cannot recognize a petitioning Tribe, it bears the burden of proof to show "through hearings and investigations, that the group *does not meet any one* of the . . . definitional factors" (482, emphasis added).

Given this quite explicit presumption in favor of Tribal recognition, it is notable that the criteria first set by the commission remained substantially unchanged for nearly thirty years. Indeed, they map almost directly onto the criteria enshrined in Section 83.7 of 25 C.F.R.—the same criteria that the VRTN were held to have failed to meet when their petition was denied by the OFA. But since the meeting of all of these factors, rather than just one, was made mandatory in their adoption by the OFA's predecessor—the Branch of Acknowledgment and Research (or BAR)—it is perhaps unsurprising that they, and the entire acknowledgment process, have come under withering (and still ongoing) criticism from the very first days of their implementation. The federal acknowledgment process has been the subject of over thirty

Senate and House subcommittee hearings, during which the regulations were revised three times (in 1994, 2007, and 2015). The OFA was restructured and renamed twice, and twelve secretaries of Indian affairs have come and gone.

The criticisms of the system and the efforts at reform run the gamut. However, three common themes of complaint emerge. Chief among them is that the petition process is an onerous burden for Tribal Nations that rarely have the resources and expertise to gather the many thousands of pages of documentary evidence necessary to adequately answer how they meet *each* of the seven mandatory criteria, as was required once these criteria became part of the official acknowledgement process. Second, the OFA is dramatically inefficient in processing petitions, with some petitioners waiting decades for their petitions to be formally considered. For example, the OFA (and the BAR before it) had held up VRTN's petition for four decades. These delays are exacerbated by the concomitant complaint that the OFA fails to provide transparency and open channels of communication about where petitions are in the internal processes, leaving Tribal Nations completely in the dark about when they might expect a decision. Finally, several complaints suggest that when a final determination is made, it almost always seems to turn on an arbitrary and capricious evaluation and application of the evaluative criteria in ways that cannot be rationalized by comparison to decisions made in other Tribal petitions.

All of these issues persisted during the time when the VRTN's petition was under consideration, and it appears the BIA had planned to address them when it adopted its 2015 revisions to the acknowledgment regulations. In the executive summary on the final rule changes it made to the criteria for acknowledgment, the BIA explained that the "rule clarifies the criteria by codifying past Departmental practice in implementing the criteria. An overriding purpose for codification is to address assertions of arbitrariness and ensure consistency."[11] The implication is arbitrariness and inconsistency remained a concern for Tribal Nations whose petitions were under evaluation up to that time, and that the problem was sufficiently serious that the BIA felt the need to address it by reforming its rules.

Arguably, problems persist after the 2015 revisions. The summary reports that the revised "rule does not substantively change the Part 83 criteria, except in two instances."[12] The first change eliminated the requirement that petitioning Tribes show evidence that it has been identified "as an Indian entity . . . by those external to the petitioner." The second change revised the ways in which Tribal members' marriages were reviewed by the OFA as evidence to

---

11. 25 C.F.R. 83 at 37863.
12. 25 C.F.R. 83 at 37863.

meet criterion 83.7(b): the existence of a "distinct Indian community."[13] Instead of counting the number of marriages in a given petition, the rule now requires that the OFA count the number of petitioner members married to those in the same group.

It is unknown what effects the revisions had on the acknowledgment process, because the OFA, by its own admission, still goes by what was required before the 2015 changes. And those changes that followed still treat Tribal norms, knowledge, and practices as interesting objects of evaluation, not as the governing logics of a sovereign that might one day be a partner in a government-to-government relationship. This is all the more ironic given that the OFA eliminated the requirement that petitioners submit evidence that they were identified as an Indian entity by those external to it. Apparently, while the judgment of a Tribe's Indian-ness by others was no longer a legitimate criterion on which to evaluate its petition, questioning the value of such evidence did not prompt any reflection that the self-same external identification is exactly the project of the OFA's entire acknowledgment process—an assessment by an entity "external to the petitioner" as to the sufficiency of its claim to Indian-ness. Of course, the argument can be made that the OFA, as representative of the US government, is not just another external petitioner, but the agency being petitioned. And as such, it has to be able to make such a judgment. And yet, there is nothing inherent to its judgment that requires it to privilege its own evaluative logics regarding Indian-ness above those of the petitioner itself, or to otherwise sidestep evaluating Tribal Nations in light of the way their norms, knowledge, and relations undergird their own Indigenous juris-dictions of CWS. Indeed, given the requirements of the federal trust responsibility, and the way in which that responsibility has been applied to other moments of interpretive and evaluative judgment, such as in the interpretation of treaties, the OFA is arguably required to give preference to petitioners' own understanding of their Indian-ness when determining whether it meets regulatory criteria for acknowledgment. At a minimum, it would seem, it should be required to follow the original recommendations of the 1977 American Indian Policy Review Commission, and shoulder the burden of proof in showing why a petitioner "does . . . not meet any one of its definitional factors" (1977, 482). Perhaps unsurprisingly, even after the 2015 revisions, the OFA has not adjusted its evaluative posture toward the petitions it receives.

In the decades since the creation of the process for federal acknowledgment, sixty petitions have been submitted to the Office of Federal Acknowledgment.

13. 25 C.F.R. 83 at 37863.

Of those petitions, thirty-four have been denied, and eight are under ongoing consideration. Only eighteen Tribes have been formally recognized as "tribal nations for federal purposes."[14] What can account for the radical and enduring failure of the recognition process in the United States, especially one that was originally recommended to give preference to and presumption of recognition?

No doubt the criticisms of recognition leveled by Povinelli, Coulthard, and others find fertile ground in the US process. But I suggest that attending to the actual details by which this failure takes place in the everyday practices of the acknowledgment process offers information that unveils what is wrong and how it might be repaired. It might be that the problem is not with "recognition" itself but with the various ways in which specific actors in the OFA actively work to produce a sense of Tribal Nations as unrecognizable.

As mentioned earlier, I turn now to the details of the technical assistance meeting that took place between VRTN officials and the OFA, as they were in the midst of preparing what would ultimately become a fifty-five-thousand-page multivolume petition.

Taking the Measure of a Tribal Nation: A Federal Acknowledgment Consultation

In anticipation of that meeting, friends in the VRTN told me they had spent countless hours consuming whatever information they could find on how to approach the development of their petition. This included turning to the acknowledgment process guidelines that the Bureau of Indian Affairs published in 1997, which were designed to help potential petitioners understand what kinds of evidence will be required for meeting the mandatory criteria outlined at 25 C.F.R. 83.7. For example, it advised Tribal groups that wanted to hire professional researchers to assist with the preparation of their petitions precisely how a combination of genealogists, historians, and anthropologists should be deployed, in a manner mirroring their use by the OFA in reviewing petitions. It explains:

> Start with the genealogy. Hire a genealogist first. They will try to trace your ancestry to a historic tribe. A historian will next build on what the genealogist has found by placing the ancestors in a historical context. Finally, the anthropologist describes the social and political entity your ancestors maintained in the past, and you maintain today. Don't hire them all at once. Stagger their

14. Website of the Office of Federal Acknowledgement, Bureau of Indian Affairs, Petitions in Process & Decided Cases, www.bia.gov/as-ia/ofa (accessed June 30, 2020).

work. This is generally how BIA researchers work too. (Bureau of Indian Affairs, Branch of Acknowledgment and Research 1997, 32)

At first glance, the suggested sequencing of expert advising from genealogist to historian to anthropologist is based on an idea of Euro-American history and sociology that doesn't necessarily reflect the way Native Nations give meaning to their own histories and social orders. It creates an image of Tribal petitioners as constituted of individuals whose various "vital records" can be mined for information tracing their paternity back in time to other individuals, to "ancestors," who, by "placing" them in a historical context, can be understood as collectively making up some larger (i.e., upscaled) group whose abstracted (i.e., upscaled again) "social and political entity" can be compared by an anthropologist to the contemporary "entity" of the petitioner. It is presumed that the evidentiary line is laid for linking the present group of individuals constituting the petitioning Tribal group to a past group of individuals known to constitute a historic Indian Tribe. Notice how this seeming lockstep scaling is different from the much messier and realistic evidentiary process. Notice the first step is to "start with *the* genealogy," suggestive that the genealogist's work is to "trace your ancestry to a historic tribe." Already unclear are the scales at which both the demonstrative noun phrase "the genealogy" and the second-person possessive noun phrase "your ancestry" are working. Given that genealogists work with records that mark relationships of individuals to others—birth certificates, baptismal records, marriage licenses, divorce decrees—it becomes apparent that both phrases could index simultaneously the records of individuals and the archive of some upscaled collective (*the* family, lineage, clan, gens, or Tribe). The net effect is a kind of evidentiary sleight of hand in which the sliding movement up the scales from individual to group that seems stepwise and rational from the perspective of different domains of scientific expertise proves much more opaque and underdetermined under closer inspection.

This opacity was evident in the face-to-face technical assistance meeting between VRTN leaders and OFA officials. The OFA solicitor opened the meeting by explaining that the office had "two areas of concern" about the evidence in the petition; namely, "genealogical issues as well as historical and documentation issues that we wanted to bring to your quick attention."[15]

In talking about these kinds of evidence as "areas of concern," the fields of information captured by the phrase "genealogical issues" are treated as

15. The quotes are from a transcript of the interaction that took place in Washington, DC. Transcript is in the author's possession.

separable and distinct from those of "historical and documentation issues."
This is a separation, I argue, that neatly matches, and implicitly works, the
scalar logic of lockstep rational fields of expertise recommended in the OFA
official guidelines. This figuring is further reinforced, elaborated, and rami-
fied to an institutional scale when the solicitor introduces two members of
the OFA's research team as "Dr. June Eddy, genealogist" and "Dr. Bill James,
historian."

Approximately twenty-two minutes into the recording of the meeting, the
conversation turns from a discussion of the *kinds* of documents relevant as
evidence of an individual member's genealogy to the *amount* of documents
that would be sufficient to establish that an individual is not just genealogi-
cally an Indian but also a member of the historical Tribe from which the contemporary group claims descent. It is precisely in this shift from the quality
to quantity of documentary evidence that the slippery scalability between genealogy and history emerges as a problem of proof.

The relevant spate of talk begins just after the OFA solicitor explains that
the office will need to have from the petitioners "copies of sample complete
membership files." Almost immediately after announcing this mandatory requirement, the VRTN Tribal chairman raises a question as to what exactly
constitutes a relevant sample of complete membership files.

In the following transcripts, TC = Tribal chairman, S = OFA solicitor, G =
OFA genealogist, and C = Tribal council member.

Transcript 1

083	TC	Now a sample of completed
		and very organized ahm membership files
		consists of what,
		Twenty?
		Fifty to a hundred?
		More?
084	S	Ah, we have ahm,
		looked at certain groups,
		and initially have requested copies of membership files
		that would represent each ancestral family,
		from ah– [(inaudible)
085	G	[Course,
		if you had twenty individuals
		from which all of your members descended,

086   TC   Mm.
087   G   Then we would like one
           from each of those descent lines.
088   TC   Okay.
089   G   At least.

Note how the Tribal chairman asks if the sample may be one of any number but the solicitor responds that it has to do with its relevance to a larger whole for which both quantity and quality have to figure. There is no uptake at turn 084 ("Ah, we have ahm, looked at certain groups"). What is offered instead is an explanation that what the OFA has requested in the past are "membership files" tied to OFA's criteria, albeit rendered in a more scalable form: of "each ancestral family." This is made more concrete when the genealogist explains that the number of files should be tied to the number of individuals from which the current members descend: "one from each of those . . . lines." Here, genealogy becomes countable as history when individual member files ("one . . . at least" [turns 087–089]) can stand as synecdochic evidence for the families that, somehow, together, constitute the Tribe both historically and as it is in the present.

The VRTN members still seem perplexed by the request for a "sample" of files, especially when the solicitor reiterates that a "random" sample will not do but only those files that show a representative descent relationship. A Tribal council member offers up a different figuration of what this might be, framing it no longer in terms of number but in terms of a metaphorical mass centrality, or what he calls a "core."

Transcript 2

104   S   So ahm,
           that's what you must consider
           in providing to us.
           Clear links going back
           through a sample representative member file.
           Or files.
           (some turns omitted)
109   C   So like,
           maybe a core?
110   G   Well, a core.
           Let me say–

one from each line.

At least.

(some turns omitted)

116   S   But each family line needs
to be represented.

117   G   Yeah.

And to have–

and make sure that

you have a complete lineage record,

you know,

in each– descent record

in each one of those files.

You know, which family

they descend from–

118   C   Got ya.

119   G   And what the links are back,

and we can see cross-links then to other lines.

If there are marriages and things like that.

The VRTN council member's proposal at turn 109 of the mass metaphor "core" in reference to the relevant "sample" implies a vision of the scalability that moves away from the count character of files and toward the image of these records as standing for a larger, undifferentiated whole within which a core is centrally nested. But this too seems unsatisfactory to OFA officials. This time it's the genealogist, who at the beginning of turn 110 starts with the discourse particle "well," which conversation analysts have argued that, at least in English conversation, signals that what the speaker is going to say deviates from the position taken in the just prior turn at talk (Heritage 2015). In the context of this exchange, that deviation conveys the sense that the council member's use of the term "core" isn't satisfactory to the genealogist, who then indeed follows with a description meant as a counterproposal to the term "core" ("Well, a core. Let me say—one from each line"). But this formulation is also a departure from the Tribal Chairman's previous proposal, at turn 083, that the relevant sample could be defined merely by recourse to a particular number of files ("Twenty? Fifty to a hundred? More"). Perhaps concerned that this latter point might be lost on the VRTN leaders, the solicitor steps in at turn 116 to amplify the point ("But each family line needs to be represented"), echoing the genealogist's use of the term "line" (turn 110). This then prompts the genealogist to agree and elaborate, at turn 117, explaining that the sample files must contain "a complete lineage record" of each family. This latter point is relevant insofar as the genealogist wants to ensure that files produced not only make possible a reckoning of individual descent but equally connections by and between the various families (so "we can see cross-links then to other lines. If there are marriages and things like that").

The net effect is a return to the mixed genealogical-historical value of membership files that stand at once for individuals and the collective group of which they are members, but never in a fully disambiguated way. As this interaction suggests, the OFA solicitor and genealogist seem to be arguing that the "sample" they require is based neither solely on number of records nor on type of sample. It cannot be a quantifiable sample because while this might establish the genealogical Indian-ness of the individuals whose files were picked, it would not work to convey how these individuals "scale up" to reflect the larger Tribal entity, past or present. At the same time, it cannot be a sample based on quality because defining the sample as simply a "core" understands the sample only in terms of its metaphorical and representative centrality to the collective Indian-ness of the whole group without sufficiently "scaling down" to establish how the core links to the Indian-ness of individual members. It is important to read this interaction against the posited rationality of a federal acknowledgment process that draws on the expertise of genealogy, history, and anthropology for establishing the "enduring Indian-ness" of a Tribal group and of its individual members. Upon closer inspection of the ways in which documents are invoked in this technical assistance interaction to stand as and for evidence of Indian-ness at these different social scales, it is shown that they constitute a mode of evidence and a standard of proof for Tribal petitioners that seems inherently ambiguous. I would argue that they constitute the elements of an evidentiary double-bind that doesn't just set an impossible hurdle for petitioners to overcome when trying to establish their Indian-ness, though it certainly does this. But even more, it actively constitutes the VRTN as unrecognizable. In so doing, it converts the inherent ambiguity in the status of Native Nations across the whole of US laws and policies toward them (as discussed in chapter 2) and weaponizes it against them. As such, the goal of VRTN to engage the US in and through their Indigenous juris-dictions of CWS is lost before it can even begin. By failing to attend to the norms, knowledge, and relations of VRTN as anything other than objects observable only through the evaluative logics of the OFA's criteria, the unrecognizability of VRTN is the bitter product of an acknowledgment process always set against them.

Conclusion

In the days following the phone call from the OFA informing the VRTN that its petition for federal acknowledgment had been denied, when the shock of the news became less sharp, the Tribe's leadership printed out the official final decision document and began poring over its text. As they did, a general consensus began to emerge objecting to what they saw as the OFA's contradictory, perhaps even duplicitous, reasoning. What the decision explained was that the OFA acknowledged that the documents submitted had established that the Tribe currently had members who were descendants of individuals who were Indian, and those and other documents also established that there was indeed a historic Indian Tribe. Yet somehow, these same documents and the other evidence they submitted had failed to establish that current members of VRTN were descendants of Indians who constituted a historic Tribe from which the VRTN—as a group—claimed succession as a distinct community, over which it had continuous political influence and authority. Despite all the discussions that seemed to rationalize a lockstep relationship between genealogy and history, and the scalability they presuppose and entail between individuals members and a Native Tribe, it was a recalcitrant nonscalability among genealogy and history and anthropology, at least as applied by the OFA to the evidence submitted by the VRTN. This ultimately convinced the OFA that the Tribe that operates today is not the "same entity" that operated historically, and thus does not exist as an Indian Tribe for federal purposes. Somehow, despite all the positive assessments of their Indian-ness, past and present, individual and group, the VRTN was unable to meet the criteria of 25 C.F.R. 83.7 in a way that could "reasonably" result in a finding of an enduring Indian Tribe.

I argue that the problems of scale that the petitioners were so desperately trying to work through with the OFA in their technical assistance meeting foreshadowed precisely the problems of scale that were attributed to their petition in the final determination. More importantly, they suggest that an interest in consulting with Native Nations about their Indigenous norms, knowledge, and relations is insufficient to take seriously the possibility that Native Nations are sovereigns with whom the US government might exercise a government-to-government relationship. Insofar as the OFA's interest in VRTN members' histories, genealogies, and political formations was to evaluate them against the regulatory criteria for acknowledgment, and not as what presumptively grounds VRTN juris-dictions of self-governance, the OFA's objectivizing interest offered no real way to enter into a genuine mutual government-to-government relationship with them. In this sense, Coulthard

(2014) and Povinelli (2002) are right when they point out the impossibility of recognition. Neither scalability nor nonscalability alone suggests the promise or problems that the federal acknowledgment process poses for Tribal Nations. There is, instead, a slippery movement between the logics of both that work as an evidentiary double bind. This allows the US government to make Indigenous juris-dictions produced by VRTN in their multivolume petition—all fifty-five-thousand pages of it—unrecognizable. This is not to say that there could not have been some amount of evidence that the VRTN proffered that would have satisfied the criteria of the federal acknowledgment process. I suspect there could have been. But the process, even after all the reforms it has undergone, remains premised on the idea that the United States can impose and evaluate as objects of their investigation a Native Nation's knowledge, relations, and norms. It remains a process that cannot produce the mutual relations of CWS that Tribal Nations are clamoring for, and which the United States, even by its own principles, is required to instantiate for a government-to-government relationship (see chapter 2). Indeed, to the extent that the acknowledgment criteria are ostensibly designed to safeguard against Tribal Nations "being Native" just for the purposes of federal acknowledgment, the criteria are undermined when OFA agents unreflexively impose them as evidentiary measures against which Tribal Nations must prove themselves to be sufficiently Native. The entire OFA process, even after the 2015 reforms, remains closed to Native juris-diction. The VRTN not only had abundant records as an ongoing Tribe, but were actively engaged as a Tribe on the day that they were told they did not exist as a Tribal Nation for federal purposes. VRTN's enactments of their sovereignty and rights to self-determination, and their petition for a government-to-government relationship premised on their modes of cooperation without submission, fell on deaf ears. Indeed, even if the OFA had acknowledged them as a Tribal Nation pursuant to 25 CFR 83.7, it remains a genuine possibility that the VRTN would be fundamentally unrecognizable by the US in ensuing government-to-government engagements, so long as their juris-dictions of CWS, and the Indigenous *insistence* it constitutes, is overlooked by the misfirings of US agencies' settler evaluative logics. And this will be true of all Tribal Nations, whether acknowledged by the US or not.

6

Taxing Relations:
Indigenous Juris-diction and the Tribal Tax
Status Act

Introduction

In the last chapter I described the unrecognizability constituted in the US federal acknowledgment process and analyzed the details of the engagement between the VRTN and the Office of Federal Acknowledgment. There are cascading perils when a Tribe's eligibility for federal acknowledgment is premised on how the United States measures Tribal "existence" rather than on the many ways in which a Native Nation exercises its Indigenous juris-diction. There is also a bitter irony in this inversion of knowledge, relations, and norms that suggests just how problematic the politics of recognition can be and the extent to which the everyday acts of Indigenous juris-diction via cooperation without submission are not just overlooked in the evaluative calculations of US regulations and implementation but stand as their antipode.

This chapter considers another area in which regulatory oversight threatens to make Native Nations' commitments to their juris-dictions unrecognizable: the US tax code. Tribal Nations fight to secure their rights to issue tax-exempt bonds, which is what other US state and municipal governments are empowered to issue when generating investment capital for large economic development projects. Rather than think of these matters as convoluted regulatory mazes or bureaucratic doublespeak, think of them as spaces in which issues of Indigenous juris-dictions of CWS, and their rendering as unrecognizable by US political and legal actors, emerge in ways both surprising and unsurprising. My goal here is to extend a substantive and analytical understanding of CWS and its role in Native Nations–US engagements to an area of federal regulation—taxation—that is not centrally concerned with Tribal-US relations, but which can pose the same promises and perils that the government-to-government relationship poses to Native Nations more generally.

This chapter considers how the rendering of Tribal norms, knowledge, and relations as unrecognizable informed a recent line-item amendment to a provision of the Indian Tribal Governmental Tax Status Act (hereafter Tribal Tax Status Act),[1] which effectively hindered sorely needed Tribal economic development projects. The amendment added a regulatory hurdle to Tribal governments being able to issue tax-exempt municipal bonds to potential investors for development projects, a hurdle not imposed on non-Native municipalities. It specifically required Tribes seeking to issue tax-exempt bonds to first show that the projects in question were ones "customarily the practice of state and municipal governance."[2]

The text of the amendment was neutral on its face, and appeared to mirror similar language in other legislation that authorized federal agencies to treat Tribal Nations as states for the purpose of implementing federally mandated regulations. Indeed, it has long been an established principle of US law and policy that Tribal Nations generally have the power to levy taxes on persons and activities on Tribal lands, whether they be Native or non-Native. What has been a stickier question is whether Tribal Nations, because they and their members are exempt from state and federal income taxation, enjoy the power to abstain from levying taxes altogether.[3] The Tribal Tax Status Act was designed to stop what was viewed as Tribes' unfair advantage, under certain conditions, over non-Native competitors to attract outside investment by issuing tax-exempt municipal bonds for economic development projects. It was the brainchild of a congressman who staunchly opposed Tribal gaming. My analyses of the act's legislative history and actions taken by political and legal actors to influence how the Internal Revenue Service (IRS) interpreted the provision reveal how, even in seemingly neutral legal texts of tax law, the evaluation of Tribal norms, knowledge, and relations can be deployed for the purposes of making Indigenous juris-dictions unrecognizable. In this chapter I also extend my arguments of CWS, Indigenous juris-diction, and the non-Native rendering of them as unrecognizable by showing that understanding the effects of this act's amendment depends on a classic theory of sociolegal analysis of legislative texts that itself has its roots in an appropriation of Native American norms, knowledge, and relations.

---

1. Indian Tribal Governmental Tax Status Act of 1982, P.L. 97-473, Title II, §202(a), 96 Stat. 2608 (1983) (codified as amended by Pub. L. No. 98-21, 97 Stat. 65, 87 [1983-1 CB 510, 511], at I.R.C. §§ 7704(a), 7871). I.R.C. refers to the Internal Revenue Code, which can be found in Title 26 of the U.S. Code. For citation purposes, and unless otherwise specified, the act will hereafter be referenced as 26 U.S.C . § 7871 or Section 7871, and include its subprovisions.

2. 26 U.S.C. § 7871(e).

3. Washington v. Confederated Tribes of Colville Indians, 477 U.S. 130 (1980).

Others have written about the unacknowledged debt owed to Native American intellectual theories by American philosophical pragmatism (Pratt 2002; Wilshire 2000). Of particular note were the approaches pragmatists used toward pluralist, relational, and imminently performative dimensions of human experience and understanding. These had an unmistakable, though usually overlooked, source in Native American theories that were developed "along the border between Native and European America as a resistance against the dominant attitudes of European colonialism" (Pratt 2002, 1).

This chapter questions an offshoot of that pragmatism, American legal realism, and specifically the work of the great legal scholar, proto-legal anthropologist, and lawyer Karl N. Llewellyn. His critique of the analytic value of "custom" in sociolegal research, as well as his theory of the "trouble case method" and his application of both in drafting the Uniform Commercial Code (hereafter the UCC) all reveal a deep debt to the Indigenous juris-dictions of CWS that he discerned in the Northern Cheyenne Nation.[4] His writings on the Northern Cheyenne would become a foundational text of modern legal anthropology (Llewellyn and Hoebel 1941), but their influence on Llewellyn's jurisprudence generally and the UCC in particular would not be appreciated until a half-century later. That Llewellyn's scholarship continues to shape contemporary sociolegal understandings of the relationship between legal language and legal action, including the effects of legislative texts and their drafting, only further suggests the enduring influence that Indigenous juris-dictions have on settler colonial law and sociolegal scholarship.

Llewellyn's work has no direct bearing on the history or implementation of the Tribal Tax Status Act. Instead, I invoke it to foreground how an analytic approach on the influence of Indigenous juris-diction offers a unique angle from which to see how the engagements producing Tribal tax status works in relation to contemporary Tribal Nations and their sovereignty. I argue that what Tribal officers wanted to learn from a conference in 2008, which I attended, were ways to counteract how tax law texts afforded federal agents the opportunity to adjudge what constitutes a Native Tribe in ways that claimed a concern for Tribal norms, knowledge, and relations but, as discussed in previous chapters, actually took these as objects of US evaluation and judgment. In assessing these calculations of interpretation and assessment, I argue that Tribal officials' eventual responses not only compelled refinements of the act's text but also, and even more significantly, the creation of a community of norming, knowing, and relating—a juris-diction of CWS—forged through

4. Llewellyn led the UCC drafting project as its chief reporter from its initiation in 1941 until his death in 1962.

their willingness to open up how Tribal Nations could act for the purposes of these taxation principles.

I describe how I first discovered complex these issues, and the rather unconventional turn I took to Llewellyn's work to start to sort them out.

On Tribal Bonds

In spring 2008 my colleague Bill Maurer and I traveled to San Diego to attend the annual conference of the Native American Finance Officers Association (NAFOA). Bill and I were considering collaborating on a project on the shifting meanings of money and investment in contemporary Native American governance. It had been two decades since passage of the Indian Gaming Regulatory Act of 1988,[5] and the cascade of transformative wealth and economic opportunities that gaming introduced in certain parts of Indian Country had already been well documented (Cattelino 2008). Nonetheless, the combination of the global economic downturn now known as the Great Recession and an increased visibility of Native Nation spending on political initiatives at municipal, state, and national levels[6] meant the matter and meaning of Native Nations, their economic fortunes, and their place in relation to non-Native social and political formations had once again raised wider interest and inquiry in the workings of contemporary Native America.

More specifically, we had learned of a growing controversy surrounding how Tribal Nations were securing investment for large-scale development projects on their reservations, such as factories, fishing and boating docks, shopping malls, hotels, conference centers, golf resorts, and casinos (Braccio 2009). They had been relying for years on the Tribal Tax Status Act to issue tax-exempt bonds to private investors to raise the capital necessary for these projects. However, the IRS had issued rulings that threw substantial new bureaucratic hurdles at Tribal issuance of tax-exempt bonds and was auditing at increased rates those Tribal projects that had already used tax-exempt bonds (Clarkson 2007). The capacity to issue tax-exempt bonds is a regular feature of the power of municipal governments in the United States, one from

---

5. Indian Gaming Regulatory Act of 1988, 25 U.S.C. ch. 29 § 2701 et seq. 102 Stat. 2467, (October 17, 1988).

6. See, for example, the Jack Abramoff lobbying scandal, in which the now-discredited Washington, DC, operative played gaming Tribal Nations against each other (Stone 2006); or the Eloise Cobell lawsuit against the United States for misappropriation and mismanagement of funds from over one hundred years of oil and mineral leases required to be set aside to individual Native citizens, and the $1.5 billion settlement of that suit signed into law by President Obama in 2010 (Carpenter and Riley 2019).

which they accrue a benefit when attempting to attract investments for major civic projects like sports arenas, public golf courses, museums, and the like.[7] Ratcheting up regulatory roadblocks on Tribes hoping to avail themselves of this routine municipal power would clearly hamstring any efforts on economic development (Braccio 2009; Clarkson 2007). This disadvantage is even more pronounced because, unlike other local governments that can also use real property holdings as collateral for securing loans, the title to Tribal reservation lands is held by the United States, not the Tribal Nations themselves (Cornell and Kalt 1992; Jorgensen 2007). With little real property to offer as security against loans, Tribes are thus doubly disadvantaged when they also cannot turn to tax-exempt bonds to entice investment (Braccio 2009). It was our interest in learning more about this controversy, how it arose, and how Tribal Nations were responding to it that prompted us to inquire about attending the NAFOA conference, and to which we were warmly welcomed.

And so Bill and I made the short trip from our university campus in Irvine, California, to San Diego. The conference was in a luxury hotel newly purchased by the Sycuan Tribal Nation.

When we arrived, wearing our professorial slacks and jackets (with more than our fair share of the wrinkles this implies, at least on my part), we quickly eyed all the smartly business-attired attendees. Being considerably underdressed—and late—we took two seats at a banquet table in the back of the cavernous conference room. Traffic on the interstate had been slow, so when we arrived the conference was already underway.

We thus walked into the middle of a complicated and impassioned debate over the tax-exempt financing vehicles that Tribes were being blocked from using. Perhaps not surprisingly for two anthropologists, as the discussion went on and became more complex and detailed, we heard echoes of other kinds of Tribal "bonds"—those of normativity, epistemology, and relationality on and through which the Tribal communities are constituted. I especially thought of the lessons I had learned from my work with Hopi on the ways in which such norms, knowledge, and relations are at once presumed and produced in the discourses of navoti (see chapter 2). The IRS's differential treatment of Tribal bonds dominated the conference program, but the word "custom" came up again and again.

We first noticed it when panelists representing a number of Tribal Nations and law firms made the case that securing a court ruling on the legitimacy of Tribal bonds should be the single most important priority of NAFOA and Native Nations more broadly. Gavin Clarkson, a member of the Choctaw

7. For a good overview, see National Association of Bond Lawyers 2017.

Nation, then a professor at the University of Michigan Law School and the director of TribalFinance.org, spoke zealously in support of using court challenges and legislation to force the IRS to change its auditing practices and to compel a new interpretation of the Internal Revenue Code Section 7871 (Clarkson 2007). The leadership of the Grand Traverse Band of Ottawa and Chippewa Indians of the Upper Peninsula of Michigan presented their plans for a marina development on their reservation that would, they hoped, spur economic investment, but which had thus far been stymied by lack of capital. The Grand Traverse Band Tribal Council had just unanimously passed a resolution to support challenges to the IRS's interpretations of Section 7871 in the United States Tax Court.

Codified in 1983, and made permanent in 1985, Section 7871 implements the Tribal Tax Status Act,[8] providing for Tribal governments to be treated as state governments for a variety of tax provisions, including the issuance of tax-exempt bonds. It was amended in 1987[9] after one member of Congress raised concerns that the provision was being interpreted by the IRS too broadly, allowing Tribes to issue tax-exempt bonds for all kinds of revenue-generating projects. The amendment provided a new definition of how the language "essential government function" was to be interpreted in the law. It reads:

> For the purposes of this section, the term "essential government function" shall not include any function which is not customarily performed by State and local governments with general taxing powers.[10]

Though appearing to merely clarify precisely the ways in which Tribal governments are empowered to act as state and local governments for taxation purposes, the amendment, Clarkson and others argued, in fact added restrictions on Tribal governments that had never been imposed on state or local governments (Aprill 1994; Clarkson 2007).

The word "custom" carries with it the legacies of long debates in the anthropology of law (Barton 1949; Llewellyn and Hoebel 1941; Malinowski [1926] 1989; Moore 1986). Being a linguistic anthropologist and lawyer attuned to Native American Tribal legal and political discourse, and collaborating with an anthropologist like Bill, who is always on the lookout for new forms of culturally embedded finance, we were particularly attuned to the ensuing discussion about bond issuances and the arcana of the tax code. But while "custom" kept coming up, we noted that in this conversation it was not being

---

8. P.L. 97-473, Title II, §202(a), 96 Stat. 2608 (1983)
9. P.L. 100-203, title X, §10632, 101 Stat. 1330 (1987)
10. 25 U.S.C. §7871(e).

invoked in relation to Indigenous norms, knowledge, or relations as it often is (albeit not unambiguously) in sociolegal discussions about and among Native Americans, but to something rather different. In the conversations at NAFOA, it referred to the practices of municipal governments, their usual duties, and the normative and evidentiary weight these should play in evaluating how the IRS should relate to and regulate Tribal governments that seek to issue tax-exempt bonds to investors and developers on projects in Indian Country.

Indeed, as we would soon discover, the meaning of the word in this particular portion of the tax code had become, yet again, a fulcrum on which balanced the teetering character of relations between Tribal Nations and the US government. The term was playing a particular role in these juris-dictions around taxation that pointed to and reproduced the enduring ambiguity of those relations, and whose meaning—and the knowledge and norms that were deployed to ground that meaning—offered both promise and peril to advocates for the rights and interests of Native Nations.

In what follows, I briefly explain the contours of the debate around what are now called tax-exempt "Tribal bonds" and how the controversial language of the Tribal Tax Status Act came into being. In particular, I show the administrative wrangling by which the term "customarily," as it appears at Section 7871(e), came to be interpreted in a manner that, according to its critics, uniquely disadvantaged Tribal Nations. I suggest that the discursive and textual sleights of hand by which this is accomplished—particularly how this prejudicial interpretation of "customarily" is pushed forward even after IRS officials point out its questionable legality—once again reveal the failure to meaningfully engage Tribal Nations in the working out of their government-to-government relationship with the United States. It thus adds yet another dimension to the argument, made throughout this book, that the question of these relations must remain an open-ended and ongoing endeavor of the sort that Tribal Nations have always insisted on, and which they enact through Indigenous juris-dictions of cooperation without submission.

It is important to note that this chapter is perhaps different from the preceding ones in that it does not center on an explicit face-to-face engagement between representatives of Tribal Nations and US counterparts. I highlight this shift particularly because my emphasis in previous chapters is on how attending to discursive dimensions of these engagements is key to understanding the juris-dictions of Tribal-US relations.

And yet the same questions of knowing, norming, and relating that undergird the meaningfulness of discursive engagement can be extended to the ways in which the language of texts—and particularly legal texts like statutes, codes, and constitutions—become the objects of legal interpretation and regulatory application.

In chapter 2, in discussing treaty-making and interpretation, I spoke of the canons of construction unique to federal Indian law. Chief among these is the idea that the terms of treaties with Tribes should be interpreted in a light most favorable to them on the presumption that the barriers of language and the strangeness of Euro-American legal culture at the time of signing would have put Indians at a disadvantage in the original face-to-face negotiations, a disadvantage that should be corrected in subsequent cases and controversies in which such terms were at issue. Indeed, this was one of the key bases for the broader idea of the federal Indian trust responsibility, an enduring element of the government-to-government relationship between Tribal Nations and the United States. It is one most Tribal leaders are keen on preserving, even if it has never insulated them from the more severe deprivations of federal law and policy.

On the other hand, there is another more complex, more profound way in which legislation comes to bear the imprimatur of the communities of meaning that contribute to it, whether as its drafters or as the subjects of its edicts, and ideally both. Interestingly, it is in Llewellyn's work that these more profound connections between community and the interpretations of code revealed themselves, at least to Bill and me when we started on this project. I say "interestingly" because Llewellyn is a unique figure whose scholarship sits at the nexus of many of the traditions that come together in this book. It is to his work I turn to explain how foundational notions of knowing, relating, and norms shape the meanings applied to legislative texts like those under consideration in the Tribal bonds debate.

From Custom to Code: Llewellyn's Juris-dictional Approach to Drafting and Analyzing Legal Texts

Karl Nickerson Llewellyn was a mid-twentieth-century American legal scholar who was a leader of the school of jurisprudence known as American legal realism. He put his theories into a body of work that sits at the intersection of legal anthropological accounts of Native American societies—through his 1941 landmark volume (*The Cheyenne Way*, coauthored with anthropologist E. Adamson Hoebel)—as well as in his efforts to codify a general law for commercial activity across the United States: the Uniform Commercial Code.

Importantly, Llewellyn was at work on both at approximately the same time, and scholars have argued that each reflects the influence of the other in compelling ways (Conley and O'Barr 2004; Papke 1999). They show Llewellyn mainly working to discern the communities—the Northern Cheyenne in anthropology and merchants of goods and services in the UCC—whose knowledge, relations, and norms could be said to be represented in the scholarly and legal texts he was producing, and thus would stand as an expression of their respective communitys' consensus (Conley and O'Barr 2004; Papke 1999).

From 1937 to 1940, Llewellyn and Hoebel wrote and revised *The Cheyenne Way* based on data collected from interviews with Cheyenne elders on what was the Tongue River (now Northern Cheyenne) Reservation near Lame Deer, Wyoming (Llewellyn and Hoebel 1941). There had been a clear division of labor in the production of book. Hoebel did the bulk of the field research in the summers of 1935 and 1936, and wrote the central data chapters. Llewellyn took charge of the framing chapters, lending his voice most loudly to the theories animating the volume's methodologies and conclusions (Conley and O'Barr 2004, 179–180). This included their now famous attention to studying trouble cases, those "crucibles of conflict" that afforded a view of "not only the making of new law and the effect of old, but the hold and thrust of all other vital aspects of the culture" (Llewellyn and Hoebel 1941, 29). It was in such moments, the authors claimed, and not in the abstract statement of normative principles, that law most realistically reveals itself in the "law-ways" with which the Cheyenne actively responded to those "tensions of the culture come to expression" (29).

For Llewellyn, putting this realism into legal action meant discerning and theorizing the manner in which law can be discovered as immanent in the patterned practices of a community. As he would write later in life, it was always his understanding that "the highest task of law-giving consists in uncovering and implementing this immanent law" (Llewellyn 1960, 122). For him, the question of what the law demanded, and what its texts meant, turned on what he called the "situation sense": that anyone seeking to apply the law must have of the particular knowledge, relations, and norms of the community whose lives were governed by that law (122). As such, for Llewellyn's legal realism, any text that claimed to represent the law of a given community would have to be one that captured the immanent meaning that informed how communities ordered themselves and their relations.

For all of Llewellyn's concerns with the immanence of law in the patterned practices of social life, *The Cheyenne Way* is also famous, at least in the anthropology of law, for rejecting the notion of custom as a useful analytic category for studying law's immanence. The reasons for this are many. One is the way it tends to create a false distinction between "civilized" state-based societies with text-based laws and societies and those with a more decentralized social organization that transmits rules and resolves conflicts through oral discourses and interactions, like the Cheyenne. Another reason, and even more problematic to Llewellyn and Hoebel, was the sheer analytic fuzziness of the notion of custom. They saw it (as well as the term "mores") as both overbroad and underinclusive, all at the same time. As they write:

> First they are ambiguous. They fuse and confuse the notion of "practice" (say, a moderately discernable line of actual behavior) with the notion of "standard" (say, an actually held ideal of what the proper line of actual behavior should be). . . . Second, such terms . . . lack edges. They diffuse their reference gently and indiscriminately over the whole of the relevant society. (Llewellyn and Hoebel 1941, 275)

The problem with the notion of custom is that it blurs the line between what is a common practice and what is the normative standard against which such practices are evaluated by authoritative members of a community. It also fails to recognize that even within a single society, there persist different and sometimes competing communities of norming, knowing, and relating, whose authoritative members evaluate the same practices according to different standards and in light of different information. Regular use of the term "custom," Llewellyn and Hoebel argued, "obscure[s] the great range of trouble in which practices . . . plus their appropriate standards . . . can conflict within a society at all complex" (Llewellyn and Hoebel 1941, 275). For them, the very stuff of law, and the trouble case method by which they thought it best discerned, required attention to the situation sense with which it was experienced, evaluated, and adjudged in sometimes conflicting ways across a given society. How those conflicts were resolved within the society, and the cooperation without submission that was immanent in those situations, is what Llewellyn believed constituted the "heart of law-work of any group and of any culture" (276).

Thus, Llewellyn and Hoebel's groundbreaking scholarship on Cheyenne law-ways might have informed how Bill and I were thinking about the NAFOA debates and the *substantive critiques* we might put to the slippery meanings of the term "customarily" as it appeared in the Tribal Tax Status Act amendment. And indeed, we did (and still do) wonder about the ambiguities of notions of custom that might get smuggled into IRS determinations about Tribal Nations' abilities to issue tax-exempt bonds like other non-Native municipalities. Once again, it is the federal government's orientation to Indigenous norms, knowledge, and relations as objects to be studied that renders them unrecognizable. This then sets the standards for their evaluations of Tribal taxation powers against the requirements of 7871(e). As such, what on its face appears to be an act designed to accommodate Indigenous commitments to their self-governance, it actually accomplishes the opposite, and does so because it fails to appreciate the Indigenous commitments to CWS that underwrite that self-governance in relation to the United States.

When Bill and I revisited Llewellyn's writings, we discerned other insights that did more than add nuance to our analysis of the Tribal Tax Status Act and its effects. They showed the lasting influence that Cheyenne norms, knowledge, and relations—their Indigenous juris-dictions—may have had on the *analytic methods* underpinning Llewellyn's work more generally, and particularly in his decades-long contributions to the reform of US commercial law. I began to get an inkling of the ways in which my own sociolegal thinking had been informed by Llewellyn's notion of law's immanence in the everyday practices of a community and its conflicts, and how a situation sense is the heart of my ideas of what an informed legal analysis ought to look like. It even got me thinking that my attunement to Indigenous juris-dictions of CWS likely owes a debt to the Northern Cheyenne, whose norms, knowledge, and relationships were the objects on which Llewellyn and Hoebel's methods and insights were first tested.

That this realization emerged in the context of our efforts to understand better the meanings and consequences of adding "customarily" to the Tribal Tax Status Act is what motivates me in this chapter to revisit my analyses and lay bare the path of my own thinking. That is, as described above, our intellectual journey into these issues started with the term "customarily" and the history of its introduction into Section 7871(e) of the Tribal Tax Status Act and how they might be understood in light of Llewellyn and Hoebel's critiques of the notion of "custom" in relation to their work with the Cheyenne. But then our interests moved to the influence that his work with the Cheyenne had on Llewellyn's efforts leading the drafting of the UCC. In particular I thought about his eschewing custom for law's immanence, and the situation sense required to analyze it as differentially distributed (in ways that sometimes lead to conflict) among various communities that differ in their norms, knowledge, and relations, and how this was not just true of Indigenous Peoples, but also of commercial actors, and even how legislation should be drafted to best reflect those meanings and practices immanent in their communities as well. As such, I think by analytic extension, these same insights can be brought to bear on understanding the history and regulatory implications of the amendments made to the Tribal Tax Status Act, an effort I undertake in this chapter. In my own small way, this is an attempt to pay forward (rather than repay) a long-standing debt I owe to the Native Nations and their Indigenous juris-dictions of CWS, from which the theoretical insights shared in this book originally spring.

Llewellyn's Situational Sense and the Drafting of the UCC

Starting in 1937, during the thick of what Llewellyn described as his "three years of puzzlement" writing the Cheyenne material (Llewellyn and Hoebel

1941, xi), he also played a key role in the efforts to reform the Uniform Sales Act of 1906. After two federal sales bill reforms failed to pass Congress, first in 1922 and then in 1937, Llewellyn, who lobbied hard for the reforms, was invited to lead the drafting of a uniform commercial code by the National Conference of Commissioners on Uniform State Law (NCCUSL). This was an association started in the 1890s by legal scholars and professionals whose chief goal was (and still is) to "provide states with non-partisan . . . legislation that brings clarity and stability to critical areas of state statutory law."[11]

Llewellyn would accept the position as chief reporter of the UCC project, and the first document he and his team would produce, a reform of the law of sales (later Article 2 of the UCC), bears the imprimatur of his legal realism in a number of ways. Most centrally, is the manner in which it departs radically from the prior commercial law of sales, which among other things required a number of formalities that had grown so convoluted and diverged so greatly from actual commercial practice across the US as to be more of an impediment than an assurance to the fair execution of enforceable contracts. Llewellyn's proposed revisions sought not just to simplify sales law, but to fundamentally open its terms up to the changing conditions of local business transactions. Thus, for example, the language of Article 2 Section 204, which describes the formation of contracts for sale of goods, provides:

(1) A contract for sale of goods may be made in any manner sufficient to show agreement, including conduct by both parties which recognizes the existence of such a contract.

(2) An agreement sufficient to constitute a contract for sale may be found even though the moment of its making is undetermined.

(3) Even though one or more terms are left open a contract for sale does not fail for indefiniteness if the parties have intended to make a contract and there is a reasonably certain basis for giving an appropriate remedy.[12]

Despite Llewellyn's assurances to colleagues that revisions in Article 2 "worked slight, if any, changes in the better case-law,"[13] the truth is that this provision guts some of the most established principles of the commercial law of sales. In the provisions above, nothing was affirmatively required for

11. Uniform Law Commissioners, National Conference of Commissioners of Uniform State Laws, http://uniformlaws.org/aboutulc/overview.

12. Uniform Commercial Code, § 2-204, Formation in General.

13. See Papke 1999 (1473n8), quoting American Law Institute, Uniform Revised Sales Act 116 (Proposed Final Draft No. 1, 1944).

finding a contract beyond establishing that there was some sort of agreement. Read on its own, its circular logic is almost breathtaking. Consider Section 2-204, which provides that a contract for a sale of goods is made when there is an agreement, and that an agreement can be established by evidence that the parties acted in such a way that suggests they had a contract. This means that they acted as if they had an agreement; which means they acted as if they had a contract. And so on.

It is this apparent circularity and (elsewhere) contradiction that attracts some of the most strident criticism of the UCC. David Melinkoff (1967), a maven of legal language and especially of that used in drafting of legislation, writes:

> When we learn from the Code that *debtor* can mean someone who is not indebted, . . . that *identification* of goods "occurs" when goods have been identified, and that you may revoke an *irrevocable credit*, it is pardonable to suspect that clarification has been junked for the illusion of uniformity. (Melinkoff 1967, 185)

Yet what Melinkoff missed was that the UCC is an effort to enshrine the ongoing character of face-to-face meaning-making that is the hallmark of Llewellyn's situation sense and which is required for understanding the basic unit of immanent contract law: the context-specific character of actual agreements. Thus, the UCC does not institute a new normative order and the knowledge and relations that are to flow from it in one stroke ("I now pronounce you . . . commercial law!") but instead defers to the new configurations of norms, knowledge, and relations as they are presupposed and produced in real time among communities of meaning and practice whose contracting is accomplished through them. The UCC is legislation that stays open to the immanent standards and practices of the communities it is designed to govern.

In this respect, Llewellyn's drafting of Article 2 seems to draw directly from the insight he and Hoebel learned from the Cheyenne trouble cases; namely, that any proclamation of legal right "never exists *en vacuo*. The particular group order which it presupposes is as much a part of it as the claimant" (Llewellyn and Hoebel 1941, 276).

To see this, consider another stretch of text in the UCC's Article 2, which states:

> (2) Between merchants the reasonableness of grounds for insecurity and the adequacy of any assurance offered shall be determined according to commercial standards.[14]

---

14. Uniform Commercial Code § 2-609, Right to Adequate Assurance of Performance, (2).

On its face, the language of the section again seems empty; the reasonableness of the assurance of an agreement between merchants (a community of knowledge and relations) is determined by reference to market standards (norms) that are left undetermined by the UCC. So how can we know them? Where should readers and interpreters of the UCC—judges deciding contract disputes, say, or people desiring to enter into a contract—go to understand the meaning of these provisions?

Well, it turns out that the *context* in which the UCC is expressed matters as much as, if not more, than the *content* of the expression itself, at least in terms of giving it meaning and effect. In this instance, the effort Llewellyn led—and in a way that echoed his work with Hoebel on *The Cheyenne Way*— entailed discerning a community of meaning whose norms, knowledge, and relations would give the UCC its content and seeing it as open and responsive to their ways of doing business. It turns out that more than drafting a law, Llewellyn's realist-oriented legislation involved making not just a law, but the contours of a community whose consensus could be said to have given the UCC its meaning and effect.

At the 1941 NCCUSL conference, at the same time that Llewellyn presented his second draft of reforms to the Article of Sales and received the full endorsement of the conference to pursue his more far-reaching reforms of other areas of commercial law, an announcement was made that discussions were being held with the American Law Institute (ALI), an influential professional legal body concerned with legal unification and reform, about making the UCC a joint drafting project. In this effort, Llewellyn had a key ally in William A. Schnaeder, former attorney general of Pennsylvania and a prominent Philadelphia attorney, who was serving simultaneously as the vice president of the ALI and the president of the National Conference of Commissioners, the umbrella organization of the NCCUSL. It was Schnaeder who had recruited Llewellyn to the effort to draft the UCC, and he saw the great value in joining the forces of the NCC and the ALI to the cause. Membership into the ALI is a professional honor restricted mainly to leaders of the legal profession, so it offered the promise of influential backing in obtaining funds, cooperation, and acceptance of the reform codes. The ALI formally named Llewellyn the chief reporter of the Uniform Commercial Code Project, a title he would hold until his death in 1962. With that endorsement, Llewellyn achieved for his reform efforts "sponsorship . . . of the two most influential bodies concerned with unification and improvement of the law" (Twining 1973, 281n22).

The founding of this community was not a rubber-stamp but a source for the norms, knowledge, and relations that the UCC would then enshrine.

Llewellyn's genius was in creating a scheme for the continuous unfolding of these norms, knowledge, and relations through the simultaneous announcement of a community of "merchants" that would give sense to and take direction from the "law." Assistant chief reporter Soia Mentschikoff (who had been Llewellyn's student at Columbia Law School when she was tapped for the position in the UCC drafting effort) explained:

> From the beginning the Code had as a baseline the underlying factual life situations exposed for discussion by everybody who was present and who was involved in the process, and a very explicit statement as to why one choice was being made rather than another. (Mentschikoff 1982, 541)

Llewellyn knew that in the end, it would be the strength of this sponsorship and the ways he could argue that their input was central to the drafting of the end product that would provide the greatest sanction—a "situation sense"—to the UCC. Indeed, Twining (1973) writes, "one of the claims most commonly advanced in favour of its adoption was that rarely, if ever, in legal history, can so many lawyers and other interested parties have been actively involved in the preparation of a single legal instrument" (271). It is precisely the strength of this interpretative community, not the language of the law itself, that continues to give the UCC its authority. As with *The Cheyenne Way*, it is not just the *substance* of the UCC (it has endured as persuasive even though it remains relatively empty) but also the *method* of its discernment, its realistic emergence, its method of methods that gives it force of law in the particular moments of actual sales transactions.

The original impetus behind Llewellyn's reform was to propose that the *relations* of commercial activity (here, contracting) both produced and required knowledge of the merchants' everyday practices and their relationships to those practices, and these are what should determine the law that the UCC would enforce. This orientation to the norms, knowledge, and relations immanent in actual commercial practice, Llewellyn argued, had been largely overlooked in the overly formalistic requirements of extant commercial law, particularly the Article of Sales (Twining 1973). The theory behind the reforms enshrined in the UCC's creation was toward bringing the codified texts of commercial law into correspondence with the norms, relations, and knowledge of the merchant community of meaning. Since it was these merchants that would be bound to adhere to this law, it was likewise important that the law itself stay open to the shifting norms, knowledge, and relations that constitute the community's juris-diction, the discursive and textual practices by which they undertook their commercial activity, and which inevitably vary across space and time. This required drafting a code that would necessarily rely on language that was indeterminate, circular, and even vacuous. But this indeterminacy is problematic only if the law is read in a manner that abstracts it from the method of its drafting, and more importantly, the actual moments of commercial activity it is meant to govern. By bringing together merchants, lawyers, and business leaders as the community of meaning that would give the terms its realist content, and who would then assent to being governed by those meanings, Llewellyn oversaw a truly unique law-making process that endeavored to keep the legal text open to the dynamic situation sense it claimed to codify. It is, in short, a model of code interpretation and code drafting that expresses a juris-diction of cooperation without submission.

When Bill and I read the UCC, we too were at first struck by the circular quality of the text. We weren't as exercised by this as (most notably) Melinkoff (1967), who warned that the "cries of despair" uttered by a UCC reader would "mingle with the shriek of the wounded draftsman who has just bitten himself squarely in the back" (192). And that is because where Melinkoff and other critics of the UCC's language saw vicious hermeneutic circles, they should have seen an effort to codify the conditions necessary for cooperation without submission; namely, a code that remains open to the actual discursive engagements by which social actors within and across different communities come together to give the law its content and grounding in the norms, knowledge, and relations shaping their situation sense.[15] It was a lesson that I knew Llewellyn had taken from his work with the Cheyenne. His treatment of Cheyenne law-ways did attend, with great sensitivity, to the ways in which their norms, knowledge, and relations effectuated their unfolding acts of self-governance. He then incorporated it into the substance and methods used for drafting the UCC.

But like other misappropriations by non-Natives, Llewellyn's had also oriented to Cheyenne juris-dictions as the objects of his US sociolegal inquiry, making them unrecognizable in the process as he deployed the lessons he learned from them for the benefit of persons other than the Cheyenne themselves. So, while Bill and I found in this openness a helpful description and analytic to understand the problems of norming, knowing, and relating that emerged in the debate over Tribal bonds, I had the dawning realization

---

15. I find inspiration for this model of the iterative spiral in the linguistic anthropologist Michael Silverstein's (1998) discussion of the metapragmatic function of language. He explains that language functions metapragmatically by regimenting the indexical character of signs-in-use as an unending process of dialectic feedback between speakers ideologies about language and their language actions. He describes it as "the actual dialectic manner in which ideology engages with pragmatic fact through metapragmatic function, in a kind of spiral figurement" of emergent, penumbral iterations of signification (130–131).

that my own sociolegal training and insights stood on the shoulders of Indigenous unrecognizability. With this in mind, I felt a renewed purpose in
analyzing the Tribal Tax Status Act amendment through a method that drew
on the lessons that Llewellyn's drafting of the UCC took from Cheyenne law-
ways. It became a kind of act, however small, of overdue reciprocity, the ful-
fillment of an obligation taken on by Llewellyn but that had never, and likely
could never, be adequately repaid.

And really, this is not about repayment, because reciprocity is never about
finally balancing ledgers. A balanced ledger ends relations. Rather, mine is
more of a next step in the ongoing arc of a relationship—a paying forward—
that endeavors to extend an understanding of the substantive and analytic
dimensions of CWS and to rely on it as a logic for understanding Tribal advocacy in matters of their tax status. It is to that which I now turn.

Tax-Exempt Bonds in Indian Country: The "Custom" of Tribal Nations

The amended part of Section 7871(e) provided that the only kinds of activities for which Tribes would be able to issue tax-exempt bonds were those that
served an "essential government function." Before the amendment, the definition of essential government function was left to interpretation by IRS agents
(Aprill 1994, 349). After 1987, however, Congress added language in an effort
to narrow the meaning of the phrase by excluding some revenue-generating
activities for which the IRS previously had allowed Tribes to issue bonds. The
new provision specified that "the term 'essential governmental function' shall
not include any function which is not *customarily* performed by State and local governments with general taxing powers" (emphasis added).[16]

The matter before the Tribal leaders and advocates attending the NAFOA
conference in 2008 was how to establish that Tribal governments, in issuing tax-exempt bonds even for revenue-generating projects, were performing functions that were "customarily" those of states and municipalities.
How could they, in other words, demonstrate under the law that by engaging in certain kinds of market-based interventions, Tribes were following the
customs of local governance? How is this use of the notion of custom to be
understood to refer to municipal governance rather than Indigenous traditional dances, dress, or knowledge? After all, Native Nations are still regularly
asked to produce their knowledge when arguing for their political rights. It
has been a central part of the politics of recognition that Coulthard (2014),
A. Simpson (2008), and so many others have descried. Custom, tradition,

16. 26 U.S.C. § 7871(e).

and culture, in the words of Povinelli (2001), are the concepts deployed by settler state legal and scientific discourses, and by which "Aboriginal peoples must produce a detailed account of the content of their traditions and the force with which they identify with them," yet always as a kind of setup for them being adjudged "failures of indigeneity as such" (34). Here, however custom refers to the practices of Euro-American social and political formations. After I re-read Llewellyn and Hoebel, demonstrating the customs of municipal governance seemed to introduce a kind of slippery ambiguity that could be used as much to undermine Tribal self-governance as to secure it. In the delicate balance of contemporary cultural politics, claims to Indigenous self-determination required Native Peoples to be different, but not too different (Povinelli 2002). I wondered about the risks for Tribes claiming to have the customs of municipal governments; if they were to be like cities or states, did they risk that the United States would no longer consider them to be sovereign nations? The answer to these questions turns on the situation sense to which the term "customarily" as used in this legislative provision is meant to apply. And that, as we saw in the example of Llewellyn's efforts in the drafting of the U.C.C., depends in no small measure on the community of meaning and practice whose norms, knowledge, and relations are presupposed in the drafting and application of the rule. As we shall see below, Native Nations were almost entirely excluded in the regulatory interactions interpreting Section 7871(e), and their norms, knowledge, and relations were treated more as the object of legal evaluation than as the elements of the juris-dictions contributing to its drafting and application.

But before turning to these questions, it is important to emphasize what makes the issue of Tribal bond initiatives so important, namely the pressing matters of economic well-being that face, and have long faced, Tribal Nations. Commentators on Tribal finance generally agree that lack of access to capital markets has greatly hindered economic development. Without a large manufacturing or revenue base, and often located in remote areas, Tribes have long faced hardship in promoting development despite desires for self-sufficiency and economic self-determination. The rise of Indian gaming is in part attributable to the lack of other alternatives. Clarkson (2007) estimates that Tribes face a deficit of $50 billion required for the construction of basic infrastructure like roads, sewage systems, and housing and business development (1009). Twenty percent of Indian households lack modern plumbing.[17]

---

17. Advisory Committee on Tax Exempt and Governmental Entities: Report of Recommendations (Public Meeting June 9, 2004), IRS Pub. No. 4344 (May 2004), at 9.

One way state, county, and municipal governments can address their needs for capital is by issuing tax-exempt bonds to investors, who supply capital in return for a guaranteed interest rate and to earn interest that is deemed non-taxable income. There are two broad types of bonds: general obligation bonds and revenue bonds. General obligation bonds are backed by the power of the government offering them to raise revenue through taxation. Revenue bonds are backed by the promise of the future revenue that the bond-financed activity will generate. In some cases, interest income earned from revenue bonds is taxable, but when the revenue bond is issued to fund an activity in the public interest, then the income is tax exempt.

Private activity bonds (PABs) are revenue bonds through which governments provide financing for private activities (generally) to charitable organizations such as hospitals or private companies managing water treatment plants, airports, and the like (Clarkson 2007; Zimmerman 1991). In these cases, there is a clear public benefit. But PABs can also be issued to fund projects where there is presumed to be a broader benefit to the community at large, such as convention centers, public golf courses, and marinas. Still, such bond issuances can become controversial if they seem to support private gain through the preferential exercise of public power.

Since the 1980s, Congress and the IRS have debated whether Tribal governments can issue tax-exempt bonds in the same manner as municipalities. As I describe below, opinions flow back and forth on interpretation of the tax code—from congressional debates on the legislative text to IRS interpretive rulings to law review commentaries analyzing the phenomenon—in what appears at first glance to be a closed loop. This parallels Llewellyn's methods and analyses of the situated sense of immanent US commercial law and the way in which the text of the UCC presupposed and produced the communities of merchants and lawyers that lent their normative, epistemological, and relational consensus to it. As Bill and I heard at the NAFOA conference, one of the key concerns and complaints of the Tribal leaders, lawyers, and legal scholars was the conspicuous absence of Tribal advocates from these discussions, despite the fact that it was the norms, knowledge, and relations of Tribal tax powers that were the object under consideration and the subject of the regulation itself.

But this is not the only issue. Recall that Llewellyn and Hoebel were careful to parse the ambiguities that the notion of custom afforded, rather than the divergences that emerge when different communities engage each other in and through legal language and texts. This is different from what transpired in the circulation of legal talk and texts concerning Tribal governments' authority to issue tax-exempt bonds. In those engagements, there are clear moments of blockage and rupture across the different communities of Tribal leaders, federal regulators, and tax scholars that substantially affect Tribes' capacity to finance their projects. In short, while it seems there ought to have been a shared community of norming, knowing, and relating being constituted around the interpretation of the term "customarily" when applied to Tribes' capacity to issue tax-exempt bonds like non-Native state and local governments, none emerged.

Instead, a familiar complaint rang out about the inherent indeterminacy of the implications that 7871(e) had for Tribal bonding powers. Consider, for example, the parallels between the insights of Ellen Aprill, a leading scholar of the Tribal Tax Status Act, and concerns we heard above being raised by Llewellyn and Hoebel about the "ambiguity" inherent in the notion of custom (Llewellyn and Hoebel 1941, 275), but also in the biting condemnations Melinkoff leveled at the language of the UCC. Aprill writes that the case of tax-exempt Tribal bonds, given the fuzziness that the term "customarily" adds to the evaluation of Tribal issuances, it "shows how difficult it is to ground positive theories empirically. Much of the empirical data will, like the facts here, be uncertain and difficult to categorize" (April 1994, 367). Compare this now to Melinkoff's critique of Llewellyn's UCC:

> The language is now clear, now mud; now grammatical, now illiterate; now consistent, now inconsistent, slapdash and slovenly. It wallows in definition it does not define, and definition that misleads—definition for the sake of forgotten definition. It includes many ways of saying the same thing, and many ways of saying nothing. (Melinkoff 1967, 185)

But recall too that at least for the UCC, a certain measure of indeterminacy of language was precisely Llewellyn's point. Could the same be true for the language of the tax code authorizing tax-exempt Tribal bonds about which Aprill was writing? That is, in the debates over these bonds, a type of productivity emerged in the accretion of legal texts and the way they are given immanent significance according to the norms, knowledge, and practices across different Tribal communities of meaning, albeit one that was being used against Tribal Nations, not for them.

The Juris-dictions of Tribal Bonds

As Llewellyn did in his drafting of the UCC, IRS regulators, legal scholars, and legislators grappled over the situational senses to be attributed to the term "customarily" in the amended text of Section 7871(e). There are, of course, sources of authority in determining tax-exempt status for any entity and in implementing those determinations. The place of "law" in these determinations, however,

Types of IRS interpretive issuances and directives

IRS directives	Source and purpose
1. Regulations	Issued by Department of the Treasury to guide application of the Internal Revenue Code.
a. Notice of Proposed Rulemaking	Issued to seek input from interested public regarding proposed regulations.
b. Treasury Decisions	Temporary or final binding regulations.
2. Revenue Rulings	Official interpretations by the IRS of the Internal Revenue Code and relevant tax treaties and rulings.
a. Revenue Procedures	Statements guiding how rulings are to be implemented.
3. Private Letter Ruling	IRS rulings to specific individual taxpayers at taxpayer's request.
4. Technical Advice Memoranda	Issued by the IRS chief counsel in response to questions from the IRS director and area directors.
5. Field Service Advisory Memoranda	Issued by the IRS chief counsel in response to specific questions from field agents.
6. Notices and Announcements	Public pronouncements of guidance on the Internal Revenue Code or provisions of the law related to federal taxation matters.

is complicated by different internal notions of what law is. Is it a statute as written as law in the books, or is it what is termed "legislative history"—that is, what was the law intended to do, how did its framers talk and write about it before it became statute, and what interpretations and documents did the framers use? (See, e.g., Riles 2008; Silverstein and Urban 1997.) The process of codifying law into regulations that can be implemented out in the "field" are complicated by another series of levels of interpretative authority and standing.

In the case of the Internal Revenue Service, there are no fewer than six different types of interpretative texts that funnel the "law" into practice. Their authoritative weight or interpretive standing relative to one another are listed in the table.

In addition, the IRS uses various stakeholder committees, or what it calls organized public forums, to provide advice to the agency on matters relevant to those stakeholders. Since 2001, the IRS has empaneled the Advisory Committee on Tax Exempt and Government Entities, which includes representatives from employee pension plans, exempt organizations, tax-exempt bond holders, and federal, state, and local governments. Representatives from Tribal governments have been included on these panels too, but as we shall see below, their contributions were muted by the efforts of a single US congressman to block Tribal development in his district.

I list these various authorities and their interpretative texts for two reasons. First, many of them have become relevant over the course of the history of Tribal bonds. Second, despite the presentation here or the official presentation by the IRS, they do not channel the power of law in any direct sense from top to bottom. There is no particular sequence from law, to regulation, to revenue ruling, to technical advice memoranda or private letter ruling (PLR). Regardless of their official weight relative to one another, they actually form a twisting maze that is visible in practice. The chain of interpretation and authority can start anywhere and need not have a statutory warrant. For example, Revenue Ruling 67-284 declared that "[i]ncome statutes do not tax Indian tribes. The tribe is not a taxable entity." As Aprill notes, however, "the ruling gave no analysis or basis for this conclusion. It cited no statutory authority" (Aprill 1994, 336).

The process, in short, is very like Llewellyn's description and plan of action for the making of the Uniform Commercial Code. As with the Article of Sales, the customs of taxation and revenue generation that are to inform the law come to have their particular meaning as immanent in the situational senses of communities whose norms, knowledge, and relations they are simultaneously understood as presupposing. Thus, the legal texts that emerged from these processes—all six of them—are deemed legitimately authorized by the communities that will ultimately be governed by those laws; in this case, including the Tribal Nations hoping to issue tax-exempt bonds. But once again, as so often in the history of Native-US relations, these particular Indigenous juris-dictions are not treated by the federal government as co-equal contributors in forming the legal texts that will govern them. Instead, they are treated as their objects.

Making Indigenous Juris-dictions Unrecognizable in the Tribal Tax Status Act

The processes just described were the reason for the furor that animated discussions on Tribal bonds at the NAFOA meeting. Prior to 1983, there were only two revenue rulings related to Tribal bond issuances, and these offered somewhat contradictory interpretations of the relevant tax provisions. The 1968 ruling held that bonds issued by Tribal governments would not be treated the same as bonds issued by state governments. The 1981 ruling held that when a Tribal corporation is governed by the Tribe itself, the corporation shares the Tribe's tax-exempt status under Revenue Ruling 67-284. A 1982 US Supreme Court decision affirmed a Tribe's authority to tax based on its sovereignty over economic activity within its territory.[18]

---

18. Merrion v. Jicarilla Apache Tribe, 455 U.S. 130 (1982).

In 1983, Congress passed the Tribal Tax Status Act,[19] which treated Tribal governments like state and local governments for a number of purposes. It allowed a federal income deduction for taxes paid to Tribal governments; it exempted Tribal governments from some federal excise taxes; and it allowed income, gift, and estate tax deductions for charitable contributions to Tribal governments. Aprill (1994) and Clarkson (2007) have each documented the behind-the-scenes congressional activities around the act, especially those of US Representative Sam Gibbons, who wanted to constrain Tribal rights to act as municipalities when issuing tax-exempt bonds. When Gibbons served in the Florida House of Representatives, he helped orchestrate a transfer of land to the Seminole Tribal Nation after ancestral human remains were unearthed at the site of a parking structure being constructed by a non-Native entity. The Tribal government permitted construction to be completed on the site (after the removal of the remains) in exchange for a different parcel of land. The Tribe re-interred the ancestors on the new land, and then built a shrine and museum adjacent to them—as well as a large bingo hall and a cigarette shop. Gibbons, objecting to the additional commercial construction as a misuse of the land and complaining that the Tribe had hidden its true intentions, became a prime mover in restricting the authority of Tribes to issue the tax-exempt bonds necessary for generating capital investment for economic development projects (Aprill 1994, 360). As a result of his efforts, the federal act included provisions prohibiting Tribal governments from issuing private activity bonds while permitting them to issue tax-exempt general obligation bonds—for activities deemed to be "essential governmental functions." Gibbons intended the law to block all Tribes from doing exactly what he accused the Seminole of doing in Florida: issuing bonds to build gaming facilities like bingo parlors and other projects that generated commercial revenue based on their exemption from state regulations (including taxes), giving them an unfair business advantage over their non-Native competitors.

Between 1983 and 1988, only seven Tribal bonds were issued across all Native Nations. One bond, for $125 million sold by the Sac and Fox Tribe of Oklahoma for purchasing oil and gas wells, was controversial because of its connection with a disgraced bond underwriting firm (Pryde 1987b; Quint 1987). The issuance led to a string of negative press reports. In a piece titled "Smoke Signals," *Forbes* magazine echoed Gibbons's sentiments about PABs, but inaccurately reported that Tribal governments would be exempt

---

19. Indian Tribal Governmental Tax Status Act, Pub. L. No. 97-473, Title II, § 202(a), 96 Stat. 2608 (1983) (codified as amended at 26 U.S.C. §§ 7701(a)(4), 7871).

from new restrictions being placed on all non-Tribal private activity bonds (Schifrin 1987). The truth was that Tribes had been forbidden by the Tribal Tax Act from issuing PABs at all. Nevertheless, the story had legs, and in 1987 Gibbons, citing the article, wrote the treasury secretary complaining that Tribes were using tax-exempt bonds inappropriately and against the intent of the Tribal Tax Status Act. As he put it, "cement plants and mirror factories are a far cry from schools, streets, and sewers" (quoted in Pryde 1987a, 1). In crafting the Omnibus Budget Reconciliation Act of 1987, Gibbons succeeded in securing passage of an amendment to the Tribal Tax Status Act, codified at Section 7871(e), that caused all the problems described above because it now modified the definition of "essential government function" to include the word "customarily."

In her interpretation of the addition, Aprill (1994) argues that whatever "customarily" might mean for legislators, the import of its addition to Section 7871(e) was to enact a constraint on Tribal governmental capacity to issue tax-exempt bonds. Unsurprisingly, the view espoused by Tribal leaders and their advocates at the NAFOA conference was that the use of the term prohibited Tribal governments from using PABs to build the very kinds of things that all municipal governments already build, "customarily." One need only think of a pro shop at a public golf course or the many vendors at municipally funded oceanside piers or sports stadiums to understand just how common such arrangements actually are. So why are Tribes excluded from doing things that other municipalities customarily do, and what is entailed by the fact that Tribes are excluded by the very use of that term?

Since passage of the amended act and promulgation of Section 7871(e), the IRS has offered some guidance on the interpretation of the regulations. The most significant of these is a field service advisory memorandum (FSA) related to Tribal bonds. In FSA 2002-47012, IRS officials consider whether construction of a golf course could be considered an essential government function of a Tribe. Consistent with the language of the amended 7871(e), the FSA defined such essential functions as "only those activities that are customarily financed with government bonds (e.g., schools, roads, government buildings, etc.)." The FSA applied two tests to the golf course example to determine whether it falls within the set of activities customarily financed with government bonds: (1) a prevalence test to determine the number of other government-financed golf courses, and (2) a commercial test to decide if the purpose of the activity was primarily private commercial or public revenue generating. The Advisory Committee on Tax Exempt and Government Entities issued a report in 2004 providing guidance to the IRS by noting that these tests introduce a "grossly subjective element into the determination of whether a particular tribal activity constitutes an essential government function."[20] Although at the time there were 2,645 publicly financed golf courses in the United States, the FSA argued that a golf course would not serve the Tribe's members and therefore was not a customary government function but a "commercial enterprise." Clarkson summarizes:

> In arguing that that the golf course was not "intended to meet the recreational needs of [the] Tribe or that it is anything other than a commercial enterprise of [the] Tribe," the IRS is apparently making another generalization that Indians do not play golf, and if they do play golf, they only play at courses that are too ugly to attract a non-Indian golfer. (Clarkson 2007, 1076)

This FSA is especially controversial because of the circumstances of its public release. When it was published on the IRS website in 2005, it contained several sentences indicating that "substantial litigating hazards" existed and urging the IRS not to pursue litigation because the courts would find in favor of the Tribe:

> It is probable that a court, faced with this fairly common activity of state and local governments, and taking into account the interpretative standard accorded Tribal governments, would conclude that the Golf Course meets the statutory standard for an essential governmental function. (quoted in Clarkson 2007, 1050)

Less than a month later, however, this version of the FSA was removed from the IRS's website and replaced with substantially redacted version. The language no longer included the name of the specific Tribe seeking the ruling in this case and more importantly, blacked out the language above that predicted that golf courses would meet the statutory standard for an essential government function if the IRS attempted to sue a Tribe in federal court on the issue. All that remained visible in the redacted version was abstract policy argumentation and an expression of the kinds of legal principles that these policies might run against if challenged in tax court.

The character of these redactions did not go unnoticed by Tribes or the bond investing community, with the daily newspaper *Bond Buyer* running a prominent story on the matter (McConnell 2006). The IRS maintains that the redactions were done in the interests of protecting the privacy of the no-longer-named parties. Yet the redactions speak to the broader issue of the kind of community of meaning that is presupposed and entailed by this particular legal, social, and commercial domain and the juris-dictions that

---

20. Advisory Committee on Tax Exempt and Governmental Entities: Report of Recommendations (Public Meeting June 9, 2004), IRS Pub. No. 4344 (May 2004).

were being used in the circulating texts contributing to its constitution. While mentioning the hazard that a court might rule in a Tribe's favor does not automatically make the FSA's stated conclusions disingenuous, the act of redaction raises the question of what kind of document the FSA is and can be, and how its circulation can be blocked. Mentioning that courts of law might rule differently from the FSA raises the possibility of alternative interpretations of the same "facts," a messy and contingent field of open-ended and pragmatic meaning-making that escapes the IRS's control. Critics of the UCC's messiness, ambiguity, and open-endedness would no doubt shudder if asked to comment on the legal and regulatory processes in evidence here. And yet, I am arguing that this is what the "law" is; or, better, this is how the relationships between commerce and custom, law and commerce, and custom and law unfold and change correspondences with one another. And in the case of the Tribal Tax Status Act, Indigenous juris-dictions of CWS were being made unrecognizable by the US lawmakers and IRS officials who were willing to go to great textual and discursive lengths to find ways to turn Tribal norms, knowledge, and relations regarding contemporary Tribal development projects into objects of their evaluative exclusions. Tribal governments couldn't possibly issue tax-exempt bonds to build golf resorts and casinos because *their* norms of, knowledge about, and relations to leisure and business development didn't "customarily" include golfing in the same way that non-Native Peoples and their municipalities "customarily" did. And with the help of a few unscrupulous redactions—echoing in some ways the fraudulent postagreement manipulations of the Jerome Commission discussed in chapter 2— the unrecognizable character of Tribal juris-dictions to share in the power of bond issuances was secured. That is, until NAFOA and the Tribal leaders Bill and I saw on that day persisted in their engagements with US officials to insist on their rights to assert this authority, and doing so by engaging their non-Native counterparts in the IRS and elsewhere in juris-dictions of CWS.

In this respect, I would argue, the Indigenous *insistence* constituted through juris-dictions of CWS in this case reveal compelling parallels to what Llewellyn was trying to insist upon in his efforts leading the drafting of the UCC. And like the merchants and lawyers of the UCC, and the Tribal governments and tax agents of the Tribal bond debates, and the legal scholars of both, close attention to their details shows just how much all of us—including Bill and me—were caught in the middle trying to understand it. The relations between commerce, custom, and their regulation are not only mutually constitutive but are also performative of each other and the communities of knowing, relating, and norming they both presuppose and entail.

Conclusion

Two events after the NAFOA conference—one administrative and one legislative—seemed directly related to the questions raised there. Bill and I were convinced that both were shaped by the discussions of Indigenous juris-diction.

First, the IRS issued a new private letter ruling on March 13, 2009, on electrical service provided by a Tribal government. It set out guidelines for the essential governmental functions test and cited an unattributed definition of *customarily* as "agreeing with custom; established by custom." It concludes:

> [A]n activity is to be considered an essential governmental function customarily performed by state and local governments only if: (1) there are numerous state and local governments with general taxing powers that have been conducting the activity and financing it with tax-exempt governmental bonds, (2) state and local governments with general taxing powers have been conducting the activity and financing it with tax-exempt governmental bonds for many years, and (3) the activity is not a commercial or industrial activity.[21]

In so doing, the private letter ruling seemed to double down on the idea that unlike states and local governments, what counts as the essential government functions of Tribal governments cannot include commercial or industrial activities. Of course, a PLR is an interesting bit of regulatory text, insofar as it is a decision that only applies to the specific dispute to which it is addressed. By definition, it does not create a precedent that IRS agents, or parties seeking a future ruling from the IRS, can rely on for guidance. What is odd is that despite this, the text quoted above uses normative language that seemingly points to knowledge and relations well beyond this one case. Holding that an activity "is to be considered" an essential government function customarily performed "only if" it meets three criteria that turn on what "numerous" other governments do, and "have been conducting" all discursively construct this definition as one that has broad application. Indeed, even the very enumeration of criteria is a discourse trope that characterizes the matter being described (here "essential government functions") as generalizable across contexts of application and use. To argue that this language would then have no force beyond the specific matter in which it is raised seems to belie the very way in which the IRS agents were exercising their jurisdiction in this case. And while neither Tribal Nations nor the IRS can invoke the PLR in

21. PLR 200911001, 3.

later actions, insofar as it seems to reveal the perspectives that IRS nonetheless holds, and can invoke again at a later time, its nonprecedential character only really disadvantages Tribal nations whose advocates might want to challenge IRS logics in later cases. That is, because it is a PLR, the IRS can disavow its relevance to those cases, however much the agency may nonetheless be relying on the self-same logic it announces. Just as with other acts of settler jurisdiction, the institutional authority of the IRS is reconstituted to the exclusion of Indigenous juris-dictions, even when the agency is announcing the limits of that authority to the case at hand.

The second event occurred in February 2010, when President Obama signed into law the American Recovery and Reinvestment Act (ARRA), which included provisions that seemed to eliminate the essential government functions test altogether. Section 1402 of the act created a new bonding instrument called a Tribal economic development bond, the interest of which would be exempt from IRS Code Section 103 and thus not subject to the limitations of Section 7871(e). Generally speaking, passage of this legislation was met with cautious optimism, tempered because the provision also contains a national bond limit of $2 billion, allocated at the discretion of the secretary of the treasury, in consultation with the secretary of the interior. Nonetheless, Tribes were encouraged by the possibility that they were no longer being yoked by the demands of "custom" and the differential treatment by the IRS.

Bill and I wondered, however, whether the terms of this provision call for even more caution, not less. In addition to the $2 billion spending cap, Section 1402 places additional limitations on the kinds of Tribal economic development activities that can be underwritten by these bonds. It prohibits their use for financing "any portion of a building in which class II or III gaming is conducted or housed or any other property actually used in the conduct of such gaming," and (2) requires that the project must not be "located outside the Indian reservation."

Exempting Tribes from the essential government function requirement did allow Tribal governments to apply for bonds to finance, say, golf courses. But by allowing golf courses but not gaming facilities, when Indian gaming has been a key economic engine in many parts of Indian Country for the past two decades, the provisions of ARRA seem to promote virtue at the expense of real economic advancement or independence. By requiring that Tribal economic development bonds only finance on-reservation facilities, ARRA reinscribes Native Nations as bound not by the customs of local governance but by the customs of the terms of the American legacy of removal and displacement onto reservations.

The aforementioned PLR thus introduced a definition of "custom" that might have made Llewellyn grin, if only sardonically. He might have appreciated how the ruling, having the status only of private advice, could, through future iterations and travels, nonetheless take on the character of public law, but without ever having to face critiques of Tribal nations. But what of the provisions in ARRA? When applied to Tribal bond issuances, do they foreclose altogether the ways in which Indigenous juris-dictions might be relevant when determining the legality of such issuances? Or maybe they re-animate the Tribal tax-exempt bonds debate, raising again the specter that the IRS will evaluate when and how Tribes can be described as acting "customarily" like municipalities, but doing so out of plain sight, thus providing Tribal advocates with little opportunity to engage in those decision-making processes or challenge their evaluative conclusions.

It is hard to say what impact these acts had on Tribal bond issuances. While some Tribal Nations did use the provisions to issue tax-exempt bonds for economic development projects, on the whole the economic downturn of the time slowed development generally. Even with the ARRA, Tribal Nations (and their norms, knowledge, and relations) remained under the evaluative gaze of US agencies rather than in government-to-government partnerships. Indigenous juris-dictions of CWS were again shunted aside by legislative texts, even those written with the best of intentions.

In this chapter, I argue that both the debate on Tribal economic development bonds and the drafting of the UCC reveal that the meaning of a community's norms, knowledge, and relations are reconfigured when drafting and writing US legislative texts and in their later interpretations. In the case of the Tribal Tax Status Act, the Native Nations to be governed by the act—and their norms, knowledge, and relations that were the text's objects of evaluation, judgment, and regulatory authority—were never consulted during the drafting of the bill, and were substantially muted in its subsequent interpretation. Their norms, knowledge, and relations were never treated as the operative elements of Indigenous juris-dictions of CWS in a manner that, as I argue throughout this book, are foundational to Native Nations in their engagements with the federal government, and which the United States is required by its own laws and policies to give preferential credence.

What I discuss in this chapter extends further the analysis of US regulatory powers and the ways they are deployed to make Indigenous juris-dictions unrecognizable. The Tribal Tax Status Act, as amended, requires Tribes to first show that the projects for which they wish to issue tax-exempt bonds are the kind that state and municipal governments customarily issue such bonds for. But it adds a regulatory hurdle—26 U.S.C. Section 7871(e)—on

Tribal governments not imposed on non-Native municipalities. The amendment, which is neutral on its face, was the brainchild of Sam Gibbons, a US congressman who staunchly opposed Tribal gaming. An analysis of the act's legislative history and of actions taken by Gibbons and others to influence IRS regulatory rulings interpreting how this provision is applied to Tribal Nations reveal how the force and authority of the text were specifically designed to use the notion of "custom" to hold Tribal Nations to a narrower and more stringent standard than non-Native governments. This tracks with the same constructions of unrecognizability observed in the Office of Federal Acknowledgment's handling of the Vernon's Ridge Tribal Nation's petition for acknowledgment (see chapter 5). But the actions behind the provisions of the Tribal Tax Status Act are more bald-faced in their bad faith (and perhaps more reminiscent of the actions taken by the Jerome Commission toward the KCA Tribes, as described in chapter 2) because they maneuvered the legislative language of the act to regulate away the rights of the Native Nations the act was ostensibly supposed to protect.

This chapter also extends previously discussed theories of Indigenous juris-diction by showing that understanding the effects of the Tribal Tax Status Act amendment depends on a classic theory of sociolegal scholarship and analysis of legislative text that has its roots in an appropriation of Native American norms, knowledge, and relations. The early American legal realism of Karl Llewellyn and his theory of the so-called trouble case method, and his application of it to the drafting of the Uniform Commercial Code, reveal a deep debt to the Indigenous jurisdictions of the Northern Cheyenne Nation that he studied and wrote about. That influence on Llewellyn's jurisprudence generally and on the UCC in particular would not be appreciated by academics until a half-century later. Llewellyn's scholarship continues to shape contemporary sociolegal understanding of the relationship between legal language and legal action, including the effects of legislative texts and their drafting, and underscores the enduring but still overlooked influence that Indigenous juris-dictions have on settler colonial law and science.

I consider Llewellyn's work to show how an analytic approach using the influence of Native American juris-diction offers a unique perspective on how the law works to make contemporary Tribal Nations and their sovereignty unrecognizable. What Tribal officers sought at the NAFOA conference in 2008 was a way to counteract how the law's texts and their particular historical development held only the appearance of government-to-government relationships between the United States and Native Nations. The conference participants were debating how they could reengage the IRS and others

responsible for the drafting and enacting of the Tribal Tax Status Act to demand that they reverse course and honor US law and policies toward Native
Nations. Their calls at the conference as well as in the years that followed
urged refinements of the relevant legal discourses and their interpretation,
and even more significantly for the creation of a community of relations,
norms, and knowing forged with Tribal Nations for the purposes of these
taxation principles. They insisted on refinements and revisions to the legislative text that went into the Tribal Tax Status Act and to the act's regulatory
interpretation by both describing their Indigenous juris-dictions and enacting them. But of course, as has been the case in all Native Nation–US engagements described in this book, there remains the grim possibility that US
federal agencies like the IRS will continue to fail to appreciate the Indigenous
sociopolitical theories of cooperation without submission—the everyday acts
of Tribal sovereignty—that underwrite Native Nations' engagements with the
United States. I suspect that this would have been expected by the Tribal leaders and advocates Bill and I heard from that day at the NAFOA conference;
and my guess is that their response would be the same, to refuse to give up on
engaging the US through their juris-dictions of CWS.

PART FOUR

Conclusion

7

Standing with Indigenous Juris-dictions

I can only sing this song to someone who understands it.

ATANARJUAT: THE FAST RUNNER[1]

Introduction

I had been planning and researching this book for some time, and I started writing it in February 2017. It was the day after the deadline given by the Army Corps of Engineers for Native Peoples to evacuate a campground named for the original Oceti Sakowin (Seven Council Fires, sometimes called the Great Sioux Nation). This was the confederation of the Lakota, Dakota, and Nakota Peoples of the Northern Plains, who stood their ground against the United States in the nineteenth century. The campground was located on the banks of the Cannonball River, at the northeastern tip of the Standing Rock Sioux Reservation, in North Dakota. In the spirit of its namesake, the campground was designed to serve as the home, gathering place, and flashpoint for the stand taken by thousands of Native and non-Native activists who, since March 2016, came to block completion of the Dakota Access Pipeline (DAPL). Those who blocked the construction were particularly concerned with that portion of the pipeline that would be laid under Lake Oahe, a dammed section of the Missouri River located immediately upstream of the Standing Rock Reservation, which served as an important water source for the Standing Rock Nation. Though the lake was not within the boundaries of the reservation, it was located squarely within a portion of their Aboriginal lands that their leaders had worked to preserve in the Treaties of Fort Laramie of 1851 and 1868. The land had never been ceded by the Nation, even after the United States unilaterally abrogated the terms of those agreements and took possession of those lands in the 1890s. Indeed, if allowed to go forward, opponents noted, construction of the pipeline would level a rise on the far side of

1. *Atanarjuat: The Fast Runner*, dir. Zacharias Kunuk (Inuk), Isuma Igloolik Productions. 2001.

the lake that was a site of deep ceremonial significance to the Nation, forever making the area unusable for traditional purposes (Estes 2019).

The effort to block the laying of the DAPL under Lake Oahe captured both national and international headlines and raised awareness of the issues surrounding the specific concerns of the Standing Rock Sioux Nation and the ongoing deprivations faced by Native Nations at the hands of US settler colonial laws and policies. It also foregrounded concerns about the environmental effects of new extractive technologies like fracking and how those effects and risks were being disproportionately imposed on Native Nation populations.[2] It was not lost on the Standing Rock Nation and other opponents of the pipeline that the US government's decision to approve laying it under Lake Oahe came only after the original plan to place it upriver near Bismarck had to be scrapped. There had been vehement opposition from local and state interests because of the risks its leaking would pose to the water sources for the predominantly Euro-American city (Estes 2019; Estes and Dhillon 2019). Why then, Standing Rock leaders and their supporters asked, had the pipeline plans been so rapidly approved by US officials when the only change was to relocate it to a spot downriver from Bismarck? Were the risks to their water resources more acceptable? Were the health and well-being of their populations less important?

While these policy issues roiled the Standing Rock Nation leadership and their supporters, who called themselves Mni Wiconi (It Gives Me Life, or Water Is Life), it was the images from the standoff that most captured national and international attention. The photographs and videos of local and state law enforcement and private security personnel standing with weapons and dogs against a mix of Native and non-Native (mostly nonwhite) advocates echoed a rising tide of concern about the use of disproportionate violence to protect economic interests and a disregard for the health and welfare of racialized black and brown peoples in the United States. It echoed other events over the previous several years, including the Missing and Murdered Indigenous Women epidemic,[3] the Idle No More movement,[4] the string of beatings and killings of young black men and women[5] at the hands of predominantly

---

2. The pipeline would bring oil from Baaken and Canadian oil sands oil efficiently to distribution centers in Chicago and other Midwest urban centers.

3. See, e.g., Deer, 2015; Coalition to Stop Violence Against Native Women, www. csvanw.org /mmiw (accessed June 30, 2020).

4. Idle No More, www.idlenomore.ca (accessed June 30, 2020).

5. Among the names of those killed by police forces in recent yearsare George Floyd, Trayvon Martin, Tamir Rice, Eric Garner, Philando Castile, Breonna Taylor, and Sandra Bland.

white police forces in Minneapolis (Minnesota), Evanston and Chicago (Illinois), Ferguson (Missouri), and elsewhere, and the galvanizing protests and outpouring of outrage captured by the Black Lives Matter movement.

The rise of explicitly racialized violence was a marked feature of our current moment even before Donald Trump's vitriolic US presidency. After those events, the Mni Wiconi/#NoDAPL movement took on yet more significance. Protests in cities across the United States increasingly mixed their criticisms of the pipeline's environmental and cultural resource effects with a more general rejection of the platform of the newly elected president. In Chicago, marches in December 2016 that were originally planned to show solidarity with water protectors standing firm against an increasingly hostile security force and an impending North Dakota winter were expanded to also protest the revanchist, white supremacist politics of the new president and the members of the Republican Party lining up behind him. And the protests seemed to have some impact. On December 4, 2016, the Army Corps of Engineers issued an order denying an easement to Energy Transfer Partners, owners of the DAPL, which was necessary to complete the pipeline. The sense of victory that swept across the campground was tempered when Standing Rock Sioux chairman David Archambault II, said, "We have to keep going. We have to persevere. Trump's right next in line."[6]

As Archambault predicted, the reversal of fortune came quickly. On January 24, 2017, just days after Trump's inauguration, in one of the quieter moves of an otherwise bombastic first week, he issued a presidential memorandum directing the Army Corps to "review and approve in an expedited manner . . . requests for approvals to construct and operate the DAPL."[7] Campground occupants were given until February 22 to abandon Oceti Sakowin, and they did so, but not before burning some of the camp structures in what was described as a ceremonial cleansing of the area.

As I watched the scenes splash across various media outlets of the smoke and flames turning the snow and signage into so much ash and mud, it was something else, and much less spectacular, that my mind kept going to. In some of the July 2016 legal filings from the then nascent movement, it was

---

For the more complete, and continuously uploaded list please consult #SayTheirName tag on Twitter.

6. Nathan Rott and Michel Martin, "In Victory for Protesters, Army Corps Denies Easement for Dakota Pipeline," National Public Radio, December 4, 2016, https://www.npr.org/2016/12/04/504352878/in-victory-for-protesters-army-corps-denies-easement-to-dakota-pipeline.

7. Administration of Donald J. Trump, "Memorandum on Construction of the Dakota Access Pipeline," January 24, 2017, 82 Federal Register 11129 (February 17, 2017)

significant to me that the original arguments against the pipeline stemmed from a very specific procedural objection leveled by the Standing Rock Sioux Tribal Nation against the expedited permitting process granted to Energy Transfer Partners by the Army Corps of Engineers. In their complaint seeking a federal injunction and declaratory relief against the Army Corps's decision, the Standing Rock Sioux Tribe argued that the agency did not fulfill its legal obligation under the National Historic Preservation Act when it failed to conduct a Section 106 consultation. This is required of all proposed federal actions that might impact sites of potential historic, traditional, religious, or cultural significance prior to completion of the federal action.[8]

Specifically, the complaint alleged that "[c]onsultation with [the Tribe], on the DAPL, which would be routed just outside the reservation boundary, on ancestral land with great cultural and religious importance to the Standing Rock Sioux Tribe, has been profoundly inadequate."[9] As a result, "the Corps' final permit decision is the product of a fundamentally flawed consultation process that does not meet the requirements" of the law.[10] Thus, "the Corps' decision that . . . consultation had been completed . . . was arbitrary, capricious, and not in accordance with law."[11]

In his statement to the court pursuant to his Tribe's lawsuit against the Army Corps, Chairman Archambault said:

> In our culture, relationships are about respect—between individuals and between governments. We acknowledge each other's value as human beings. We do not impose on each other. Everyone's opinion matters. The pipeline proponent and the Army Corps came up with plans to build a pipeline that would threaten our water and culture, without consulting us on the creation or implementation of the plans, and wanted us to just sign off. That is neither respect nor consultation.[12]

---

8. "Protection of Historic Properties," Code of Federal Regulations, Title 36, Parks, Forests, and Public Property; Chapter VIII, Advisory Council on Historic Preservation, §§ 800.1–800.2(c) (2) "Purposes and Participants"; §§ 800.3–800.13, "The section 106 Process."

9. Standing Rock Sioux Tribe v. Army Corp of Engineers, Complaint for Declarative and Injunctive Relief, Case No. 1:16-cv-01534 (July 27, 2016, DC Circuit) at 23.

10. *Standing Rock Sioux Tribe* Complaint for Declarative and Injunctive Relief (July 27, 2016 DC Circuit) at 39.

11. *Standing Rock Sioux Tribe* Complaint for Declarative and Injunctive Relief (July 27, 2016 DC Circuit) at 40.

12. Declaration of Dave Archambault II in Support of Motion for Preliminary Injunction, Standing Rock Sioux Tribe vs. Army Corps of Engineers, Case No. 1:16-cv-1534-JEB, (August 3, 2016), 5.

★

INTERLUDE: A LESSON FROM ATANARJUAT

The epigraph for this chapter is the opening line of the 2001 movie *Atanarjuat: The Fast Runner*, written, directed, and produced by Inuk filmmaker Zacharias Kunuk. It is the retelling of a traditional Inuk song-story about the introduction of evil into its society, and is the first film shot entirely in the Inuktitut language, on Inuk land, by an all-Inuk cast and crew. But as the narrator says, at the very outset, it is a song that can only be sung to audiences who already understand it. What kind of song is that? What insight might this provide in understanding the kinds of knowledge that at least some Indigenous Peoples' singing and storytelling convey and the relations and norms such transmissions presume and produce? For whom are such songs sung, and to what ends?

I think about these opening words of *Atanarjuat* in relation to the complaints leveled by the Standing Rock Sioux Tribe against the Army Corps that led to the events of 2016 and 2017. I also think about the manner and meaning of Archambault's complaint that the Army Corps' efforts to engage them were "profoundly inadequate." Was the problem less about failing to consult—indeed, the Sioux Tribe did not contest the claim that the Army Corps met with them on numerous occasions over the life of the project— than about the quality of those consultations? Was Archambault speaking in particular about the failures that the Standing Rock Sioux leaders, advocates, and citizens saw in efforts by the Army Corps? Did the Army Corps not even attempt to build a relationship when the Standing Rock Tribal Nation sought to share its knowledge, relations, and norms? Could this be what Archambault meant when he explained that for the Sioux, "relationships are about respect—between individuals and between governments" but that there was "neither respect nor consultation" in this case?

Or perhaps the problem was the inability of the federal agency to appreciate what a meaningful consultation was for the Standing Rock Nation. Perhaps it was a complaint that the Army Corps failed to understand that the consultation was not just about information or knowledge but about forging a relationship and appreciating the norms, knowing, and relationships that make mutual respect possible. This harks back to the 2012 National Congress of American Indians report on the progress of implementing procedures for "meaningful tribal consultation," pursuant to an executive order and presidential memo from Clinton and Obama, respectively, in which Tribal Nations demand the United States move "beyond dialogue" and take real action (National Congress of American Indians 2012, 2; see chapter 2).

Indeed, is this not what government-to-government relationships with Tribal Nations and the United States should be? Does this explain the enduring failures of federal Indian law and policy as evidenced not only in the long arcs of history but also in various everyday current engagements between Native Nations and US officials? Could this be why so many Indigenous advocates, activists, and leaders from across the United States still choose to engage US officials, undertaking acts akin to what Emory Sekaquaptewa called the central tenet of Hopi sociocultural order, namely, cooperation without submission? Could it be that they refuse to give up on the possibility that their non-Native counterparts may one day relate to them and their stories as if "they already understand them."

*

Conclusion: Cooperation without Submission

I have endeavored in this book to answer these questions through a novel approach for understanding the contemporary shape of Tribal Nation–US relations through a close examination of the actual language used in specific acts of engagement. I have drawn on my twenty-five years of experience and training as a law scholar and linguistic anthropologist engaged with the everyday practices of Native American law and politics. Specifically, I relied on theories and methods of ethnography to explain the effects of social norms, structures, and practices, including those of US law and policy. This demands attention to the empirical details with which these effects are invoked (and to what end) by social actors engaging each other in and through their everyday work. I analyzed more than thirty hours of transcribed audio recordings and observations I made between 2007 and 2016 of meetings between US agencies (and institutions supported by them) and Native American actors as they advocate for their legal claims and interests. I have shown that the legal and political texts and discourses coming out of Washington, DC, always take on a life of their own during actual enactment. They are shaped by the considerations, commitments, and concessions that Native Nations, their advocates, and their communities—both Native and non-Native—make in real-time, and which can lead the two sides to orthogonal perspectives on the goals and aims of these enactments. Native Nations have a commitment to cooperation without submission and a model of government-to-government interdependency and relation building. This differs from US agents' commitment to federal control. It is this difference that unfolds in the details of Native Nations' talk and texts in these engagements. The acts of Indigenous juris-diction are expressions of their spheres of legal and political authority (i.e., the speaking of Indigenous law) that both presume and enact their sovereignty, even if non-Natives fail to appreciate them as such.

The chapters have detailed that these types of engagement can be understood as sites in which, in real time, the relationship between the US government (which ostensibly recognizes government-to-government relationships) and Native Nations play out. They are also sites of legal interaction in which Native Nation and US cultural norms and practices of governance are held up, compared, and made to confront each other as various proponents address the specific, concrete policies and legal issues that brought them together. *Cooperation without Submission* offers new ground from which to ask about the relationship between Native Nations and the US and those engaged in its making. The actual enactment process is often overlooked by scholars and advocates on all sides who debate over the enduring challenges faced by those who work in, on, and through these relationships. I suggest that ethnography is particularly suited to the study of legal and other phenomena that straddle nature and norm, matter and culture, and object and subject.

This book examines a range of such engagements through an integrative linguistic, anthropological, and legal academic approach to posit a way forward for understanding what engagements like these mean for the Tribal actors who undertake them and for their understanding and expectations of the government-to-government relationship more generally. I have offered arguments through instances of key Tribal-US interactions and a close study of their discourses. Native American leaders and advocates orient to engagements as opportunities for respectful relations between two sovereign (but interdependent) nations, but too often find their federal counterparts orient to these engagements only as bureaucratic hurdles. This explains why Native actors party to these interactions so often express frustration at the outcomes of their engagements yet feel it is essential to make attempts again and again. Moreover, given that US policy has long been to recognize the "unique relationship" that it has with Native Americans—whether in the form of a "trust responsibility" or a government-to-government relationship—I have argued that it is long past due for the scope and contours of that relationship to reflect how Native Americans orient to and execute that relationship.

I may harbor my own skepticism about whether the US, through its agents and by its policies and procedures, might ever be willing or able to appreciate the meanings that Native Nations bring to meaningful Tribal consultation and other modes of everyday engagement with them. But it is not really my view that matters. And I hope that after reading this book it becomes clear to the reader that it isn't really the US view on Native Nations and their relations with them that matters either. If I have learned anything from my time working with and for Native Nations, including in some of the scenes I have related in the pages above, it is that Tribal leaders undertaking the everyday work of their Nation's sovereignty and self-determination are doing so through juris-dictions of CWS that trace arcs of significance that almost always both speak to but also shoot past the particular moments of political engagement in which they are enacted. They are, much as the narrator in *Atanarjuat* says, songs that are sung for those who already understand them. Of course, whether or not the settler state will ever catch their drift is another matter entirely. If they do, it will depend on their ability to appreciate Indigenous jurisdictions of cooperation without submission.

Acknowledgments

This manuscript was a long time in the making. As my three sons have re-minded me at different times over the years the unfinished book has been on my desk, they don't even remember a time when I *wasn't* working on this project. That always stops me in my tracks. Mostly it reminds me of all the many people, institutions, and occasions—both large and small—that have played an important role in the development of the book that sits before you now. First and foremost, I must thank the Native people, professionals, and advocates whom I have had the immense privilege to work with and for over the past twenty-five years. It is hard to overstate the generosity, good humor, patience, and fair share of straight-talk that I have been fortunate to be the recipient of in that time. Many of you prefer to remain unnamed, and I am happy to honor that preference, but please know how grateful I am to each and every one of you for allowing me to share a good laugh, shed some tears, furrow some brows, but always come away having learned something. There are a few of you who I hope won't mind being named here. They include Patricia Sekaquaptewa, to whom I owe incalculable amounts of gratitude for introducing me to her family and being an unwavering colleague, friend, and partner on the Hopi Appellate Court for so many years now. I am so lucky that you have let me ride your long coattails all this time, and I have no plans of getting off anytime soon. Thanks as well to Susan Sekaquaptewa, Selwyn Sekaquaptewa, Stewart Koyiyumptewa, Leigh Kuwanwisiwma, Lee Wayne Lomayestewa, Joel Nicholas, and Terry Morgart for allowing me the opportu-nity to work with you and learn from you and to call you my friends. I hope you'll see at least some of what you have taught me reflected in these pages. I also must thank the Kewanimptewa family—Leroy, Emory, Dianna, Bobby, Jared, Arlinda, Paulette, Sunny, Kenzer, and Andre—there are not enough words to express the warmth I feel for you and your mom, and the honor at having my family welcomed by yours. We treasure our connection to all of you and look forward to continuing to share it as often as we can in the days, months, and years to come.

The scholarly work undertaken for this book was supported by a number of sources. They include a 2011 grant from the National Science Foundation, Law and Social Sciences & Cultural Anthropology Programs (Award #106106, Co-PI with Susan Coutin, UCI), as well as a 2015 Humanities Without Walls, Global Midwest Mellon Fellowship (Co-PI with Frederick Hoxie, UIUC). Additional support was provided by a grant from the Chauncey and Marion D. McCormick Family Foundation and a John Simon Guggenheim Fellowship, both awarded in 2016. Most recently, I have been able to supplement and extend my understanding of the many nuances of the federal Tribal consultation regulatory scheme through a generous grant in 2019 from the Henry Luce Family Foundation, support that will also allow me to complete a handbook for practitioners working with Native Nations and US agencies on how to navigate the consultation process in a way that better meets the goals of Native Nation self-governance.

The first inklings of this book began to emerge for me in essays I have written that have appeared in other publications. In particular, portions of chapters 1 and 3 have appeared in articles published as the following essays, respectively: "Jurisdiction: Law's Grounding in Language," *Annual Review of Anthropology* 42 (2013): 209–226; and "Hopi Sovereignty as Epistemological Limit," *Wicazo Sa Review* 24, no. 1 (2009): 89–112. Likewise, an earlier version of chapter 4 appeared as an essay in "Jurisdictions of Significance: Narrating Time-Space in a Hopi-US Tribal Consultation," *American Ethnologist* 45, no. 2 (2018): 268–280. I am grateful to the editors and reviewers who worked with me on those publications.

Likewise, I have to thank Charles Myers, John Conley, the anonymous reviewers, and others at the University of Chicago Press who have helped to bring this volume to print with critically important feedback. I must also thank Lila Stormer and Michael Koplow, both editors extraordinaire, who each made my ideas sound so much better with their careful attention to various drafts of the manuscript. I thank Julie Shawvan for her expertly crafted Index.

I have shared drafts of the chapters at a variety of speaking engagements over the years and have benefited greatly from the interactions with the audiences at those events. The first time all of these essays came together in anything like the collection you see here was in the summer of 2016, when I was invited to deliver the Adolph E. Jensen Gedächtnis-Vorlesung/Memorial Lectures at the Frobenius Institute for Cultural Anthropological Research at Goethe University Frankfurt, in Germany. The six-part lecture series is funded by a generous gift of the Frobenius Society and the Hahn-Hissink'sche Frobenius Foundation under the direction of acting president Dr. Eberhard Mayer-Wegelin. I am particularly grateful to Prof. Karl-Heniz Kohl, former director of the Frobenius Institute, for extending the invitation to me, and to Dr. Markus Lindner, my friend and colleague now for many years, who has served as such a generous host every time I get the chance to visit him. I also send my warmest thanks to all the colleagues and students who engaged me in this work during my stay in Frankfurt.

I was equally fortunate to give versions of these lectures to colleagues in a 2017 lecture to the UCLA Center for Language, Interaction and Culture, as a conference keynote to the 2017 Ways of Knowing Annual Graduate Student Conference of the Program in Science, Religion and Culture at Harvard University, and as another conference keynote at the 2018 Annual Conference of the Enthographic Praxis in Industry Community/EPIC. Finally, in 2019 I was given three unique opportunities to explore these ideas in a lecture to the Department of Anthropology at the University of Michigan, as a participant in the 2019 Sawyer Seminar on Race and Indigeneity in the Americas at Brown University, and at a 2019 Workshop of the Critical Indigenous Studies Program at the University of British Columbia. My thanks to the many colleagues and students who helped me through the trickier parts of my thinking, and who were sure to not let me skate by with sloppy reasoning.

In these and other contexts, I would be remiss if I did not call out by name certain key interlocutors whose insights and perspectives are most certainly reflected in the pages of this book. They include many of my friends and colleagues at UC Irvine, most notably Keith Murphy, Bill Maurer, Susan Coutin, Tom Boellstorff, Eve Darian-Smith, and Lee Cabatingan. It includes colleagues and students from whom I learned so much during my seven years as faculty in anthropology at the University of Chicago—including Hussein Agrama, Sean Brotherton, Julie Chu, John Comaroff, Shannon Dawdy, Ray Fogelson, Darryl Li, Joe Masco, William Mazzarella, Stefan Palmie, Eugene Raikhel, François Richard, Marshall Sahlins, and Alice Yao. I must also make special note of the many wonderful conversations I had with my linguistic anthropology colleagues—Sue Gal, Costas Nakassis, and Michael Silverstein, whose thoughtful and often hilarious engagement with my work will stand as one of the highlights of my time in Chicago. Of course I must also thank my incredible graduate students, past and present, who always have always helped move my thinking forward—Karma Frierson, Rob Gelles, Grigory Gorbun, Eric Hirsch, Megan Morris, Stephen Schwartz, and Anna Weichselbraun. I must specifically thank Hannah McElgunn and Joey Weiss, whose deeply ethical and intellectually stimulating engagement with the peoples of the Hopi and Haida Nations, as well as so many others across the landscape of advocacy and scholarship with and for Indigenous peoples, continues to inspire me in my own work.

My time in Chicago also gave me the chance to forge important connections to the faculty at the American Bar Foundation, where I served as Research Faculty and now as Faculty Fellow, and at the Field Museum. I must thank the ABF's director, Ajay Mehrotra, as well as Bernadette Atuahene, Traci Burch, Steve Daniels, Tom Ginsberg, Terence Halliday, Carol Heimer, Beth Mertz, Bob Nelson, Laura Beth Nielsen, Jothie Raja, Chris Schmidt, and Susan Shapiro, for all the vibrant sociolegal conversations that inspired me to think about law, language, and society in the most fruitful of ways. At the Field Museum, I must especially thank Alaka Wali, curator of anthropology, who is an indefatigable advocate for opening up what a natural history museum can and should be and whose ability to reach out to contemporary Native artists, advocates, and communities proved to be the prime mover that has finally made the much-overdue renovation of the Field Museum's North American Anthropology Hall a very near reality. I also must thank Chris Pappan, Debra Yepa-Pappan, and Ji Hae Pappan, a trio of extraordinary artists and incredible colleagues, who have shown me, time and again, the ways in which cooperation without submission can underwrite deep and lasting friendships. It is their artistry that informs this book through and through, and it is why I am so very honored that they have allowed me to reproduce some of their artwork for its cover art.

Beyond colleagues at my various home institutions, there are many fellow travelers in the worlds of Indigenous studies, law, anthropology, and philosophy whose support and perspectives I have continuously drawn on and whose professionalism, brilliance, and integrity will always stand as the very ideal of what it means to me to be an engaged scholar. They include: Jane Anderson, Jason Bartulis, John Borrows, Kristen Carpenter, Rob Collins, Marianne Constable, Rosemary Coombe, Erin Debenport, Philip J. Deloria, Jennifer Denetdale, Alessandro Duranti, Ethan Elkind, Matthew Fletcher, Ilana Gershon, Carol Greenhouse, Christie Henry, Fred Henry, Greg Johnson, David Kamper, Paul Kroskrity, Jonathan Lear, Maggie McKinley Blackhawk, Barbra Meek, Bruce G. Miller, Paul Nadasdy, Larry Nesper, Jeanie O'Brien, Elinor Ochs, Raymond Orr, Annelise Riles, Angela Riley, Ty Tengan, Jason Throop, Mariana Valverde, and Peter Whiteley. A special note of thanks goes to my mentor, colleague, and aunt-in-law, Sally Engle Merry. If I can look back on my career and achieve at least a portion of the impact, productivity, generosity, and humility that Sally has displayed over hers, and instilled in her students and colleagues, I will count myself as having succeeded in accomplishing the best of what it means to be a public intellectual. Which is just a long way of offering my deepest thanks to Sally for modeling how to be both a genuinely good scholar and a genuinely good human being.

This manuscript would never have happened without the wellspring of support I receive from my incredible wife and companion—Lindsey Engle Richland. I cannot begin to describe the awe I have for you and your bottomless reserves of intellectual energy, patience, wit, and determination. I marvel at the fact that, as I was grapping for years with writing this one book, you were leading the way in raising our three incredible boys, while enduring two cross-country moves, three home purchases, multiple school changes, and, at the same time carried on your own wildly successful academic career. Since I don't really know how you do it all, the only thing I can say is, simply, thank you, for all of it. I am still gobsmacked at my luck in having you as my partner.

Thanks as well go to Barbara and Kent Richland, my mom and dad, and my sister Sara, for always knowing when to laugh at my jokes, and when to take me seriously, even if I don't. I am so glad you taught me how to care about others while staying vigilant against the self-importance that can come when one thinks their caring ought to count as an end in itself. It is a delicate balance, and I don't always get it right, but I thank you for always helping me steer myself back on course.

Finally, to my three sons, Silas, Graham, and Hale, I thank you guys for putting up with me during this period. I am sorry this dang book took so long to get done. But in reality, you three are the creations for which I am most proud. I am already so impressed by your kindness, poise, good humor, and intelligence. I can't wait to see what comes next.

References

Agamben, Giorgio. 1998. *Homo Sacer: Sovereign Power and Bare Life*. Translated by Daniel Heller-Roazen. Stanford, CA: Stanford University Press.

———. 2005. *State of Exception*. Translated by Kevin Attell. Chicago: University of Chicago Press.

American Indian Movement. 1972. "Trail of Broken Treaties 20-Point Position Paper," October 27. http://www.aimovement.org/archives/.

Aprill, Ellen P. 1994 "Tribal Bonds: Indian Sovereignty and the Tax Legislative Process." *Administrative Law Review* 46: 333–368.

Bakhtin, Mikhail M. 1981. *The Dialogic Imagination*. Translated by M. Holquist. Austin: University of Texas Press.

Barker, Joanne, ed. 2017. *Critically Sovereign: Indigenous Gender, Sexuality and Feminist Studies*. Durham, NC: Duke University Press.

Baron, Jane B. 1999. "Law, Literature and the Problems of Interdisciplinarity." *Yale Law Journal* 108 (5): 1059–1085.

Barton, Roy F. 1949. *The Kalingas, Their Institutions and Custom Law*. Chicago: University of Chicago Press.

Basso, Keith. 1996. *Wisdom Sits in Places: Landscape and Language among the Western Apache*. Albuquerque: University of New Mexico Press.

Benveniste, Émile. 1973. *Indo-European Language and Society*. London: Faber and Faber.

Berman, Paul Schiff. 2002. "The Globalization of Jurisdiction." *University of Pennsylvania Law Review* 151 (2): 311–545.

Blackhawk, Maggie. 2019. "Federal Indian Law as Paradigm within Public Law." *Harvard Law Review* 132 (7): 1787–1877.

Blommaert, Jan. 2007. "Sociolinguistic Scales." *Intercultural Pragmatics* 4 (1): 1–19.

Braccio, Audrey Bryant. 2009. "How the Anti-gaming Backlash Is Redefining Governmental Functions." *American Indian Law Review* 34 (1): 171–201.

Brandt, Elizabeth A. 1980. "On Secrecy and Control of Knowledge." In *Secrecy: A Cross-cultural Perspective*, edited by Stanton K. Tefft, 123–146. New York: Human Sciences Press.

———. 1994 "Egalitarianism, Hierarchy, and Centralization in the Pueblos." In *The Ancient Southwestern Community*, edited by Wirt H. Wills and Robert D. Leonard, 9–24. Albuquerque: University of New Mexico Press.

Brandt, Richard B. 1954. *Hopi Ethics: A Theoretical Analysis.* Chicago: University of Chicago Press.

Brooks, Peter. 2006. "Narrative Transactions: Does the Law Need a Narratology?" *Yale Journal of Law & the Humanities* 18 (1): 1–28.

Brooks, Peter, and Paul Gerwitz. 1996. *Law's Stories: Narrative and Rhetoric in the Law.* New Haven: Yale University Press.

Bruyneel, Kevin. 2007. *The Third Space of Sovereignty: The Postcolonial Politics of U.S.-Indigenous Relations.* Minneapolis: University of Minnesota Press.

Bureau of Applied Research in Anthropology. 1977. *Hopìikwa Lavàytutuveni: A Hopi Dictionary of Third Mesa Dialect.* Tucson: University of Arizona Press.

Bureau of Indian Affairs, Branch of Acknowledgment and Research. 1997. "Official Guidelines to the Federal Acknowledgment Regulations, 25 C.F.R 83." Washington, DC: Government Printing Office.

Byrd, Jodi. 2011. *The Transit of Empire: Indigenous Critiques of Colonialism.* Minneapolis: University of Minnesota Press.

Cabatingan, Lee. 2016. "Time and Transcendence: Narrating Higher Authority at the Caribbean Court of Justice." *Law & Society Review* 50 (3): 674–702.

Carpenter, Kristen A. 2005. "A Property Rights Approach to Sacred Site Cases: Asserting a Place for Indians as Nonowners." *UCLA Law Review* 52: 1061–1148.

———. 2008. "Interpretive Sovereignty: A Research Agenda." *American Indian Law Review* 33: 111–152.

Carpenter, Kristen A., and Angela R. Riley. 2019. "Privatizing the Reservation?" *Stanford Law Review* 71: 791–878.

Carr, E. Summerson, and Michael Lempert, eds. 2016. *Scale: Discourse and Dimensions of Social Life.* Los Angeles: University of California Press.

Cattelino, Jessica. 2008. *High Stakes: Florida Seminole Gaming and Sovereignty.* Durham, NC: Duke University Press.

Clark, Blue. 1994. *Lone Wolf v. Hitchcock: Treaty Rights & Indian Law at the End of the Nineteenth Century.* Lincoln: University of Nebraska Press.

Clark, Jeffery J. 2001. *Tracking Prehistoric Migrations: Pueblo Settlers among the Tonto Basin Hohokam.* Tucson: University of Arizona Press.

Clarkson, Gavin. 2007. "Tribal Bonds: Statutory Shackles and Regulatory Restraints on Tribal Economic Development." *North Carolina Law Review* 85: 1009–1085.

Clemmer, Richard O. 1978. *Continuities of Hopi Culture Change.* Ramona, CA: Acoma Books.

———.1995. *Roads in the Sky: The Hopi Indians in a Century of Change.* Denver: Westview Press.

Clifford, James. 2013. *Returns: Becoming Indigenous in the 21st Century.* Cambridge, MA: Harvard University Press.

Clifton, James A. 1989. *Being and Becoming Indian: Biographical Studies of North American Frontiers.* Chicago: Dorsey Press.

Cohen, Felix S. 1958. *Handbook of Federal Indian Law.* Albuquerque: University of New Mexico Press.

Coke, Lord Edward. [1644] 2002. *The Fourth Part of the Institutes of the Laws of England: Concerning the Jurisdiction of Courts.* Clark, NJ: Lawbook Exchange Ltd.

Colwell-Chanthaphonh, Chip, and T. J. Ferguson. 2008. *Collaboration in Archaeological Practice: Engaging Descendant Communities.* New York: Alta Mira Press.

Conley, John M., and William M. O'Barr. 2004. "A Classic in Spite of Itself: The Cheyenne Way and the Case Method in Legal Anthropology." *Law and Social Inquiry* 29 (1): 179–217.

Conley, John M., William M. O'Barr, and Robin Conley Riner. 2019. *Just Words: Law, Language and Power*. 3rd ed. Chicago: University of Chicago Press.

Conley, Robin. 2016. *Confronting the Death Penalty: How Language Influences Jurors in Capital Cases*. New York: Oxford University Press.

Constable, Marianne. 2010. "Speaking the Language of Law: A Juris-dictional Primer." *English Language Notes* 48 (2): 9–14.

———. 2014. "Law as Language." *Critical Analysis of Law and the New Interdisciplinarity* 1 (1): 63–74.

Cormack, Bradin. 2007. *A Power to Do Justice: Jurisdiction, English Literature, and the Rise of Common Law*. Chicago: University of Chicago Press.

Cornell, Stephen J., and Joseph P. Kalt. 1992. *What Can Tribes Do? Strategies and Institutions in American Indian Economic Development*. Los Angeles: University of California Los Angeles, American Indian Studies Center.

Coulthard, Glen S. 2014. *Red Skins, White Masks: Rejecting the Colonial Politics of Recognition*. Minneapolis: University of Minnesota Press.

Cover, Robert M. 1983. "Foreword: Nomos and Narrative. The Supreme Court, 1982 Term." *Harvard Law Review* 97 (1): 4–76.

———. 1993. *Narrative, Violence and the Law. The Essays of Robert Cover*. Edited by Martha Minow, Michael Ryan, and Austin Sarat. Ann Arbor: University of Michigan Press.

Cramer, Renée A. 2005. *Cash, Color, and Colonialism: The Politics of Tribal Acknowledgement*. Norman: University of Oklahoma Press.

Debenport, Erin. 2015. *Fixing the Books: Secrecy Literacy and Perfectibility in Indigenous New Mexico*. Santa Fe: School of Advanced Research Press.

Deer, Sarah. 2015. *The Beginning and End of Rape: Confronting Sexual Violence in Native America*. Minneapolis: University of Minnesota Press.

Deloria, Philip J. 1998. *Playing Indian*. New Haven, CT: Yale University Press.

———. 2004. *Indians in Unexpected Places*. Lawrence: University of Kansas Press.

Deloria, Vine, Jr. 1969. *Custer Died for Your Sins: An Indian Manifesto*. Norman: University of Oklahoma Press.

———. 1974. *Behind the Trail of Broken Treaties. An Indian Declaration of Independence*. Norman: University of Oklahoma Press.

Deloria, Vina, Jr., and Clifford M. Lytle 1983. *American Indians, American Justice*. Austin: University of Texas Press.

DeMallie, Raymond J. 1980. "Touching the Pen: Plains Indian Treaty Councils in Ethnohistorical Perspective." In *Ethnicity on the Great Plains*, edited by Frederick C. Luebke, 38–51. Lincoln: University of Nebraska Press.

Dombrowski, Kirk. 2001. *Against Culture: Development, Politics and Religion in Indian Alaska*. Lincoln: University of Nebraska Press.

Dorsett, Shaunnagh, and Shaun McVeigh. 2012. *Jurisdiction*. London: Routledge.

Douzinas, Costas. 2007. "The Metaphysics of Jurisdiction." In *The Jurisprudence of Jurisdiction*, edited by Shaun McVeigh, 19–31. London: Routledge-Cavendish.

Duranti, Alessandro. 1997. *Linguistic Anthropology*. Cambridge: Cambridge University Press.

Eggan, Frederick R. 1950. *Social Organization of the Western Pueblos*. Chicago: University of Chicago Press.

Eitner, Michael. 2014. "Meaningful Consultation with Tribal Governments: A Uniform Standard to Guarantee that Federal Agencies Properly Consider Their Concerns." *University of Colorado Law Review* 85 (3): 867–900.

Eisenberg, Avigail, Jeremy Webber, Glen Coulthard, and Andrée Boisselle, eds. 2015. *Recognition versus Self-Determination: Dilemmas of Emancipatory Politics*. Vancouver: University of British Columbia Press.

Estes, Nick. 2019. *Our History Is the Future: Standing Rock versus the Dakota Access Pipeline, and the Long Tradition of Indigenous Resistance*. New York: Verso.

Estes, Nick, and Jaskiran Dhillon. 2019. *Standing with Standing Rock: Voices from the #NoDAPL Movement*. Minneapolis: University of Minnesota Press.

Fanon, Frantz. 1967. *Black Skin, White Masks*. Translated by Charles Lam Markmann. New York: Grove Press.

Ferguson, Thomas J., Kurt Dongoske, and Leigh Kuwanwisiwma. 2001. "Hopi Perspectives on Southwestern Mortuary Studies." In *Ancient Burial Practices in the American Southwest: Archaeology, Physical Anthropology, and Native American Perspectives*, edited by Douglas R. Mitchell and Judy L. Brunson-Hadley. Albuquerque: University of New Mexico Press, pp. 9–26.

Ferguson, Thomas J., Leigh Jenkins, and Kurt Dongoske. 1996. "Managing Hopi Sacred Sites to Protect Religious Freedom." *Cultural Survival Quarterly* 19 (4): 53–59.

Ferguson, Thomas J., Stewart Koyiyumptewa, and Maren P. Hopkins. 2015. "Co-creation of Knowledge by the Hopi Tribe and Archaeologists." *Advances in Archaeological Practices* 3 (3): 249–262.

Ferrero, Pat. 1984. *Hopi: Songs of the Fourth World*. Documentary, 58 min. New Day Films.

Fewkes, Jesse Walter. (1900). 1987. *The Snake Ceremonials at Walpi*. New York: AMS Press.

Fletcher, Matthew L. M. 2016. *Hornbook on Federal Indian Law*. New York: West Academic Publishing.

Fox, Katsitsionni. 2013. "Two Row Wampum Renewal Campaign Completes Journey to United Nations." *Indian Time*, August 22, 2013. http://www.indiantime.net/story/2013/08/22/news/two-row-wampum-renewal-campaign-completes-journey-to-united-nations/11091.html.

Fixico, Donald L. 2008. *Treaties with American Indians: An Encyclopedia of Rights, Conflicts, and Sovereignty*. New York: ABC-CLIO.

Ford, Richard T. 1999. "Law's Territory (A History of Jurisdiction)." *Michigan Law Review* 97 (4): 843–930.

Geertz, Armin. 1994. *The Invention of Prophecy: Continuity and Meaning in Hopi Indian Religion*. Berkeley: University of California Press.

Getches, David H., Charles E. Wilkinson, Robert A. Williams Jr., Matthew L. M. Fletcher, and Kristen A. Carpenter. 2016. *Cases and Materials on Federal Indian Law*. New York: West Publishing.

Goldberg, Carole E., Rebecca Tsosie, Robert N. Clinton, and Angela R. Riley. 2015. *American Indian Law: Native Nations and the Federal System*. New York: LexisNexis.

Haas, Angela M. 2007. "Wampum as Hypertext: An American Indian Intellectual Tradition of Multimedia Theory and Practice." *Studies in American Indian Literatures* 19 (4): 77–100.

Hagan, William T. 2003. *Taking Indian Lands: The Cherokee (Jerome) Commission, 1889–1893*. Norman: University of Oklahoma Press.

Hale, Sir Matthew. 1971. *The History of the Common Law in England*. Edited by Charles M. Gray. Chicago: University of Chicago Press.

Hanson, Allan F. 1997. "Empirical Anthropology, Postmodernism, and the Invention of Tradition." In *Present Is Past: Some Uses of Tradition in Native Societies*, edited by Marie Mauze, 195–214. New York: University Press of America.

Haskew, Derek C. 2000. "Federal Consultation with Indian Tribes: The Foundation of Enlightened Policy Decisions, or Another Badge of Shame." *American Indian Law Review* 24 (1): 21–74.

Hedquist, Saul L., and Stewart B. Koyiyumptewa. 2013. "Hopi Traditional Cultural Properties Investigation for the Proposed Payson Ranger District Administration Site Sale." Submitted by the Hopi Cultural Preservation Office and the Hopi Tribe to the Tonto National Forest, US Department of Agriculture, Phoenix, AZ, August 2.

Hedquist, Saul L., Stewart B. Koyiyumptewa, Peter Whiteley, Leigh J. Kuwanwisiwma, Kenneth C. Hill, and T. J. Ferguson. 2014. "Recording Toponyms to Document the Endangered Hopi Language." *American Anthropologist* 116 (2): 324–331.

Heritage, John. 2015. "*Well*-prefaced Turns in English Conversation: A Conversation Analytic Perspective." *Journal of Pragmatics* 88: 804.

Hopkins, Maren P., Stewart B. Koyiyumptewa, Saul L. Hedquist, T. J. Ferguson, and Chip Colwell. 2017. "Hopisinmuy Wu'ya'mat Hisat Yang Tupqa'va Yeesiwngu (Hopi Ancestors Lived in These Canyons)." In *Legacies of Space and Intangible Heritage: Archaeology*, edited by Fernando Armstrong-Fumero and Julio Holi Gutierrez, 33–52. Boulder: University of Colorado Press.

Indian Health Services. 2019. *Indian Health Disparities*. Washington, DC: Indian Health Services.

Ishii, Lomayumtewa C. 2001. "Voices from Our Ancestors: Hopi Resistance to Scientific Historicide." Ph.D. diss., Northern Arizona University.

Hoxie, Frederick E. 1984. *A Final Promise: The Campaign to Assimilate the Indians, 1880–1920.* Lincoln: University of Nebraska Press.

Jenkins, Leigh, T. J. Ferguson, and Kurt Dongoske. 1994. "A Reexamination of the Concept of *Hopitutsqwa.*" Paper presented at the Annual Meeting of the American Society for Ethnohistory, Tempe, Arizona, November 11 (on file with the Hopi Cultural Preservation Office).

Jorgensen, Miriam, ed. 2007. *Rebuilding Native Nations: Strategies for Governance and Development.* Tucson: University of Arizona Press.

Kahn, Jeffrey S. 2017. "Geographies of Discretion and the Jurisdictional Imagination." *PoLAR: Political and Legal Anthropology Review* 40: 5–27.

———. 2019. *Islands of Sovereignty: Haitian Migration and the Borders of Empire.* Chicago: University of Chicago Press.

King, C. Richard, and Charles Fruehling Springwood. 2001. *Team Spirits: The Native American Mascots Controversy.* Lincoln: University of Nebraska Press.

Koyiyumptewa, Stewart, and Chip Colwell-Chanthaphonh. 2011. "The Past Is Now: Hopi Connections to Ancient Times and Places." In *Movement, Connectivity, and Landscape Change in the Ancient Southwest (Proceedings of the Southwest Symposium)*, edited by Margaret C. Nelson and Colleen Strawhacker, 443–455. Boulder: University Press of Colorado.

Kroskrity, Paul V. 1993. *Language, History and Identity: Ethnolinguistic Studies of the Arizona Tewa.* Tucson: University of Arizona Press.

Kuwanwisiwma, Leigh J. 2002. "Hopi Navtiat. Hopi Knowledge of History: Hopi Presence on Black Mesa." In *Prehistoric Culture Change on the Colorado Plateau: Ten Thousand Years on Black Mesa*, edited by Shirley Powell and Francis E. Smiley, 161–163. Tucson: University of Arizona Press.

———. 2008. "Collaboration Means Equality, Respect, Reciprocity: A Conversation about Archaeology and the Hopi Tribe." In *Collaboration in Archaeological Practice: Engaging Descendant Communities*, edited by Chip Colwell-Chanthaphonh and Thomas J. Ferguson, 151–167. Walnut Creek, CA: Alta Mira Press.

Kuwanwisiwma, Leigh, T. J. Ferguson, and Chip Colwell, eds. 2018. *Footprints of Hopi History: Hopihiniwtiput Kukveni'at.* Tucson: University of Arizona Press.

La Farge, Oliver. 1937. "Notes for Hopi Administrators, February 1937." Typescript. Library of Department of the Interior, Washington D.C., Catalogue number E99.H7L2.

Latour, Bruno. 2005. *Reassembling the Social: An Introduction to Actor-Network-Theory*. London: Oxford University Press.

Le Duc, Thomas. 1957. "The Work of the Indian Claims Commission under the Act of 1946." *Pacific Historical Review* 26 (1): 1–16.

Lempert, Michael. 2012. "Interaction Rescaled: How Monastic Debate Became a Diasporic Pedagogy." *Anthropology & Education Quarterly* 43 (2): 138–156.

Levy, Jerrold. 1992. *Orayvi Revisited: Social Stratification in an "Egalitarian" Society*. Santa Fe: School of American Research Press.

Llewellyn, Karl N. 1960. *The Common Law Tradition: Deciding Appeals*. Boston: Little, Brown & Co.

Llewellyn, Karl N., and E. Adamson Hoebel. 1941. *The Cheyenne Way: Conflict and Case Law in Primitive Jurisprudence*. Norman: University of Oklahoma Press.

Lyons, Scott Richard. 2010. *X-Marks: Native Signatures of Assent*. Minneapolis: University of Minnesota Press.

Lurie, Nancy Oestreich. 1978. "The Indian Claims Commission." *Annals of the American Academy of Political and Social Science*. 436 (1): 97–110.

Malinowski, Bronislaw. [1926] 1989. *Crime and Custom in Savage Society*. Totowa, NJ: Rowman & Littlefield.

Malotki, Ekkehart, and Michael Lomatuway'ma. 1987. *Stories of Maasaw, A Hopi God*. Lincoln: University of Nebraska Press.

Maurer, Bill. 2013. "Jurisdictions in Dialect: Sovereignty Games in the British Virgin Islands." In *European Integration and Postcolonial Sovereignty Games: The EU Overseas Countries and Territories*, edited by Rebecca Adler-Nissen and Ulrik Pram Gad, 120–144. London: Routledge.

McConnell, Alison. 2006. "IRS: 'Essential Governmental Function' Needed for Conduit Debt." *Bond Buyer*, January 23, 5.

McVeigh, Shaun. 2007. *Jurisprudence of Jurisdiction*. London: Routledge-Cavendish.

Melinkoff, David. 1967. "The Language of the Uniform Commercial Code." *Yale Law Journal* 77 (2): 185–227.

Mentschikoff, Soia. 1982. "Reflections of a Drafter: Soia Mentschikoff." *Ohio State Law Journal* 43 (3): 534–544.

Meriam, Lewis. 1928. *The Problem of Indian Administration: Report of a Survey made at the Request of Honorable Hubert Work, Secretary of the Interior, and Submitted to Him, February 21, 1928*. Baltimore: The Johns Hopkins Press.

Mertz, Elizabeth. 1994. "Legal Language: Pragmatics, Poetics, and Social Power." *Annual Reviews of Anthropology* 23: 435–55.

———. 2007. *The Language of Law School: Learning to "Think like a Lawyer."* London: Oxford University Press.

Miller, Bruce G. 2003. *Invisible Indigenes: The Politics of Nonrecognition*. Lincoln: University of Nebraska Press.

Miller, Cary. 2002. "Gifts as Treaties: The Political Use of Received Gifts in Anishinaabeg Communities." *American Indian Quarterly* 26 (2): 221–245.

Miller, Mark E. 2004. *Forgotten Tribes: Unrecognized Indians and the Federal Acknowledgement Process*. Lincoln: University of Nebraska Press.

Miller, Robert J. 2015. "Consultation or Consent: The United States' Duty to Confer with American Indian Governments." *North Dakota Law Review* 91: 37–94.

National Association of Bond Lawyers. 2017. *Federal Taxation of Municipal Bonds.* Deskbook, 3rd ed. New York: LexisNexis.

Moore, Sally F. 1986. *Social Facts and Fabrications: "Customary" Law on Kilimanjaro, 1880–1980.* Cambridge: Cambridge University Press.

National Congress on the American Indian. 2012. *Consultation With Tribal Nations: An Update on Implementation of Executive Order 13175.* www.ncai.org/resources/consultation-support.

———. 2019. "Indian Country Demographics." National Congress of American Indians. http://www.ncai.org/about-tribes/demographics.

Nagata, Shuichi. 1970. *Modern Transformations of Moenkopi Pueblo.* Urbana: University of Illinois Press.

Ochs, Elinor, and Lisa Capps. 2001. *Living Narrative.* Cambridge, MA: Harvard University Press.

Ochs, Elinor, and Bambi B. Schieffelin. 1984. "Language Acquisition and Socialization: Three Developmental Stories and Their Implications." In *Culture Theory: Essays on Mind, Self and Emotion,* edited by Richard A. Shweder and Robert A. LeVine, 276–320. New York: Cambridge University Press.

Orr, Raymond I. 2017. *Reservation Politics: Historical Trauma, Economic Development, and Intratribal Conflict.* Norman: University of Oklahoma Press.

Ortiz, Alfonso. 1969. *The Tewa World: Space, Time, Being and Becoming in a Pueblo Society.* Chicago: University of Chicago Press.

———. 1972. "Ritual Drama and the Pueblo World View." In *New Perspectives on the Pueblos,* edited by Alfonso Ortiz, 135–162. Albuquerque: University of New Mexico Press.

Otis, Delos Sacket. 1973. *The Dawes Act and the Allotment of Indian Lands.* Norman: University of Oklahoma Press.

Owungule, Stella. 2006. *We the People: American Indians and Alaska Natives in the United States.* Census 2000 Special Report 2B. Washington, DC: US Census Bureau.

Papke, David Ray. 1999. "How the Cheyenne Indians Wrote Article 2 of the Uniform Commercial Code." *Buffalo Law Review* 47 (3): 1457–1485.

Parker, Patricia L., and Thomas F. King. 1990. "Guidelines for Evaluating and Documenting Traditional Cultural Properties." *National Register Bulletin* 38: 1–22.

Perry, Steven W. 2004. *American Indians and Crime. A Bureau of Justice Statistical Profile 199002.* Washington, DC: United States Department of Justice, Office of Justice Programs. ·

Pommersheim, Frank M. 2009. *Broken Landscapes: Indians, Indian Tribes and the Constitution.* Oxford: Oxford University Press.

Povinelli, Elizabeth A. 2002. *The Cunning of Recognition: Indigenous Alterities and the Making of Australian Multiculturalism.* Durham, NC: Duke University Press.

———. 2011. *Economies of Abandonment: Social Belonging and Endurance in Late Liberalism.* Durham, NC: Duke University Press.

Pratt, Scott L. 2002. *Native Pragmatism: Rethinking the Roots of American Philosophy.* Bloomington: Indiana University Press.

Proctor, Bernadette D., et al. 2016. *Income and Poverty in the United States, 2015: Current Population Reports.* Washington, DC: United States Census Bureau.

Prucha, Francis Paul. 1984. *The Great Father: The United States Government and the American Indians.* Lincoln: University of Nebraska Press.

———. 1997. *American Indian Treaties: The History of a Political Anomaly*. Los Angeles: University of California Press.

———, editor. 2000. *Documents of United States Indian Policy*. 3rd ed. Lincoln: University of Nebraska Press.

Pryde, Joan. 1987a. "Two Bond Issues Sold by Tribes May Face Review by Congress." *Bond Buyer*, June 9, p. 1.

———. 1987b. "Legislator Urges Repeal of Portion of Rules on Bond Sales by Indians." *Bond Buyer*, September 14, p. 1.

Quint, Michael. 1987. "Questionable Municipal Bonds." *New York Times Business Day*, July 27, p. D1.

Richland, Justin B. 2005. "What Are You Going to Do with the Village's Knowledge? Talking Tradition, Talking Law in Hopi Tribal Court." *Law and Society Review* 39: 235–271.

———. 2010. "'They Did It Like a Song': Ethics, Aesthetics, and Tradition in Hopi Legal Discourse." In *Ordinary Ethics: Anthropology, Language, and Action*, edited by Michael Lambek, 249–270. New York: Fordham University Press.

———. 2013. "Jurisdiction: Grounding Law in Language." *Annual Review of Anthropology* 42: 209–226.

Rifkin, Mark. 2010. *The Erotics of Sovereignty: Queer Native Writing in the Era of Self-Determination*. Minneapolis: University of Minnesota Press.

———. 2017. *Beyond Settler Time. Temporal Sovereignty and Indigenous Self-Determination*. Durham, NC: Duke University Press.

Riles, Annelise. 2008. "Introduction: In Response." In *Documents: Artifacts of Modern Knowledge*, edited by Annelise Riles, 1–38. Ann Arbor: University of Michigan Press.

Riley, Angela R. 2007a. "(Tribal) Sovereignty and Illiberalism." *California Law Review* 95: 799–849.

———. 2007b. "Good (Native) Governance." *Columbia Law Review* 107 (5): 1049–1125.

———. 2017. "Native Nations and the Constitution: An Inquiry into 'Extra-constitutionality.'" *Harvard Law Review Forum* 130 (6): 173–199.

Routel, Colette, and Jeffery Holth. 2013. "Toward Genuine Tribal Consultation in the 21st Century." *University of Michigan Journal of Law Reform* 46 (2): 417–475.

Rosser, Ezra. 2006. "Ambiguity and the Academic: The Dangerous Attraction of Pan-Indian Legal Analysis. Replying to Philip P. Frickey, Native American Exceptionalism in Federal Public Law, 118 Harvard L. Rev. 431 (2005)." *Harvard Law Review Forum* 119: 141–147.

Schifrin, Matthew. 1987. "Smoke Signals." *Forbes*, June 15, pp. 42–53.

Schmitt, Carl. 2006. *Political Theology: Four Chapters on the Concept of Sovereignty*. Chicago: University of Chicago Press.

Scalia, Antonin. 1997. *A Matter of Interpretation: Federal Courts and the Law*. Princeton, NJ: Princeton University Press.

Sekaquaptewa, Emory. 1972. "Preserving the Good Things of Hopi Life." In *Plural Society in the Southwest*, edited by Edward Spicer and Raymond Thompson, 239–260. Albuquerque: University of New Mexico Press.

Shaul, David L. 2002. *Hopi Traditional Literature*. Albuquerque: University of New Mexico Press.

Silverstein, Michael. 1998. "Utility of Ideology: A Commentary." In *Language Ideologies: Practice and Theory*, edited by Bambi B. Schieffelin, Kathryn A. Woodard, and Paul V. Kroskrity, 123–145. Oxford: Oxford University Press.

Silverstein, Michael, and Greg Urban. 1997. *Natural Histories of Discourse*. Chicago: University of Chicago Press.

Simpson, Audra. 2007. "Ethnographic Refusal: Indigeneity, 'Voice' and Colonial Citizenship." *Junctures: The Journal for Thematic Dialogue* 9: 67–80.

———. 2008. "Subjects of Sovereignty: Indigeneity, the Revenue Rule, and Juridics of Failed Consent." *Law and Contemporary Problems* 71 (3): 127–215.

———. 2014. *Mohawk Interruptus: Political Life Across the Borders of Settler States.* Durham, NC: Duke University Press.

Simpson, Leanne Betasamosake. 2017. *As We Have Always Done: Indigenous Freedom through Radical Resistance.* Minneapolis: University of Minnesota Press.

Singer, Joseph William. 2002. "*Lone Wolf*, Or How to Take Property by Calling It a 'Mere Change in the Form of Investment.'" *Tulsa Law Review* 38: 37–48.

Stone, Peter H. 2006. *Heist: Superlobbyist Jack Abramoff, His Republican Allies, and the Buying of Washington.* New York: Farrar, Straus and Giroux.

Taylor, Charles. 1994. *Multiculturalism: Examining the Politics of Recognition.* Princeton, NJ: Princeton University Press.

Tiersma, Peter. 2010. *Parchment, Paper, Pixels: Law and the Technologies of Communication.* Chicago: University of Chicago Press.

Titiev, Mischa. 1944. *Old Oraibi: A Study of the Hopi Indians of Third Mesa.* Papers of the Peabody Museum of American Archaeology and Ethnology, Harvard University, 22 (1).

Tsing, Anna L. 2012. "Nonscalability: The Living World Is Not Amenable to Precision-Nested Scales." *Common Knowledge* 18 (3): 505–524.

Twining, William J. 1973. *Karl Llewellyn and the Realist Movement.* Cambridge: Cambridge University Press.

US Forest Service Southwest Region Tonto National Forest. 2013. "Findings of No Significant Impact (FONSI), Decision Notice and Non-significant Plan Amendment." Payson Ranger District Administrative Site Sale and Facilities (August 09, 2013).

Valverde, Mariana. 2015. *Chronotopes of Law: Jurisdiction, Scale and Governance.* Oxford, UK: Routledge.

Veracini, Lorenzo. 2010. *Settler Colonialism: A Theoretical Overview.* London: Palgrave MacMillan.

———. 2015. *The Settler Colonial Present.* London: Palgrave MacMillan.

Vizenor, Gerald. 1999. *Manifest Manners: Narratives on Postindian Survivance.* Lincoln: University of Nebraska Press.

———. 2008. *Survivance: Narratives of Native Presence.* Lincoln: University of Nebraska Press.

———. 2019. *Native Provenance: The Betrayal of Cultural Creativity.* Lincoln: University of Nebraska Press.

Voth, Heinrich R. [1903] 1968. "The Oraibi Summer Snake Ceremony: The Stanley McCormick Hopi Expedition." *Chicago Field Columbian Museum, Anthropological Series* 3 (4): 267–358.

Weiss, Joseph. 2018. *Shaping the Future on Haida Gwaii: Life beyond Settler Colonialism.* Vancouver: University of British Columbia Press.

Whiteley, Peter. 1985. "Unpacking Hopi 'Clans': Another Vintage Model Out of Africa?" *Journal of Anthropological Research* 41: 359–374.

———. 1986. "Unpacking Hopi 'Clans' II: Further Questions about Hopi Descent Groups." *Journal of Anthropological Research* 42: 69–79.

———. 1988. *Deliberate Acts: Changing Hopi Culture through the Oraibi Split.* Tucson: University of Arizona Press.

———. 1998. *Rethinking Hopi Ethnography.* Washington, DC: Smithsonian Institution Press.

Whorf, Benjamin L. 1956. *Language, Thought, Reality: Selected Writings.* Edited by J. B. Carroll. Cambridge, MA: MIT Press.

Wilkins, David E., and K. Tsianina Lomawaima. 2002. *Uneven Ground: American Indian Sovereignty and Federal Law.* Norman: University of Oklahoma Press.

Wilkins, David E., and Heidi K. Stark. 2018. *American Indian Politics and the American Political System.* 4th ed. New York: Rowman & Littlefield Press.

Wilkinson, Charles F. 1987. *American Indians, Time and the Law.* New Haven, CT: Yale University Press.

———. 1999. *Fire on the Plateau: Conflict and Endurance in the American Southwest.* Washington, DC: Island Press.

———. 2005. *Blood Struggle: The Rise of Modern Indian Nations.* New York: W. W. Norton.

Wilkinson, Charles F., and John M. Volkman. 1975. "Judicial Review of Indian Treaty Abrogation: 'As Long as Water Flows, or Grass Grows Upon the Earth'—How Long a Time Is That?" *California Law Review* 63: 601–661.

Williams, Robert A. 1997. *Linking Arms Together: American Indian Treaty Visions of Law and Peace, 1600–1800.* London: Oxford University Press.

Wilshire, Bruce. 2000. *The Primal Roots of American Philosophy: Pragmatism, Phenomenology, and Native American Thought.* University Park: Penn State University Press.

Wolfe, Patrick. 1999. *Settler Colonialism and the Transformation of Anthropology.* London: Cassell Press.

———. 2006. "Settler Colonialism and the Elimination of the Native." *Journal of Genocide Research* 8 (4): 387–409.

Zimmerman, Dennis. 1991. *The Private Use of Tax-Exempt Bonds: Controlling Public Subsidy of Private Security.* Washington, DC: Urban Institute Press.

Legislation, Executive Orders, Federal Regulations

Advisory Committee on Tax Exempt and Governmental Entities: Report of Recommendations (Public Meeting June 9, 2004). IRS pub. no. 4344 (May 2004).

American Indian Policy Review Commission. May 1977. *Final Report.* Vols. 1 and 2. Washington, DC: US Government Printing Office.

Dawes Severalty Act of 1887 (General Allotment Act) Pub. L. No. 49-119, 25 U.S.C. ch. 9 §331 et seq. (February 23, 1887).

Executive Order 13,175, Consultation and Coordination with Tribal Governments. 65 Fed. Reg. 67,249, November 6, 2000. https://www.fws.gov/nativeamerican/pdf/executive-order-13175.pdf.

Executive Order of President Chester A. Arthur, December 16, 1882; Moqui (or Hopi) Reserve. In *Executive Orders Relating to Indian Reserves from May 14, 1855 to July 1, 1902.* Compiled by the Indian Office under Authority of Act of Congress Approved May 17, 1882, Washington, DC: Government Printing Office, 1902, g. 9.

Federal Acknowledgment of American Indian Tribes. 25 C.F.R. 83, 80 Fed. Reg. 37861 (July 1, 2015).

Hopi Village of Shungopavi v. United States of America. Docket No. 196, 210, Indian Claims Commission Records, RG 33494-23-054, National Archives, Washington, DC.

Hopi Tribal Resolution, H-70-94, May 23, 1994. On file with the Hopi Tribe.

Improving Tribal Consultation and Tribal Involvement in Federal Infrastructure Decisions. US Department of the Interior, US Department of the Army, and US Department of Justice. January 2017. https://www.achp.gov/sites/default/files/reports/2018-06/ImprovingTribalConsul tationandTribalInvolvementinFederalInfrastructureDecisionsJanuary2017.pdf.

Indian Appropriations Act of 1871. 41st Congress, Sess. III, Ch. 119–120, §1, 16 Stat. 566, 25 U.S.C. ch. 3 § 71 (March 3, 1871).

Indian Claims Commission Act of 1946. 60 Stat. 1050, 25 U.S.C. § 70(a) et seq.

Indian Claims Commission. 1979. *Final Report of the United States Indian Claims Commission, August 13, 1946 to September 30, 1978*. Washington, DC: Government Printing Office, 1979.

Indian Entities Recognized by and Eligible to Receive Services from the Bureau of Indian Affairs 84 Fed. Reg. 1200 (January 30, 2020).

Indian Entities Recognized by and Eligible to Receive Services from the United States Bureau of Indian Affairs. 83 Fed. Reg. 141, 34863 (July 23, 2018).

Indian Gaming Regulatory Act of 1988. 25 U.S.C. ch. 29 § 2701 et seq. 102 Stat. 2467 (October 17, 1988).

Indian Self Determination and Education Assistance Act of 1975. Pub. L. No. 93-638, 25 U.S.C. ch. 14, subch. II § 5301 et seq. (January 4, 1975).

Indian Tribal Governmental Tax Status Act of 1982. Title II of Pub. L. No. 97-473, 966 Stat. 2605, 2607, as amended by Pub. L. No. 98-21, 97 Stat. 65, 87 (1983-1 CB 510, 511), codified at 26 U.S.C. § 7871.

Joint Resolution to Provide for the Establishment of the American Indian Policy Review Commission. Pub. L. No. 93-580, 25 U.S.C. § 174 (1975).

Letter from the Secretary of the Interior, in response to Resolution of the Senate of January 13, 1899, Relative to Condition and Character of the Kiowa, Comanche, and Apache Indian Reservation, and the Assent of the Indians to the Agreement for the Allotment of Lands and the Ceding of Unallotted Lands, S. Doc. No. 77, at 2, 8, 55th Cong. (3d. Sess. 1899) (referring to copy of a report of the proceedings of the councils held by the commission, which made the agreement of 1892).

National Environmental Protection Act, Council on Environmental Regulations. 40 Code of Federal Regulations, §1500–1518.

National Historic Preservation Act of 1966 (As Amended 1992). Pub. L. No. 89-665, 54 U.S.C. § 300101 et seq. (June 18, 1934).

National Register of Historic Places. 36 Code of Federal Regulations, § 60.

Native American Graves Protection and Repatriation Act. Pub. L. No. 101-601, 25 U.S.C. 3001 et seq., 104 Stat. 3048 (1990).

Petition of the Hopi Leaders of the Village of Shungopavi. Indian Claims Commission Docket No. 210, Aug. 8, 1951, 1.

Presidential Memorandum for the Heads of Executive Departments and Agencies on Tribal Consultation. 74 Fed. Reg. 57,881 (November 5, 2009).

Presidential Memorandum on Government-to-Government Relations with Native American Tribal Governments. 59 Fed. Reg. 22951-2 (April 29, 1994).

Procedures for Establishing that an American Indian Group Exists as an Indian Tribe. 25 C.F.R. 83, 59 Fed. Reg. 9293 (February 25, 1994).

Pub. L. No. 83-280, 18 U.S.C. § 1162, 28 U. S. C. § 1360, and 25 U.S.C. §§ 1321–1326.

Tribal Consultation: Additional Federal Actions Needed for Infrastructure Projects. March 2019 (GAO-19-22). Government Accountability Office. https://www.gao.gov/assets/700/697694. pdf.

2017 IAJ Report on Tribal Consultation. See *Improving Tribal Consultation*.

2019 GAO Report. See *Tribal Consultation.*

Wheeler-Howard Act of 1934 (Indian Reorganization Act) Pub. L. No. 73-383, 25 U.S.C. ch. 14, subch. V. § 461 et seq.

Court Cases

Cherokee Nation v. Georgia, 30 U.S. (5 Pet.) 1, (1831).

Jones v. Meehan, 175 U.S. 1, 11 (1899).

Lone Wolf v. Hitchcock, 187 U.S. 503 (1903).

Marbury v. Madison, 5 U.S. (1 Cranch) 137 (1803).

Merrion v. Jicarilla Apache Tribe, 455 U.S. 130 (1982).

Minnesota v. Milles Lacs Band of Chippewa Indians, 562 U.S. 172 (1999).

Tax Analyst v. Internal Revenue Service, 117 F.3d 607 (D.C. Cir. 1997).

Washington v. Confederated Tribes of Colville Indians, 477 U.S. 130 (1980).

Worcester v. Georgia, 31 U.S. (6 Pet) 515 (1832).

Index

A page number in italics refers to an illustration.

Abramoff, Jack, 165n6
acknowledgment process: enduring failures of, 151–54; Euro-American norms of law and science in, 140, 155; evidentiary criteria for, 141, 150–51; history and operation of, 148–52; Indigenous insistence during, 147–48, 161; number of Tribal Nations acknowledged, 23, 36n4, 41; presumption of recognition in, 151, 153, 154; reluctance to give concrete evidentiary recommendations in, 142–43, 144, 148; unrecognizability in, 31–32, 140, 142–43, 144, 147–48, 154, 159, 161. *See also* Office of Federal Acknowledgment (OFA); recognition
Agamben, Giorgio, 28
Alcatraz occupation in 1969, 22
Allotment Era, 74, 80. *See also* Dawes Severalty Act; KCA (Kiowa-Comanche-Apache)
American Indian Movement, 22, 24
American Indian Policy Review Commission, 148–51, 153
American Law Institute (ALI), 175
American Recovery and Reinvestment Act (ARRA), 189–90
Anishinaabeg, and texts of treaties, 60
anthropologists: First Nations' evasive responses to, 11; Hopi consideration of ending research by, 104; Hopi society according to, 96–101; protesting the Jerome Agreement, 44
anthropology, linguistic, 24–25; Silverstein's metapragmatic function in, 177n
Aprill, Ellen, 181, 183, 184, 185
archaeologists: Hopi consideration of ending research by, 104; Kuwanwisiwma's partnering

with, 104–5. *See also* US Forest Service consultation with HCPO
Archambault, David, II, 197, 198, 199
Arthur, Chester, 94
Article of Sales, 175, 176, 183
askwali (thanks), 116
assimilation: Australian Native title rights and, 145; end of policies of, 7, 150–51; forced cultural policies of, 6, 8, 151; forced removal of Native children and, 74; Native Nations blamed for, 145; Native Nations not yielding to, 70
Assimilation and Allotment Era, 74, 80
Atanarjuat (film), 199, 202
Australian politics of recognition, 144–45, 147
Australian settler colonialism, 7

bait-and-switch: in acknowledgment process, 143; in archaeological consultation, 121; by Jerome Commission, 121
Bakhtin, Mikhail, 124, 125, 130
Basso, Keith, 119
Behind the Trail of Broken Treaties (Deloria), 21
Benveniste, Émile, 27
"best interests" of Tribes: Dawes Act supposedly passed in, 46; as domestic dependent nations, 54; federal Indian trust relationship and, 71; losses inflicted by US policies in the name of, 6–7, 39, 79
"beyond dialogue," 35–36, 39, 40–41, 43, 52, 80, 124, 199
Black Lives Matter movement, 197
Boston Tea Party, 8
Boyden, John S., 87, 88–89, 90–92, 93, 110
Boy Scouts of America, 8

The Chicago Series in Law and Society
Edited by John M. Conley, Charles Epp, and Lynn Mather